Fodor's 92
Italy's
Great Cities

D0943233

Reprinted from *Fodor's Italy '92*.

Fodor's Travel Publications, Inc.
New York & London

Fodor's Italy's Great Cities

Editor: Conrad Little Paulus
Area Editor: Barbara Walsh Angelillo
Editorial Contributors: Barbara Lazear Ascher, Bob Blake, Sheila Brownlee, Harry Eyres, Ruth Gruber, Tara Hamilton, Andrew Heritage, Holly Hughes, Amanda Jacobs, Guy Lesser, Tony Peisley, Carolyn Price, Claudia Rader, George Sullivan, Phoebe Tait, Robert Tine
Art Director: Fabrizio La Rocca
Cartographer: David Lindroth
Illustrator: Karl Tanner
Cover Photograph: Michaelangelo Gratton

Design: Vignelli Associates

Special Sales

Contents

Maps

Foreword

We would like to express our gratitude to Barbara Walsh Angelillo for her patience, enthusiasm, and hard work in preparing this new edition.

While every care has been taken to ensure the accuracy of the information in this guide, the passage of time will always bring change, and consequently, the publisher cannot accept responsibility for errors that may occur.

All prices and opening times quoted here are based on information supplied to us at press time. Hours and admission fees may change, however, and the prudent traveler will avoid inconvenience by calling ahead.

Fodor's wants to hear about your travel experiences, both pleasant and unpleasant. When a hotel or restaurant fails to live up to its billing, let us know and we will investigate the complaint and revise our entries where the facts warrant it.

Send your letters to the editors of Fodor's Travel Publications, 201 E. 50th Street, New York, NY 10022.

Highlights '92 and Fodor's Choice

Highlights '92

This is a year of commemorations in Italy, with the biggest event being the 500th anniversary of **Columbus's discovery of America.**

The heartland of Tuscany from Florence to Arezzo and beyond to the little town of Sansepolcro is the center of celebrations of the 500th anniversary of the death of one of Italy's greatest artists, **Piero della Francesca,** an early Renaissance painter whose importance was inexplicably overlooked by art historians until the mid-20th century. Piero's works in the **Uffizi** in Florence, his frescoes of the Legend of the True Cross in **Arezzo,** and his paintings in his home town of **Sansepolcro** and in the Ducal Palace of **Urbino** will be the subjects and center of commemorative appraisals of his genius during 1992.

Throughout Italy, hotels are being refurbished and upgraded; though this makes them pleasanter places to stay, it also means that their new rates may be out of reach of the budget-minded. Many hotels covet the business-traveler trade and are offering secretarial services, faxes and such. Among noteworthy new hostelries are the five-star **Majestic** in Rome and the five-star **Sheraton** in Florence. Unfortunately, hotel rates in general continue to be steep, especially when compared for value with U.S. rates. The same is true of prices in restaurants. The budget-conscious will be glad to hear that more and more McDonald's are opening up; there are four in Rome alone.

Growing public awareness and denunciation of urban air pollution, caused mainly by automobile and bus exhaust fumes, may force procrastinating city administrators to place strict limitations on traffic in downtown areas. Particularly in Rome, where pollution levels during the winter of 1990–91 forced enactment of stopgap measures, cleaner air would make city streets much pleasanter for tourists.

By the end of 1992 further steps toward European unification will have been taken, and life in Italy is bound to reflect changes and liberalization in travel and trade. Consumers may find goods from other European countries at competitive prices in Italian shops. While problems of funds and staff continue to limit opening hours at many Italian museums, there's good news from Florence, where the **Uffizi Gallery** is being enlarged so that even more of its fabulous collections can be exhibited to the million-or-so visitors it attracts every year. Work will continue for several years.

Fodor's Choice

No two people will agree on what makes a perfect vacation, but it's fun and helpful to know what others think. We hope you'll have a chance to experience some of Fodor's Choices yourself while visiting Italy. For detailed information about each entry, refer to the appropriate chapters (given in parentheses) within this guidebook.

Hotels

Hassler (Rome) *Very Expensive*

Baglioni (Florence) *Expensive*

Accademia (Venice) *Moderate*

Internazionale (Rome) *Moderate*

Restaurants

El Toulà (Rome) *Very Expensive*

Fiaschetteria (Venice) *Expensive*

Beccherie, Treviso (10 mi north of Venice) *Moderate*

Cafés

Florian (Venice)

Tre Scalini (Rome)

Classical Sites

Fiesole (Florence)

Ostia Antica (Rome)

Roman Forum (Rome)

Works of Art

Donatello's *Judith and Holofernes* (Florence)

Michelangelo's *David* and *Slaves* (Florence)

Michelangelo's newly restored Sistine Chapel ceiling (Rome)

Raphael's Vatican *Stanze* (Rome)

Titian's *Martyrdom of St. Lawrence* (Venice)

Veronese's *Feast at the House of Levi* (Venice)

Churches

Frari (Venice)

Il Gesù (Rome)

San Miniato al Monte (Florence)

Santa Maria Maggiore (Rome)

St. Mark's (Venice)

Museums

Accademia (Venice)

Galleria degli Uffizi (Florence)

Vatican Museums (Rome)

Villa Giulia (Rome)

Architectural Gems

Baptistry (Florence)

Palazzo Barberini (Rome)

Palazzo Ducale (Venice)

Taste Treats

Bistecca alla Fiorentina (Florence)

Gnocchi alla Romana (Rome)

Tiramisù (Venice)

Times to Treasure

Cheering for the boats in Venice's Historic Regatta (Venice)

Peeping through the Knights of Malta keyhole to see St. Peter's dome (Rome)

The sleepy view of Florence and the Arno valley from Via San Francesco, Fiesole (Florence)

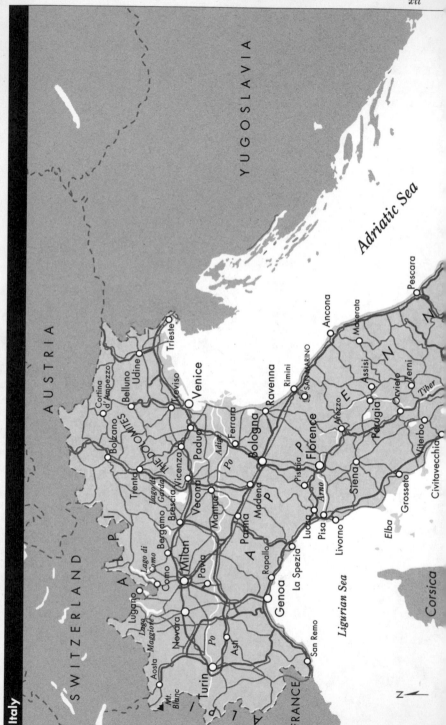

Italy

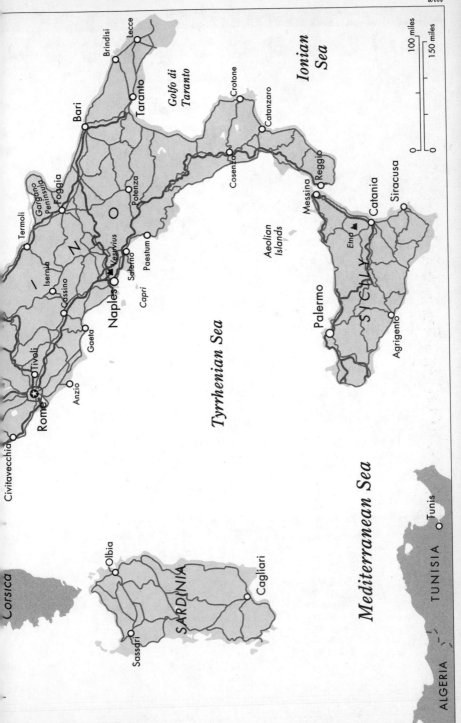

World Time Zones

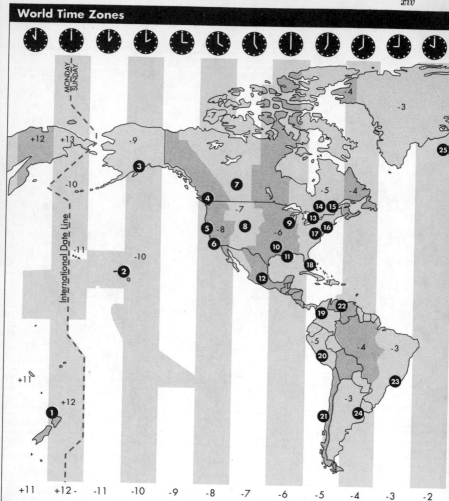

Numbers below vertical bands relate each zone to Greenwich Mean Time (0 hrs.).
Local times frequently differ from these general indications,
as indicated by light-face numbers on map.

Algiers, **29**
Anchorage, **3**
Athens, **41**
Auckland, **1**
Baghdad, **46**
Bangkok, **50**
Beijing, **54**

Berlin, **34**
Bogotá, **19**
Budapest, **37**
Buenos Aires, **24**
Caracas, **22**
Chicago, **9**
Copenhagen, **33**
Dallas, **10**

Delhi, **48**
Denver, **8**
Djakarta, **53**
Dublin, **26**
Edmonton, **7**
Hong Kong, **56**
Honolulu, **2**

Istanbul, **40**
Jerusalem, **42**
Johannesburg, **44**
Lima, **20**
Lisbon, **28**
London (Greenwich), **27**
Los Angeles, **6**
Madrid, **38**
Manila, **57**

9:00

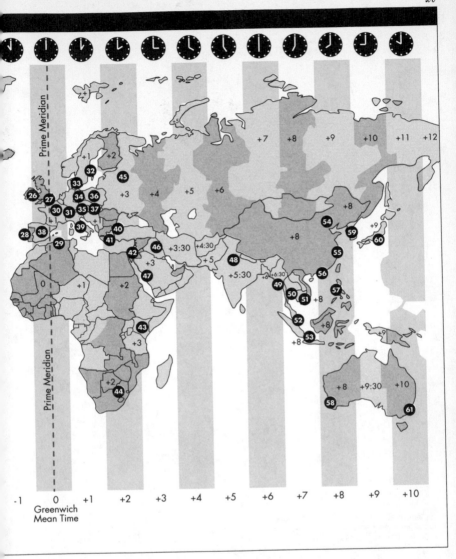

1 Essential Information

Before You Go

Government Tourist Offices

In the U.S. Contact the Italian National Tourist Offices at 630 5th Ave., Suite 1565, New York, NY 10111, tel. 212/245–4822; 500 N. Michigan Ave., Chicago, IL 60611, tel. 312/644–0990; 360 Post St., Suite 801, San Francisco, CA 94108, tel. 415/392–6206.

In Canada 1 Place Ville Marie, Montreal, Quebec H3B 2E3, tel. 514/866–7667.

In the U.K. 1 Princes St., London W1R 8AY England, tel. 071/408–1254.

Tour Groups

Tour groups are not just for beginners anymore. While the whistle-stop express tour of all the most famous sights is still around—and still a good introduction for those making a first visit—there are a growing number of more focused and more sophisticated packages. In fact, considering the wealth of options available, the toughest part of your vacation may well be to find the tour that best fits your personal style. Listed below is a sampling of programs to give you an idea of what is available. For more information, contact your travel agent and/or the Italian National Tourist Office.

When considering a tour, be sure to find out exactly what expenses are included (particularly tips, taxes, side trips, additional meals, and entertainment); government ratings of all hotels on the itinerary and the facilities they offer; and, if you are traveling alone, what the single supplement is. Note whether the tour operator reserves the right to change hotels, routes, or even prices after you've booked, and ask about its policy regarding cancellations, complaints, and trip-interruption insurance. Most tour operators request that bookings be made through a travel agent—there is no additional charge for doing so.

General-Interest Tours **CIT Tours** (594 Broadway, Suite 307, New York, NY 10012, tel. 212/274–0593 or 800/223–7987) offers several popular packages that benefit from the operator's extensive support network of 47 offices throughout Italy. **Central Holiday** (206 Central Ave., Jersey City, NJ 07307, tel. 201/798–5777 or 800/526–6045) can be counted on for solid, reasonably priced tours. **Maupintour** (Box 807, Lawrence, KS 66044, tel. 913/843–1211 or 800/255–4266) runs 12-day "Italy's Famous Places" tours that visit Milan, Venice, Florence, and Rome; and 19-day "Italy Grand and Leisurely" tours that include Venice, Florence, Rome, Assisi, and Capri. **American Express Vacations** (Box 5014, Atlanta, GA 30302, tel. 800/241–1700 or, in Georgia, 800/282–0800) is a veritable supermarket of tours—you name it, they've either got it packaged or will customize a package for you.

Other major operators to Italy include **Globus-Gateway/Cosmos** (150 S. Los Robles Ave., Suite 860, Pasadena, CA 91101, tel. 818/449–0919 or 800/556–5454), **Donna Franca Tours** (470 Commonwealth Ave., Boston, MA 02215, tel. 617/227–3111), **Perillo Tours** (577 Chestnut Ridge Rd., Woodcliff Lake, NJ 07675, tel. 201/307–1234 or 800/431–1515) and **Italiatour** (666 5th Ave., New York, NY 10103, tel. 212/765–2183 or 800/237–0517).

Special-Interest Tours *Wine/Cuisine*	**Connaissance & Cie** (790 Madison Ave., New York, NY 10021, tel. 212/472–5772) offers a wine and food tour of Italy, including Florence, with Melissa Sere, noted wine educator.
Art/Architecture	There is a staggering wealth of both in Italy, and **Esplanade Tours** (581 Boylston St., Boston, MA 02116, tel. 617/266–7465) delves into much of it. Tours include "Renaissance Italy" and "Villas and Gardens of Italy."
Singles and Young Couples	**Trafalgar Tours** (21 E. 62nd St., New York, NY 10010, tel. 212/689–8977 or 800/854–0103) offers "Club 21–35," faster-paced tours for travelers unafraid of a little physical activity—whether it's bike riding, or discoing the night away in the cities.
Music	**Dailey-Thorp Travel** (315 W. 57th St., New York, NY 10019, tel. 212/307–1555) offers deluxe opera and music tours, including "Opera Capitals of Italy" (Rome, Naples, Florence, Bologna, Milan). Itineraries vary, according to available performances.

Package Deals for Independent Travelers

Italiatour, Alitalia's in-house tour operator, offers the "Italian Honeymoon" series of tours, which will melt the heart of any romantic couple, with candlelit dinners and a host of special treats. It also has more traditional air/hotel packages, as do **Central Holiday** and **CIT Tours. TWA Getaway Vacations** (tel. 800/GETAWAY) has a reasonably priced eight-day "Roman Holiday." **TourCrafters** (30 S. Michigan Ave., Chicago, IL 60603, tel. 312/726–3886 or 800/621–2259) offers city tours and self-drive tours of the countryside. **Pan Am Holidays** (tel. 800/THE TOUR) provides special rates at select hotels in Rome, Milan, Florence, and Venice when you fly roundtrip on Pan Am. **American Airlines Fly AAway Vacations** (tel. 800/433–7300 or 817/355–1234) lets you design your own fly/drive itinerary from a selection of hotels, rental cars, and rail passes.

When to Go

The main tourist season runs from mid-April to the end of September. The best months for sightseeing are April, May, June, September, and October, when the weather is generally pleasant and not too hot. In general, the northern half of the peninsula and the entire Adriatic Coast, with the exception of Apulia, are rainier than the rest of Italy. Foreign tourists crowd the major art cities at Easter, when Italians flock to resorts and to the country. From March through May, bus loads of eager schoolchildren on excursions take cities of artistic and historical interest by storm.

If you can avoid it, don't travel at all in Italy in August, when much of the population is on the move. The heat can be oppressive, and vacationing Italians cram roads, trains, and planes on their way to shore and mountain resorts. All this is especially true around the August 15 national holiday, when cities such as Rome and Milan are deserted and many restaurants and shops are closed.

The hottest months are July and August, when brief afternoon thunderstorms are common in inland areas. Winters are relatively mild in most places on the main tourist circuit but always include some rainy spells.

Major cities, such as Rome, Florence, and Milan, have no off-season as far as hotel rates go, though some hotels will reduce rates during the slack season upon request. You can save considerably on hotel rooms in Venice and in such resorts as Sorrento and Capri during their off-seasons.

You may want to plan your trip to take in some spectacular *festas* (local festivals) or satisfy special interests, such as opera festivals or wine tours. From May through September the calendar is dotted with festas. Outdoor music and opera festivals are held mainly in July and August (*see* Festivals and Seasonal Events, below).

Climate The following are average daily maximum and minimum temperatures for Italy.

Florence								
Jan.	48F	9C	May	73F	23C	Sept.	79F	26C
	36	2		54	12		59	15
Feb.	52F	11C	June	81F	27C	Oct.	68F	20C
	37	3		59	15		52	11
Mar.	57F	14C	July	86F	30C	Nov.	57F	14C
	41	5		64	18		45	7
Apr.	66F	19C	Aug.	86F	30C	Dec.	52F	11C
	46	8		63	17		39	4

Rome								
Jan.	52F	11C	May	74F	23C	Sept.	79F	26C
	40	5		56	13		62	17
Feb.	55F	13C	June	82F	28C	Oct.	71F	22C
	42	6		63	17		55	13
Mar.	59F	15C	July	87F	30C	Nov.	61F	16C
	45	7		67	20		49	10
Apr.	66F	19C	Aug.	86F	30C	Dec.	55F	13C
	50	10		67	20		44	6

Venice								
Jan.	42F	6C	May	70F	21C	Sept.	75F	24C
	33	1		56	13		61	16
Feb.	46F	8C	June	76F	25C	Oct.	65F	19C
	35	2		63	17		53	12
Mar.	53F	12C	July	81F	27C	Nov.	53F	12C
	41	5		66	19		44	7
Apr.	62F	17C	Aug.	80F	27C	Dec.	46F	8C
	49	10		65	19		37	3

Current weather information for more than 750 cities around the world may be obtained by calling **WeatherTrak** information service at 900/370–8728 or in TX, 900/575–8728. A taped message will tell you to dial the three-digit access code for the destination you're interested in—either the area code (in the United States) or the first three letters of the foreign city. For a list of all access codes, send a stamped, addressed envelope to Cities, Box 7000, Dallas, TX 75209. For further information, phone 800/247–3282.

Festivals and Seasonal Events

Top seasonal events in Italy include carnival celebrations in January and February; Epiphany celebrations in January; Easter celebrations in Rome and Florence; the Florence May Music Festival; The Maritime Republics Regatta in June, alternatively in Venice, Genoa, Amalfi, or Pisa; and the Venice Film Festival in late August. Contact the **Italian National Tourist Office** for exact dates and further information.

January 5–6	**Epiphany Celebrations.** Roman Catholic Epiphany celebrations and decorations are evident throughout Italy. Notable is the Epiphany Fair at Piazza Navona in Rome.
Mid-February	**Carnival in Venice** includes plays, masked balls, fireworks, and more in Venice's squares and in sites throughout the city.
April 17	The **Good Friday Procession** in Rome is led by the Pope, from the Colosseum past the Forum and up the Palatine Hill. This nighttime parade is torchlit.
Easter Sunday (April 19)	The **Scoppio del Carro,** or "Explosion of the Cart," in Florence, is a pyramid of fireworks in the Cathedral Square, set off by a mechanical dove released from the altar during High Mass.
Late April-Early July	The **Florence May Music Festival** is the oldest and most prestigious Italian festival of the performing arts.
	The **Flower Festival,** in Genzano (Rome), is a religious procession along streets carpeted with flowers in magnificent designs.
	The **Regatta of the Great Maritime Republics** sees keen competition among the four former maritime republics—Amalfi, Genoa, Pisa, and Venice.
Late June	**Soccer Games in 16th-Century Costume,** in Florence, commemorate a match played in 1530. Festivities include fireworks displays.
Mid-July	The **Feast of the Redeemer** is a procession of gondolas and other craft, commemorating the end of the epidemic of 1575 in Venice. The fireworks over the lagoon are spectacular.
Late August-Early September	The **Venice Film Festival,** oldest of the international film festivals, takes place mostly on the Lido.
	The **Historic Regatta** includes a traditional competition between two-oar gondolas in Venice.

What to Pack

The weather is considerably milder in Italy all year round than it is in the north and central United States or Great Britain. In summer, stick with clothing that's as light as possible; women should carry a scarf, light stole, or jacket to cover bare arms and shoulders when visiting churches or the Vatican Museums. Shorts or otherwise revealing clothes—on women or men—are taboo in churches; Italians are very strict about this in St. Peter's in Rome and St. Mark's in Venice and in other churches in general. A sweater or woolen stole is a must for the cool of the evening, even during the hot months. In summer, brief afternoon thunderstorms are common in Rome and inland cities, so carry a folding plastic raincoat. And if you go into the mountains, you will find the evenings there quite chilly. During the winter a medium-weight coat and a raincoat will stand you in good stead in Rome and farther south; Northern Italy calls for heavier clothes, gloves, hats, and boots. You'll probably need an umbrella, too, but you can pick it up on the spot (or invest in a good folding one). Pack comfortable, sturdy shoes. Cobblestones are murder on the feet; crepe soles are a help.

In general, Italians dress well and are not sloppy. They usually don't wear shorts in the city, unless longish bermudas happen to be in fashion at the time. Even when dressed casually or informally, they are careful about the way they look; that's why so few restaurants establish dress codes. Men aren't required to wear ties or jackets anywhere, except in some of the grander hotel dining rooms and top-level restaurants. Formal wear is the exception rather than the rule at the opera nowadays, though people in expensive seats usually do get dressed up. For the huge general papal audiences, no rules of dress apply other than those of common sense. For other types of audience, the Vatican Information Office will give requirements.

To guard against purse snatchers and pickpockets, take a handbag with long straps that you can sling across your body and with a zippered compartment for money and other valuables. Beware of aggressive groups of thieving children.

You'll need an electrical adapter for hair dryers and other small appliances. The current is 220 volts and 50 cycles. If you stay in budget hotels, take your own soap. Many do not provide soap or else give guests only one tiny bar per room.

Taking Money Abroad

Traveler's checks and major U.S. credit cards, particularly Visa and American Express, are accepted in larger cities and resorts. In smaller towns and rural areas, you'll need cash. Small restaurants and shops in the cities also tend to operate on a cash basis. You won't get as good an exchange rate at home as abroad, but it's wise to change a small amount of money into Italian lire before you go, to avoid long lines at airport currency-exchange booths. Most U.S. banks will change U.S. money into lire. If your local bank can't provide this service, you can exchange money through **Thomas Cook Currency Service.** To find the office nearest you, contact them at 29 Broadway, New York, NY 10006, tel. 212/757–6915.

For safety and convenience, it's always best to take traveler's checks. The most recognized traveler's checks are **American Express, Barclay's, Thomas Cook,** and those issued through major commercial banks such as **Citibank** and **Bank of America.** Some banks will issue the checks free to established customers, but most charge a 1% commission fee. Buy part of the traveler's checks in small denominations to cash toward the end of your trip. This will save you from having to cash a large check and ending up with more foreign money than you need. You can also buy traveler's checks in lire—a good idea if the dollar is falling and you want to lock in the current rate. Remember to take the address of offices where you can get refunds for lost or stolen traveler's checks.

Banks and bank-operated exchange booths at airports and railroad stations are the best places to change money. Hotels and privately run exchange firms will give you a significantly lower rate.

American Express allows cardholders to withdraw up to $1,000 in a seven-day period from their personal checking accounts at Express Cash machines at American Express offices in Florence, Milan, Rome, and Venice. (Gold cardmembers can receive up to $2,500 in a seven-day period.) Express Cash is not a cash advance service; only money already in the linked checking account can be withdrawn. Every transaction carries a 2% fee, with a minimum charge of $2 and a maximum of $6. Apply for a PIN (Personal Identification number) and to link your accounts at least two to three weeks before departure. Call 800/227–4669 to receive an application or a list locating the nearest Express Cash machine.

Italian Currency

The unit of currency in Italy is the lira. There are bills of 500,000, 100,000, 10,000, 5,000, 2,000 and 1,000 lire. Coins are 1,000, 500, 100, 50, 20, and 10 (the last two are hardly ever used because cashiers often round out sums). At press time (mid-May 1991) the exchange rate was about 1,239 lire to the U.S. dollar, 1,063 to the Canadian dollar, and 2,075 to the pound sterling.

What It Will Cost

Italy's prices are in line with the rest of Europe, with costs comparable to those in other major capitals, such as Paris and London. Its days as a country with a low Mediterranean price tag are over. With the cost of labor and social benefits rising and in the face of a persistently weak dollar, Italy is no longer a bargain. Travelers are finding hotels and restaurants much more expensive than they used to be, and many are opting for lower-category hotels and giving up such luxuries as cars with drivers. Package tours, group or individual, remain the best way to beat increasing costs. Everywhere in Italy, if you want the luxury of a five-star hotel, be prepared to pay top rates—and likewise with many four-star first-class hotels.

Taxes are usually included in hotel bills, but some five-star hotels quote rates not inclusive of the whopping 18.6% IVA (VAT) for that category. There are several direct taxes in Italy that affect the tourist, such as the 19% IVA on car rentals.

Passports and Visas

Americans A visa is not required of U.S. citizens for stays up to three months. Check with the Italian Embassy, 2700 16th St., N.W., Washington, DC 20009, tel. 202/328–5500, or with the nearest consulate for longer stays. Passports are required for all U.S. citizens.

Canadians Visas are not required of Canadian citizens for stays of up to three months in Italy. Check with the nearest Italian consulate for longer stays. Passports are required for all Canadian citizens.

Britons Visas are not required of British citizens staying in Italy for up to three months.

Customs and Duties

On Arrival Non-European visitors can bring into Italy duty-free 400 cigarettes or 200 cigarillos or 100 cigars or 500 grams of tobacco, 1 liter of alcohol or 2 liters of wine, 50 grams of perfume, and ¼ liter of toilet water. European visitors can bring in duty-free 300 cigarettes or 150 cigarillos or 75 cigars or 400 grams of tobacco, 1.5 liters of alcohol or 3 liters of sparkling wine and 3 liters of table wine, and 90 cc of perfume. Officially, 10 rolls of still camera film and 10 reels of movie film may be brought in duty-free. Other items intended for personal use are generally admitted, as long as the quantities are reasonable.

On Departure   **U.S. Customs.** If you are bringing any foreign-made equipment from home, such as a camera, it's wise to carry the original receipt with you or register it with U.S. Customs before you leave (Form 4457). Otherwise, you may end up paying duty upon your return. For each 30-day period, U.S. residents may bring home duty-free up to $400 worth of foreign goods, as long as they have been out of the country for at least 48 hours. Each member of the family is entitled to the same exemption, regardless of age, and exemptions can be pooled. For the next $1,000 worth of goods, a flat 10% rate is assessed; above $1,400, duties vary with the merchandise. Included for travelers 21 or older are one liter of alcohol, 100 cigars (non-Cuban), and 200 cigarettes. Only one bottle of perfume trademarked in the United States may be brought in. However, there is no duty on antiques and art more than 100 years old. Anything exceeding these limits will be taxed at the port of entry and may be taxed additionally in the traveler's home state. Gifts valued at under $50 may be mailed to friends or relatives at home duty-free, but not more than one package per day to any one addressee, and packages may not include perfumes costing more than $5, tobacco, or liquor.

Canadian Customs. Exemptions for returning Canadians range from $20 to $300, depending on length of stay out of the country. For the $300 exemption, you must have been out of the country for one week. For any given year, one $300 exemption is allowed. You may bring in duty-free up to 50 cigars, 200 cigarettes, 2.2 pounds of tobacco, and 40 ounces of liquor, provided these are declared in writing to customs on arrival and accompany the traveler in hand or in checked baggage. Personal gifts should be mailed as "Unsolicited Gift—Value under $40." For further details, request the Canadian customs brochure "I Declare."

British Customs. Since Italy is an EC country, British residents have the following exemptions, provided the items were not bought in a duty-free shop: 300 cigarettes or 150 cigarillos or 75 cigars or 400 grams of tobacco and 5 liters of table wine. In addition, they may bring in 1.5 liters of alcohol over 22% volume (most spirits) or 3 liters of alcohol under 22% volume (fortified or sparkling wine), 90 milliliters of perfume, 375 ml of toilet water, or other goods totaling a value of £250. No animals or pets of any kind can be brought into the United Kingdom without a lengthy quarantine. The penalties are severe and strictly enforced.

Traveling with Film

If your camera is new, shoot and develop a few rolls of film before you leave home. Pack some lens tissue and an extra battery for your built-in light meter. Invest about $10 in a skylight filter and screw it onto the front of your lens. It will protect the lens and also reduce haze.

Film doesn't like hot weather. If you're driving in summer, don't store film in the glove compartment or on the shelf under the rear window. Put it behind the front seat on the floor, on the side opposite the exhaust pipe.

On a plane trip, never pack unprocessed film in check-in luggage; if your bags get X-rayed, you can say good-bye to your pictures. Always carry undeveloped film with you through security, and ask to have it inspected by hand. (It helps to isolate your film in a plastic bag, ready for quick inspection.) Inspectors at American airports are required by law to honor requests for hand inspection; abroad, you'll have to depend on the kindness of strangers.

The old airport scanning machines—still in use in some countries—use heavy doses of radiation that can turn a family portrait into an early morning fog. The newer models—used in all U.S. airports—are safe for many more scans, depending on the speed of your film. The effects are cumulative; you can put the same roll of film through several scans without worry. After five scans, though, you're asking for trouble.

If your film gets fogged and you want an explanation, send it to the **National Association of Photographic Manufacturers** (550 Mamaroneck Ave., Harrison, NY 10528). They will try to determine what went wrong. The service is free.

Language

In the main tourist cities, language is no problem. You can always find someone who speaks at least a little English, albeit with a heavy accent; remember that the Italian language is pronounced exactly as it is written (many Italians try to speak English as it is written, with disconcerting results). If you run into a language barrier remember that a phrase book and close attention to the Italians' astonishing use of pantomime and expressive gestures will go a long way.

Try to master a few phrases for daily use, and familiarize yourself with the terms you'll need to decipher signs and museum labels. You will find the basics in the Vocabulary and Menu Guide in the back of this book.

The exhortation, "Va via!" (Go away!) is useful in warding off beggars.

Staying Healthy

There are no serious health risks associated with travel to Italy. However, the Centers for Disease Control (CDC) in Atlanta caution that most of Southern Europe is in the "intermediate" range for risk of contacting traveler's diarrhea. Part of this risk may be attributed to an increased consumption of olive oil and wine, which can have a laxative effect on stomachs used to a different diet. The CDC also advises all international travelers to swim only in chlorinated swimming pools, unless they are absolutely certain the local beaches and fresh-water lakes are not contaminated.

If you have a health problem that might require purchasing prescription drugs while in Italy, have your doctor write a prescription using the drug's generic name or bring a supply with you. Brand names vary widely from country to country.

If you wear glasses or contact lenses, take along a spare pair or the prescription.

The **International Association for Medical Assistance to Travelers (IAMAT)** is a worldwide association offering a list of approved English-speaking doctors whose training meets British and American standards. For a list of Italian physicians and clinics that are part of this network, contact IAMAT, 417 Center St., Lewiston, NY 14092, tel: 716/754–4883. In **Canada:** 40 Regal Rds., Guelph, Ontario N1K 1B5. In **Europe:** 57 Voirets, 1212 Grands—Lancy, Geneva, Switzerland. Membership is free.

Shots and Medications Inoculations are not needed for entering Italy. The American Medical Association (AMA) recommends Pepto Bismol for minor cases of traveler's diarrhea.

Insurance

Travelers may seek insurance coverage in three areas: health and accident, loss of luggage, and trip cancellation. Your first step is to review your existing health and home-owner policies; some health insurance plans cover health expenses incurred while traveling, some major medical plans cover emergency transportation, and some home-owner policies cover the theft of luggage.

Health and Accident Several companies offer coverage designed to supplement existing health insurance for travelers:

Carefree Travel Insurance (Box 310, 120 Mineola Blvd., Mineola, NY 11501, tel. 516/294–0220 or 800/323–3149) provides coverage for emergency medical evacuation and accidental death and dismemberment. It also offers 24-hour medical phone advice.
International SOS Assistance (Box 11568, Philadelphia, PA 19116, tel. 215/244–1500 or 800/523–8930), a medical assistance company, provides emergency evacuation services, worldwide medical referrals, and optional medical insurance.
Travel Guard International, underwritten by Transamerica Occidental Life Companies (1145 Clark St., Stevens Point, WI 54481, tel. 715/345–0505 or 800/782–5151), offers reimbursement for medical expenses with no deductibles or daily limits and emergency evacuation services.
Wallach and Company (243 Church St. NW, Suite 100D, Vienna, VA 22180, tel. 703/281–9500 or 800/237–6615) offers comprehensive medical coverage, including emergency evacuation services worldwide.

Lost Luggage Loss of luggage is usually covered as part of a comprehensive travel insurance package that includes personal accident, trip cancellation, and sometimes default and bankruptcy insurance. Several companies offer comprehensive policies: **Access America Inc.,** a subsidiary of Blue Cross–Blue Shield (Box 11188, Richmond, VA 23230, tel. 800/334–7525 or 800/284–8300); **Near Services** (450 Prairie Ave., Suite 101, Calumet City, IL 60409, tel. 708/868–6700 or 800/654–6700); and **Travel Guard International** (*see* above).

On international flights, airlines are responsible for lost or damaged property up to $9.07 per pound (or $20 per kilo) for checked baggage and up to $400 per passenger for unchecked baggage. If you're carrying any valuables, either take them with you on the airplane or purchase additional lost-luggage insurance. Not all airlines sell you this added insurance. Those that do will sell it to you at the counter when you check in, but you have to ask for it. Others will refer you to the insurance booths located throughout airports, which are operated by **Tele-Trip** (tel. 800/228–9792), a subsidiary of Mutual of Omaha. They will insure your luggage for up to 180 days. Rates vary according to the length of the trip. **The Travelers Insurance Corporation** (Ticket and Travel Dept., 1 Tower Square, Hartford, CT 06183, tel. 203/277–0111 or 800/243–3174) will insure checked or hand baggage for $500–$2,000 valuation per person, up to 180 days. Rates for 1–5 days for $500 valuation are $10; for 180 days, $85. Check with your travel agent or the travel section of your Sunday newspaper for the names of other insurance companies. Itemize the contents of each bag in case you need to file a claim. If your lost luggage is recovered, the airline will deliver it to you at your home. There will be no charge to you.

Trip Cancellation Flight insurance is often included in the price of a ticket when paid for with American Express, Visa, and other major credit and charge cards. It is usually included in combination travel insurance packages available from most tour operators, travel agents, and insurance agents.

Renting Cars

Renting If you're flying into a major Italian city and planning to spend some time there, save money by arranging to pick up your car in the city the day you depart; otherwise, arrange to pick up and return your car at the airport. You'll have to weigh the added expense of renting a car from a major company with an airport office against the savings on a car from a budget company with offices in town. If you're arriving and departing from different airports, look for a one-way car rental with no return fees. If you're traveling to more than one country, make sure your rental contract permits you to take the car across borders and that the insurance policy covers you in every country you visit. Be prepared to pay more for a car with an automatic transmission, and reserve them in advance. Rental rates vary widely, but in most cases, rates quoted include unlimited free mileage and standard liability protection. Not included are a collision damage waiver (CDW), which eliminates your deductible payment should you have an accident; personal accident insurance; gasoline; and European value-added taxes (IVA). Again, the IVA in Italy is 19%.

Driver's licenses issued in the United States, Canada, and Britain are valid in Italy. You might also take out an International Driving Permit before you leave, to smooth out difficulties if you have an accident, or as additional identification. Permits are available for a small fee through local offices of the American Automobile Association (AAA) and the Canadian Automobile Association (CAA), or from their main offices: **AAA**, 1000 AAA Dr., Heathrow, FL 32746, tel. 800/336–4357; **CAA**, 2 Carlton St., Toronto, Ontario M5B 1K4, tel. 416/964–3170).

It's best to arrange a car rental before you leave. Rental companies usually charge according to the exchange rate of the dollar at the time the car is returned or when the credit card payment is processed. Two companies with special programs to help you hedge against the falling dollar, by guaranteeing advertised rates if you pay in advance, are **Budget Rent-a-Car** (3350 Boyington St., Carrollton, TX 75006, tel. 800/527–0700) and **Connex Travel International** (23 N. Division St., Peekskill, NY 10566, tel. 800/333–3949). Other budget rental companies serving Italy include **Europe by Car** (1 Rockefeller Plaza, New York, NY 10020, tel. 800/223–1516 or, in New York, 212/245–1713 or 212/581–3040, in California, 800/252–9401); **Auto Europe** (Box 1097, Camden, ME 04843, tel. 207/236–8235; in Canada, 800/548–9503); **Foremost Euro-Car** (5430 Van Nuys Blvd., Van Nuys, CA 91401–5680, tel. 800/272–3299; in Canada 800/253–3876); and **Kemwel** (106 Calvert St., Harrison, NY 10528, tel. 914/835–5449 or 800/678–0678).

Other companies include **Avis** (tel. 800/331–1212); **Hertz** (tel. 800/654–3131 or, in New York, 800/654–3001); and **National** or **Europcar** (tel. 800/227–3876).

Rail Passes

For those planning on doing a lot of traveling by train, the **Italian RailPass** is an excellent value because it covers the entire system, including Sicily. The pass is available in first class for periods of 8 days ($206), 15 days ($258), 21 days ($298), and 30 days ($360). In second-class the prices for the same periods are $136, $172, $198, and $240. There is also a $10 processing fee.

Also available is the **Italy Flexi Railcard,** which entitles purchasers to travel to 4 destinations within 9 days; 8 destinations within 21 days; and 12 destinations within 30 days. Rates for first-class travel are $154, $226, and $284; for second-class travel, rates are $104, $148, and $190. To all rates you must add a $10 processing fee.

Although you can buy the passes at major train stations in Italy, you'll save about 30% by buying them before you leave. They can be bought through travel agents or through CIT, representative for **Italian State Railways** (594 Broadway, Suite 307, New York, NY 10012, tel. 212/274–0593).

The **EurailPass,** valid for unlimited first-class train travel through 17 countries, including Italy, is an excellent value if you plan on traveling around the Continent. The ticket is available for periods of 15 days ($390), 21 days ($498), one month ($616), two months ($840), and three months ($1,042). For two or more people traveling together, a 15-day rail pass costs $298. Between April 1 and September 30, you need a minimum of three in your group to get this discount. For those under 26, there is the **Eurail Youthpass,** for one or two months' unlimited second-class train travel at $425 and $560.

For travelers who like to spread out their train journeys, there is the **Eurail Flexipass.** With the 15-day Flexipass ($230), travelers get 5 days of unlimited first-class train travel, but they can spread that travel out over 15 days; a 21-day pass gives you 9 days of travel ($398), and a one-month pass gives you 14 days ($498). The **Eurail Youth Flexipass** permits 15 days of second-class travel within three months for $340 or 30 days within three months for $540.

Ask also about the **Eurail Drive** Pass, which lets you combine train and car travel.

The EurailPass does not cover Great Britain and is available only if you live outside Europe or North Africa. The pass must be bought from an authorized agent before you leave for Europe. Apply through your travel agent or **Italian State Railways** (*see* above).

Travelers under 26 who have not invested in a **Eurail Youthpass,** or any of the other rail passes, should inquire about discount travel fares under the Billet International Jeune (BIJ) scheme. The special one-trip tickets are sold by **EuroTrain International,** (no connection with Eurailpass) at its offices in London, Dublin, Paris, Madrid, Lisbon, Rome, Zurich, Athens, Brussels, Budapest, Hanover, Leiden, Vienna, and Tangier, and at travel agents, mainline rail stations, and youth-travel specialists.

Student and Youth Travel

The **International Student Identity Card (ISIC)** entitles students to youth rail passes, special fares on local transportation, intra-European Student Charter flights, and discounts at museums, theaters, sports events, and many other attractions. If purchased in the United States, the $14 ISIC also includes $3,000 in emergency medical insurance, plus $100 a day for up to 60 days of hospital coverage and a collect phone number to call in case of emergency. Apply to the **Council on International Student Exchange** (CIEE), 205 E. 42nd St., 16th Floor, New York, NY 10017, tel. 212/661–1414. In Canada, the ISIC is available for CN$12 from **Travel Cuts** (187 College St., Toronto, Ont. M5T 1P7, tel. 416/979–2406).

The **Youth International Educational Exchange Card** (YIEE), issued by the Federation of International Youth Travel Organizations (FIYTO), 81 Islands Brugge, DK-2300 Copenhagen S, Denmark, provides similar services to nonstudents under age 26. In the United States, the card is available from CIEE (*see* above). In Canada, the YIEE is available from the Canadian Hostelling Association (CHA), 1600 James Naismith Dr., Suite 698, Gloucester, Ont. K1B 5N4, tel. 613/748–5638.

An **International Youth Hostel Federation** (IYHF) membership card is the key to inexpensive dormitory-style accommodations at thousands of youth hostels around the world. Hostels provide separate sleeping quarters for men and women at rates ranging from $7 to $20 a night per person and are situated in a variety of facilities, including converted farmhouses, villas, and restored castles, as well as specially constructed modern buildings. There are more than 5,000 hostel locations in 68 countries around the world. IYHF memberships, which are valid for 12 months from the time of purchase, are available in the United States through American Youth Hostels (AYH; Box 37613, Washington, DC 20013, tel. 202/783–6161). The cost for a first-year membership is $25 for adults 18 to 54. Renewal thereafter is $15. For youths (17 and under) the rate is $10 and for seniors (55 and older) the rate is $15. Family membership is available for $35. Every national hostel association arranges special reductions for members visiting their country, such as discounted rail fare or free bus travel, so be sure to ask for an international concessions list when you buy your membership.

Council Travel, a CIEE subsidiary, is the foremost U.S. student travel agency, specializing in low-cost charters and serving as the exclusive U.S. agent for many student airfare bargains and student tours. (CIEE's 80-age *Student Travel Catalog* and "Council Charter" brochure are available free from any Council Travel office in the United States (enclose $1 postage if ordering by mail). In addition to CIEE headquarters at 205 E. 42nd St. and a branch office at 35 W. 8th St. in New York City, there are Council Travel offices in Berkeley, La Jolla, Long Beach, Los Angeles, San Diego, and San Francisco, California; Chicago, Illinois; Amherst, Boston, and Cambridge, Massachusetts; Portland, Oregon; Providence, Rhode Island; Austin and Dallas, Texas; and Seattle, Washington, to name a few.

The **Educational Travel Center,** another student travel specialist worth contacting for information on student tours, bargain fares, and bookings and may be reached at 438 N. Frances St., Madison, WI 53703, tel. 608/256–5551.

Students who would like to work abroad should contact *CIEE's Work Abroad Department* (at 205 E. 42nd St. in New York City; see above). The council arranges various types of paid and volunteer work experiences overseas for up to six months. CIEE also sponsors study programs in Europe, Latin America, and Asia and publishes many books of interest to the student traveler; these include *Work, Study, Travel Abroad: The Whole World Handbook* ($10.95 plus $1 book-rate postage or $2.50 first-class postage) and *Volunteer! The Comprehensive Guide to Voluntary Service in the U.S. and Abroad* ($6.95 plus $1 book-rate postage or $2.50 first-class postage).

The Information Center at the **Institute of International Education** has reference books, foreign university catalogues, study-abroad brochures, and other materials that may be consulted by students and nonstudents alike, free of charge. The Information Center (809 UN Plaza, New York, NY 10017, tel. 212/984–5413) is open Monday–Friday 10–4. It is not open on weekends or holidays.

IIE administers a variety of grant and study programs offered by U.S. and foreign organizations and publishes a well-known annual series of study-abroad guides, including *Academic Year Abroad* and *Vacation Study Abroad*. The institute also publishes *Teaching Abroad*, a book of employment and study opportunities overseas for U.S. teachers. For a current list of IIE publications with prices and ordering information, write Publications Service, Institute of International Education, 809 UN Plaza, New York, NY 10017. Books must be purchased by mail or in person; telephone orders are not accepted.

General information on IIE programs and services is available from its regional offices in Atlanta, Chicago, Denver, Houston, San Francisco, and Washington, DC.

For information on the Eurail Youthpass, *see* Rail Passes, above.

Traveling with Children

Publications *Family Travel Times* is a newsletter published 10 times a year by **TWYCH** (Travel with Your Children, 80 8th Ave., New York, NY 10011, tel. 212/206–0688). A subscription includes access to back issues and twice-weekly opportunities to call in for specific advice.

Hotels **CIGA** Hotels (reservations: tel. 800/221–2340) have 22 properties in Italy, all of which welcome families. Notable are the two on the Lido in Venice: They are right on the beach and have a parklike area for children to enjoy. **Club Med** (40 W. 57th St., New York, NY 10019, tel. 800/CLUB–MED) has a "Mini Club" (for ages 4–6) and "Kids Club" (for ages 8 and up during school holidays) at its resort village in Sestriere.

Villa Rentals Contact **At Home Abroad, Inc.** (405 E. 56th St., Suite 6H, New York, NY 10022, tel. 212/421–9165); **Villas International** (71 W. 23rd St., New York, NY 10010, tel. 212/929–7585 or 800/221–2260); **Hideaways Int'l** (Box 1270, Littleton, MA 01460, tel. 508/486–8955); **Vacanze in Italia** (Box 297, Falls Village, CT 06031; tel. 203/824–5155 or 800/533–5405); or **Italian Villa Rentals** (Box 1145, Bellevue, WA 98009, tel. 206/827–3694).

Home Exchange Exchanging homes is a surprisingly low-cost way to enjoy a vacation abroad, especially a long one. The largest home-exchange service, **International Home Exchange Service** (Box 190070, San Francisco, CA 94119, tel. 415/435–3497) publishes three directories a year. Membership costs $45 and entitles you to one listing and all three directories. **Loan-a-Home** (2 Park Lane, Apt. 6E Mount Vernon, NY 10552, tel. 914/664–7640) is popular with the academic community on sabbatical and businesspeople on temporary assignment. There's no annual membership fee or charge for listing your home; however, one directory and a supplement costs $45.

Getting There On international flights, children under two not occupying a seat pay 10% of adult fare. Various discounts apply to children two to 12 years of age. Regulations about traveling with infants on airplanes are in the process of changing. Until they do, however, if you want to be sure your infant is secure and traveling in his or her own safety seat, you must buy your baby a separate ticket and bring your own infant car seat. (Check with the airline in advance; certain seats aren't allowed.) Some airlines allow babies to travel in their own car seats at no charge if there's a spare seat available; otherwise safety seats will be stored, and the child will have to be held by a parent. (For the booklet *Child/Infant Safety Seats Acceptable for Use in Aircraft*, write to the Federal Aviation Administration, APA–200, 800 Independence Ave., SW, Washington DC 20591 tel. 202/267–3479.) If you opt to hold your baby on your lap, do so with the infant outside the seatbelt so he or she won't be crushed in case of a sudden stop.

Also inquire about special children's meals or snacks. The February 1990 and 1992 issues of *Family Travel Times* include TWYCH's Airline Guide, which contains a rundown of the children's services offered by 46 airlines.

Hints for Disabled Travelers

The **Information Center for Individuals with Disabilities** (Fort Point Pl., 27–43 Wormwood St., Boston, MA 02210, tel. 617/727–5540; TDD 617/727–5236) offers useful problem-solving assistance, including lists of travel agents that specialize in tours for the disabled.

Moss Rehabilitation Hospital Travel Information Service (1200 West Tabor Rd., Philadelphia, PA 19141–3009, tel. 215/456–9600; TDD 215/456–9602) provides information on tourist sights, transportation, and accommodations in destinations around the world for a small fee.

Mobility International USA (Box 3551, Eugene, OR 97403, tel. 503/343–1284) coordinates exchange programs for disabled people and offers information on accommodations and organized study programs around the world.

The **Society for the Advancement of Travel for the Handicapped** (26 Court St., Penthouse, Brooklyn, NY 11242, tel. 718/858–5483) offers access information. Annual membership costs $45, or $25 for senior travelers and students. Send a stamped, self-addressed envelope.

The Itinerary (Box 2012, Bayonne, NJ 07002, tel. 201/858–3400) is a bimonthly travel magazine for the disabled.

Nautilus Tours (5435 Donna Ave., Tarzana, CA 91356, tel. 818/343–6339) has for nine years operated international trips and cruises for the disabled. **Travel Industry and Disabled Exchange** (TIDE, at the same address, tel. 818/368–5648), an industry-based organization with a $15 annual membership fee, which provides a quarterly newsletter and information on travel agencies and tours.

Access to the World: A Travel Guide for the Handicapped, by Louise Weiss offers tips on travel and accessibility around the world. It is available from Henry Holt & Co. for $12.95 (tel. 800/247–3912; the order number is 0805001417).

Italy has only recently begun to provide for handicapped travelers, and facilities such as ramps, telephones, and toilets for the disabled are still the exception, not the rule. Seats are reserved for the disabled on public transportation, but buses have no lifts for wheelchairs. High, narrow steps for boarding trains create additional problems. In many monuments and museums, even in some hotels and restaurants, architectural barriers make it difficult, if not impossible, for handicapped to gain access. In Rome, however, St. Peter's, the Sistine Chapel, and the Vatican Museums are all accessible by wheelchair.

Hints for Older Travelers

The **American Association of Retired Persons** (AARP, 1909 K St. NW, Washington, DC 20049, tel. 202/662–4850) has two programs for independent travelers: (1) The Purchase Privilege Program, which offers discounts on hotels, airfare, car rentals, and sightseeing, and (2) the AARP Motoring Plan, provided by Amoco, which offers emergency aid and trip routing information, for an annual fee of $33.95 per couple. The AARP also arranges group tours, including apartment living in Europe, through **American Express Vacations** (*see* Tour Groups, above). AARP members must be 50 or older. Annual dues are $5 per person or per couple.

When using an AARP or other identification card, ask for a reduced hotel rate at the time you make your reservation, not when you check out. At participating restaurants, show your card to the maitre d' before you're seated, since discounts may be limited to certain set menus, days, or hours. When renting a car, be sure to ask about special promotional rates which might offer greater savings than the available discount.

Elderhostel (75 Federal St., Boston, MA 02210–1941, tel. 617/426–7788) is an innovative educational program for people 60 and older. Participants live in dorms on some 1,200 campuses around the world. Mornings are devoted to lectures and seminars; afternoons, to sightseeing and field trips. The all-inclusive fee for two- to three-week trips, including room, board, tuition, and round-trip transportation, ranges from $1,800 to $4,500.

Saga International Holidays (120 Boylston St., Boston, MA 02116, tel. 800/343–0273) specializes in group travel for people over age 60. A selection of variously priced tours allows you to choose the package that meets your needs.

National Council of Senior Citizens (925 15th St. NW, Washington, DC 20005, tel. 202/347–8800) is a nonprofit advocacy group with some 5,000 local clubs across the country. Annual membership is $2 per couple. Members receive a monthly newspaper with travel information and an ID card for reduced-rate hotels and car rentals.

Mature Outlook (6001 N. Clark St., Chicago, IL 60660, tel. 800/336–6330), a subsidiary of Sears Roebuck & Co., is a travel club for people over 50 that offers hotel and motel discounts and a bimonthly newsletter. Annual membership is $9.95 per couple. Instant membership is available at participating Holiday Inns.

The **Inter-Rail** senior discount is the only discount available in Italy of interest to older visitors. Older travelers planning to visit Italy during the hottest months should be aware that few public buildings, restaurants, and shops are air-conditioned. Public toilets are few and far between, other than those in coffee bars, restaurants, and hotels. Older travelers may find it difficult to board trains and some buses and trams with very high steps and narrow treads.

Further Reading

To read about other American tourists in Italy, look for *The Enchanted Ground: Americans in Italy, 1760–1980* (1980), by Erik Amfitheatrof. *The Italians*, by Luigi Barzini, is a comprehensive and lively analysis of the Italian national character.

For some good historical fiction set in Italy, pick up Samuel Shellabarger's *Prince of Foxes* (1947), about Renaissance Venice. Irving Stone's *Agony and the Ecstasy* (Doubleday, 1961) is based on the life of Michelangelo. For World War II historical fiction, look for *History: A Novel* by Elsa Morante (Random House); *Two Women* by Alberto Moravia; Walter F. Murphy's *The Roman Enigma* (Macmillan, 1981); John Hersey's *A Bell for Adano* (Knopf, 1944); or *Bread and Wine* (New American Library, 1987) by Ignazio Silone, a novel about Italian peasants under the control of the Fascists. Also, *Century* (NAL, 1981), by Fred M. Stewart, spans several generations of an Italian family.

Adventure novels set in Italy include *Any Four Women Could Rob the Bank of Italy* (Penguin, 1984) by Ann Cornelisen, Helen MacInnes's *North From Rome* (1958) and *The Venetian Affair* (Fawcett, 1963), Ngaio Marsh's *When in Rome* (Amereon Ltd., 1971), Evelyn Anthony's *The Company of Saints* (Putnam, 1984), Daphne DuMaurier's *The Flight of the Falcon* (Avon, 1965), and *Peter's Pence* (1974), by Jon Cleary.

Magdalen Nabb's entertaining thrillers such as *Death in Autumn* (1984) and *Death of a Dutchman* (1982) are set in Florence.

Other recommended titles include *Death in Venice* (Random House, 1965) by Thomas Mann, *Room with a View* (Random House, 1923) by E. M. Forster; Joseph Heller's *Catch-22* (Simon & Schuster, 1961); *A Farewell to Arms* (Scribner's, 1929) by Ernest Hemingway, *The Stories of Elizabeth Spencer* (Penguin, 1981), and *Italian Days* (Weidenfeld and Nicolson, 1989) by Barbara Grizzuti Harrison.

Arriving and Departing

From North America by Plane

Since the air routes between North America and Italy are heavily traveled, the passenger has many airlines and fares from which to choose. Fares change with stunning rapidity, so consult your travel agent on which bargains are currently available.

Be certain to distinguish among nonstop flights (no changes, no stops); direct flights (no changes but one or more stops); and connecting flights (two or more planes, two or more stops).

Airlines The airlines that serve Italy from the United States are **TWA** (tel. 800/892–4141), **Pan Am** (tel. 800/221–1111), and **Alitalia** (tel. 800/442–5860). All fly to Rome and Milan.

Flying Time The flying time to Rome from New York is 8½ hours; from Boston, 7½ hours; Chicago, 10–11 hours; Los Angeles, 12–13 hours.

Discount Flights The major airlines offer a range of tickets that can increase the price of any given seat by more than 300%, depending on the day of purchase. As a rule, the further in advance you buy the ticket, the less expensive it is and the greater the penalty (up to 100%) for canceling. Check with airlines for details.

The best buy is not necessarily an APEX (advance purchase) ticket on one of the major airlines. APEX tickets carry certain restrictions: They must be bought in advance (usually 21 days); they restrict your travel, usually with a minimum stay of seven days and a maximum of 90; and they penalize you for changes—voluntary or not—in your travel plans. But if you can work around these drawbacks (and most travelers can), they are among the best-value fares available.

Travelers willing to put up with some restrictions and inconveniences in exchange for a substantially reduced airfare may be interested in flying as air couriers, to accompany shipments between designated points. For a telephone directory listing courier companies by the cities to which they fly, send $5 and a self-addressed, stamped, business-size envelope to Pacific Data Sales Publishing, 2554 Lincoln Blvd., Suite 275-F, Marina Del Rey, CA 90291. For "A Simple Guide to Courier Travel," send $14.95 (postpaid). Box 2394, Lake Oswego, OR 97035. For more information, call 800/344–9375.

Charter flights offer the lowest fares but often depart only on certain days, and seldom on time. Though you may be able to arrive at one city and return from another, you may lose all or most of your money if you cancel your ticket. Don't sign up for a charter flight unless you've checked with a travel agency about the reputation of the packager. It's particularly important to know the packager's policy concerning refunds. One of the most popular charter operators is **Council Charter** (tel. 212/661–0311 or 800/223–7402), a division of CIEE (Council on International Educational Exchange). Other companies advertise in the Sunday travel section of newspapers.

Somewhat more expensive—but up to 50% below the cost of APEX fares—are tickets purchased through companies known as consolidators that buy blocks of tickets on scheduled airlines and sell them at wholesale prices. Here again, you may lose all or most of your money if you change plans, but at least you will be on a regularly scheduled flight with less risk of cancellation than a charter. Once you've made your reservation, call the airline to make sure you're confirmed. Among the best-known consolidators are **UniTravel** (Box 12485, St. Louis, MO 63132, tel. 314/569–2501 or 800/325–2222) and **Access International** (101 W. 31st St., Suite 1104, New York, NY 10001, tel. 212/465–0707 or 800/825–3633). Others advertise in the Sunday travel section of newspapers as well.

Yet another option is to join a travel club that offers special discounts to its members. Three such organizations are **Moment's Notice** (425 Madison Ave., New York, NY 10017, tel. 212/486–0503); **Discount Travel International** (114 Forrest Ave., Suite 205, Narberth, PA 19072, tel. 215/668–7184); **Traveler's Advantage** (CVC Travel Svce., 40 Oakview Dr., Trumbull, CT 06611, tel. 800/648–4037); and **Worldwide Discount Travel Club** (1674 Meridian Ave., Suite 300, Miami Beach, FL 33139, tel. 305/534–2082). These cut-rate tickets should be compared with APEX tickets on the major airlines.

Enjoying the Flight If you're lucky enough to be able to sleep on a plane, it makes sense to fly at night. Many experienced travelers, however, prefer to take a morning flight to Europe and arrive in the evening, just in time for a good night's sleep. Since the air on a plane is dry, it helps, while flying, to drink a lot of nonalcoholic liquids; drinking alcohol contributes to jet lag, as does eating heavy meals on board. Feet swell at high altitudes, so it's a good idea to remove your shoes while in flight. Sleepers usually prefer window seats to curl up in; those who like to move about the cabin should ask for aisle seats. Bulkhead seats (located in the front row of each cabin) have more legroom, but seat trays are attached to the arms of your seat rather than to the back of the seat in front.

From the U.K. by Plane, Car, Train, and Bus

By Plane **Alitalia** (tel. 01/081/745–8200) and **British Airways** (tel. 01/897–4000) operate direct flights from London (Heathrow) to Rome, Milan, Venice, Pisa, and Naples. Flying time is 2½ to three hours. There's also one direct flight a day from Manchester to Rome. Standard fares are extremely high. Several less expensive tickets are available. Both airlines offer APEX tickets (usual booking restrictions apply) and PEX tickets (which don't have to be bought in advance). The Eurobudget ticket (no length-of-stay or advance-purchase restrictions) is another option. Air Europe offers low fares.

Less expensive flights are available: It pays to look around in the classified advertisements of reputable newspapers and magazines such as *Time Out*. But remember to check the *full* price, inclusive of airport taxes, fuel, and surcharges. Some of the bargains are not as inexpensive as they seem at first glance.

By Car The distance from London to Rome is 1,124 miles via Calais/Boulogne/Dunkirk and 1,084 miles via Oostende/Zeebrugge (excluding sea crossings). Milan is about 400 miles closer. The drive from the Continental ports takes about 24 hours; the trip in total takes about three days. The shortest and quickest channel crossings are via Dover or Folkestone to one of the French ports (Calais or Boulogne); the ferry takes around 75 minutes and the Hovercraft just 35 minutes. Crossings from Dover to the Belgian ports take about four hours, but Oostende and Zeebrugge have good road connections. The longer crossing from Hull to Zeebrugge is useful for travelers from the north of England. The Sheerness-Vlissingen (Holland) route makes a comfortable overnight crossing; it takes about nine hours.

Fares on the cross-channel ferries vary considerably from season to season. Until the end of June and from early September onward, savings can be made by traveling midweek. Don't forget to budget for the cost of gas and road tolls, plus a couple of nights' accommodations, especially if crossing in daytime.

Roads from the channel ports to Italy are generally good and are mostly toll-free. The exceptions are the road crossing the Ardennes, the Swiss superhighway network (for which a special tax sticker must be bought at the frontier or in advance), the St. Gotthard Tunnel, and the road between the tunnel and the Italian superhighway system. Remember that the Italian government offers special packages of reduced-price petrol coupons (15%–20% off) and highway toll vouchers. They must be bought in advance from the **AA, RAC,** or **CIT** (50 Conduit St., London W1R 9FB, tel. 071/434–3844). These are available to personal callers only; the driver must produce his or her passport and vehicle registration document when applying.

If these distances seem to great to drive, there's always the Motorail from the channel ports. However, no car/sleeper expresses run beyond Milan, 390 miles north of the capital.

By Train Visitors traveling to Italy by train have several options. You can leave London's Victoria train station at 11:30 AM for Folkestone and Boulogne; from Boulogne Maritime, you take the train to Gare du Nord in Paris and then a taxi or metro across town to Gare de Lyons. From there, you pick up the "Napoli Express" for Rome. There are first- and second-class sleeping cars and second-class couchettes for the overnight run into Italy. From Paris to Dijon there's a refreshment service, and a buffet car is attached in the morning. The train reaches Turin at 5:46 AM and Rome about 1:35 PM the next day.

Alternatively, the 10 AM train from Victoria meets the Hovercraft in time for a crossing to Paris via Boulogne. It arrives at 4:30 PM, which gives you plenty of time to cross Paris by metro or taxi to catch the 6:47 PM Paris–Rome "Palatino" service. If you don't like the Hovercraft, the 9:15 AM Victoria service catches the Dover–Calais ferry crossing; arrival time in Paris is 5:20 PM. The "Palatino" leaves Paris at Gare de Lyons and travels via Chambéry and the Mont Cenis tunnel to Turin, arriving about 2:50. You reach Rome by 9:35 AM. The train has first- and second-class sleepers and second-class couchettes, but no ordinary day cars for sitting up overnight. There's a buffet car from Paris to Chambéry and from Genoa to Rome.

A year-round service leaves Victoria at 1:30, catching the Jetfoil for Oostende in plenty of time to take the 8:53 PM train to Basel. Change there and take the 7:22 AM train, which gets you to Rome by 6:05 PM.

Train, ferry, and hovercraft schedules are subject to change, so consult with **French Railways** (tel. 071/493–9731) and **British Rail** (tel. 071/928–5151) before you leave.

By Bus **Eurolines** (13 Lower Regent St., London SW1Y 4LR, tel. 071/730–0202, or any National Express agent) runs a weekly bus service to Rome that increases to three times a week between June and September. Buses leave on Sunday, Wednesday, and Friday over the summer, and on Sunday the rest of the year. The trip takes about 2½ days. Buses travel via Dover, Calais, Paris, and Lyon. Have a few French francs for spending en route. Fares are quite high, especially when you consider the long and tiring overnight journey and compare the price with that of a charter flight. Further details are available from National Express, at the Eurolines address (*see* above).

Staying in Italy

Getting Around

By Plane **Alitalia** and its domestic affiliates **ATI** and **Aermed,** in addition to smaller, privately run companies such as **Aliblu,** complete an extensive network of internal flights in Italy. Apart from the major international airports, you can find frequent flights between airports serving smaller cities, such as Bologna, Genoa, Naples, Palermo, Turin, and Verona. Flight times are never much more than an hour (long flights usually are those going from the extreme north to Naples or Sicily), and most of these smaller airports are close to the cities and linked by good bus services. Italian travel agents will inform you of the discounts available, some of which include a 50% family reduction for a spouse and/or children traveling with you, or up to 30% for certain night flights.

By Train The fastest trains on the **FS**, the state-owned railroad, are *Intercity* and *Rapido* trains, for which you pay a supplement and for which seat reservations may be required and are always advisable. *Espresso* trains usually make more stops and are a little slower. *Diretto* and *Locale* are the slowest.

To avoid long lines at station windows, buy tickets and make seat reservations at least a day in advance at travel agencies displaying the FS emblem. If you have to reserve at the last minute, reservation offices at the station accept reservations up to three hours before departure. You can also get a seat assignment just before boarding the train; look for the conductor on the platform near the train. Trains can be very crowded on weekends and during holiday and vacation seasons; we strongly advise reserving seats in advance or, if the train originates where you get on, getting to the station early to find a seat. Carry compact bags for easy overhead storage. You can buy train tickets for destinations close to main cities at tobacconists.

Note that in some Italian cities (including Milan, Turin, Genoa, Naples, and Rome) there are two or more main-line stations, although one is usually the principal terminus or through-station. Be sure of the name of the station at which your train will arrive, or from which it will depart.

There is refreshment service on all long-distance trains, with mobile carts and a cafeteria or dining car. Tap water on trains is not potable.

Rail Passes For those planning on doing a lot of traveling by train, the **Italian RailPass** is an excellent value. (*See* Rail Passes in Before You Go, above.)

By Bus Italy's bus network is extensive, although not as attractive as those in other European countries, partly because of the low cost of train travel. Buses operated by members of **ANAC** (Piazza Esquilino 29, Rome, tel. 06/463383) travel the length of the country, and most are air-conditioned and comfortable. An up-to-date timetable, published by ANAC, is available from the above address or from most tourist information offices within Italy. **SITA** (Viale Cadorna 105, Florence, tel. 055/278611) operates a similar service, and its schedule is available at tourist offices or at its office at the address above.

Local bus companies operate in many regions (*see* Getting Around By Bus in most chapters). In the hillier parts of Italy, particularly in the Alpine north, they take over when the gradients become too steep for train travel. A village shop or café will sometimes double as the ticket office and bus stop for these services. You should have your ticket before you board.

Most of the major cities have urban bus services, usually operating on a system involving the prepurchase of tickets (from a machine or a tobacco store). These services are inexpensive, but the buses can become unbearably jammed at rush hours. Remember that there are also lunchtime rush hours in the hotter periods, particularly in the south, when people go home for a siesta.

By Car There is an extensive network of *autostrade* (toll highways), complemented by equally well-maintained but free *superstrade* (expressways). All are clearly signposted and numbered. The ticket you are issued upon entering an autostrada must be returned when you exit and pay the toll. On some shorter autostrade, mainly connecting highways, you pay the toll upon entering. A *raccordo* is a connecting expressway. *Strade statali* (state highways) may be single-lane roads, as are all secondary roads; directions and turnoffs are not always clearly marked. You can obtain a good road map from **ACI** (Automobile Club of Italy, Via Marsala 8, 00185 Rome, tel. 06/49981 and from other offices throughout Italy).

Rules of the Road Driving is on the right, as in the United States. Regulations are largely as in Britain and the United States, except that the police have the power to levy on-the-spot fines. In most Italian towns the use of the horn is forbidden in certain, if not all, areas; a large sign, *Zona di Silenzio*, indicates where. Speed limits are 130 kmh (80 mph) on autostrade and 110 kmh (70 mph) on state and provincial roads, unless otherwise marked. Fines for driving after drinking are heavy, with the additional possibility of six months' imprisonment, but there is no fixed blood-alcohol regulation and no official test.

Parking   In most cities, parking space is at a premium; historic town centers are closed to most traffic, and peripheral parking areas are usually full. Parking in *Zona Disco* is allowed for limited periods. It's advisable to leave your car in a guarded parking area; many are run by ACI. Unofficial parking attendants can help you find a space but offer no guarantees. In major cities your car may be towed away if illegally parked.

Gas   Gas costs the equivalent of about $5 a U.S. gallon, or about 1,596 lire a liter. Only a few gas stations are open on Sunday, and most close for a couple of hours at lunchtime and at 7 PM for the night. Self-service pumps may be few and far between outside major cities. Gas stations on autostrade are open 24 hours.

Breakdowns   **ACI Emergency Service** (Servizio Soccorso Stradale, Via Solferino 32, 00185 Rome, tel. 06/475–5251) offers 24-hour road service. Dial 116 from any phone to reach the nearest ACI service station.

Telephones

Local Calls   Pay phones take either a 200-lire coin, two 100-lire coins, or a *gettone* (token). If you happen upon an older phone that takes only tokens, insert the token (which doesn't drop right away), dial your number, wait for an answer, then complete the connection by pushing the knob at the token slot. The token drops, and the other party can hear you. Buy tokens from the nearest cashier or the token machine near the phone. In some airports and railway stations, you will also find the new *scheda* phones, which take cards instead of coins. You buy the card at Telefoni offices, for 3,000, 6,000, or 10,000 lire. Insert the card as indicated by the arrow on it, and you will see the value of the card in the window. After the call, hang up, and the card will be returned. It can be used until its value runs out. For long-distance direct dialing (*teleselezione*), insert at least five coins and have more handy. Unused coins will be returned. It's easier to use the card.

International Calls   Since hotels tend to overcharge, sometimes exorbitantly, for long-distance and international calls, it is best to make such calls from Telefoni offices, where operators will assign you a booth, help you place your call, and collect payment when you have finished, at no extra charge. There are Telefoni offices, designated *SIP* (sometimes also *ASST*), in all cities and towns. In major cities you can charge calls, using AT&T or similar cards. You can make collect calls from any phone by dialing tel. 170, which will get you an English-speaking operator. Rates to the United States are lowest round the clock on Sunday and 11 PM–8 AM, Italian time, on weekdays.

Operators and Information   For general information in English on calling in Europe and the Mediterranean area, dial 176. For operator-assisted service in those areas, dial 15. For operator-assisted service and information regarding intercontinental calls, dial 170.

Mail

Postal Rates   Airmail letters (lightweight stationery) to the United States and Canada cost 1,100 lire for the first 19 grams and an additional 1,700 lire for up to 50 grams. Airmail postcards cost 950 lire if the message is limited to a few words and a signature; otherwise, you pay the letter rate. Airmail letters to the United Kingdom cost 750 lire; postcards, 650 lire. You can buy stamps at tobacconists.

Receiving Mail   Mail service is generally slow; allow up to 14 days for mail from Britain, 21 days from North America. Correspondence can be addressed to you care of the Italian post office. Letters should be addressed to your name, "c/o Palazzo delle Poste," with the name of the city, and should be marked *Fermo Posta*. You can collect mail at the central post office by showing your passport or photo-bearing ID and paying a small fee. American Express also has a general-delivery service for clients. There's no charge for cardholders, holders of American Express Traveler's checks, or anyone who booked a vacation with American Express.

Tipping

Tipping practices vary, depending on where you are. The following guidelines apply in major cities, but Italians tip smaller amounts in smaller cities and towns. Tips may not be expected in cafés and taxis north of Rome.

In restaurants a service charge of about 15% usually appears as a separate item on your check. A few restaurants state on the menu that cover and service charge are included. Either way, it's customary to leave an additional 5%–10% tip for the waiter, depending on the service. Checkroom attendants expect 500 lire per person. Restroom attendants are given from 200 lire in public restrooms, and more in expensive hotels and restaurants. Tip 100 lire for whatever you drink standing up at a coffee bar, 500 lire or more for table service in a smart café, and less in neighborhood cafés. At a hotel bar tip 1,000 lire for a round or two of cocktails.

Taxi drivers are usually happy with 5%–10% of the meter amount. Railway and airport porters charge a fixed rate per bag. Tip an additional 500 lire per person, but more if the porter is very helpful. Theater ushers expect 500 lire per person, but more for very expensive seats. Give a barber 1,000–2,000 lire and a hairdresser's assistant 2,000–5,000 lire for a shampoo or cut, depending on the type of establishment.

On sightseeing tours, tip guides about 1,000 lire per person for a half-day group tour, but give them more if they are very good. In some museums and other places of interest, admission is free, but an offering is expected; anything from 500 to 1,000 lire for one or two persons is usually welcome, but you may wish to give more if the guardian has been especially helpful. Service station attendants are tipped only for special services.

In hotels, give the *portiere* about 15% of his bill for services, or 5,000–10,000 lire if he has been generally helpful. For two people in a double room, leave the chambermaid about 1,000 lire per day, or about 4,000–5,000 a week, in a Moderate hotel (*see* Dining and Lodging in individual chapters for a definition of price categories); tip a minimum of 1,000 lire for valet or room service. Increase these amounts by one-half in an Expensive hotel, and double them in a Very Expensive hotel. Tip doormen in a Very Expensive hotel 1,000 lire for calling a cab and 2,000 lire for carrying bags to the check-in desk. In a Moderate hotel, if there is a doorman, tip 500 and 1,000 lire for these services. In a Very Expensive hotel tip a bellhop 2,000–5,000 lire for carrying your bags to the room and 2,000–3,000 lire for room service. In a Moderate hotel tip a bellhop 1,000–2,000 lire for carrying your bags and 1,000–2,000 for room service.

Opening and Closing Times

Banks Branches are open weekdays 8:30–1:30 and 2:45–3:45.

Churches Most are open from early morning until noon or 12:30, when they close for two hours or more; they open again in the afternoon, closing about 7 PM or later. Major cathedrals and basilicas, such as St. Peter's, are open all day. Sightseeing in churches during religious rites is usually discouraged. Be sure to have a fistful of 100-lire coins handy for the *luce* (light) machines that illuminate the works of art in the perpetual dusk of ecclesiastical interiors. A pair of binoculars will help you get a good look at painted ceilings and domes.

Museums Hours vary and may change with the seasons. Many important national museums have short hours and are closed one day a week, often on Monday. They are open on some holidays, closed on others. Check individual listings in the individual chapters and always check locally. Remember that ticket offices close from 30 minutes to one hour before official closing time.

Shops There are individual variations, depending on climate and season, but most are open 9:30–1 and 3:30 or 4–7 or 7:30. Food shops open earlier in the morning and later in the afternoon. In all but resorts and small towns, shops close on Sunday and one half-day during the week. Some tourist-oriented shops in places such as Rome and Venice are open all day, as are some department stores and supermarkets. Post offices are open 8–2; central and main district post offices stay open until 8 or 9 PM for some operations. Barbers and hairdressers, with some exceptions, are closed Sunday and Monday.

National Holidays New Year's Day (Epiphany, January 6); Easter Sunday and Monday (April 19, 20); Liberation Day (April 25); May Day (May 1); Republic Day (June 2); the Assumption of Mary, also known as Ferragosto (August 15); All Saints Day (November 1); Immaculate Conception (December 8); Christmas (December 25, 26). In addition, there are local holidays for patron saints and festivals.

Shopping

The best buys in Italy are leather goods of all kinds—from gloves to bags to jackets—in addition to silk goods, knitwear, gold jewelry, ceramics, and local handicrafts. Every region has its local specialties. Venice is known for glassware, lace, and velvet; and Florence for straw goods, gold jewelry, and leather.

Unless your purchases are too bulky, avoid having them shipped home; if the shop seems extremely reliable about shipping, get a written statement of what will be sent, when, and how. (*See* Shopping in individual chapters for details.)

IVA (VAT) Refunds Unless you are planning to spend more than 605,000 lire in one shop, the IVA refund system is too complex and time consuming to be feasible.

Bargaining The notice *Prezzi fissi* (fixed prices) means just that; in shops displaying this sign it's a waste of time to bargain unless you're buying a sizable quantity of goods or a particularly costly object. Always bargain, instead, at outdoor markets and when buying from street vendors.

Participant Sports

Italians are sports lovers, and there are several daily newspapers devoted solely to sports. The climate makes it almost impossible to resist the temptation to try a cannonball serve on the red-clay tennis courts, sink a birdie putt on a scenic green, or just hike up a hill to savor the fresh air and views.

Golf Relatively new to Italy, golf is catching on, and more courses are being laid out near major cities. For information, contact **Federazione Italiana Golf** (Via Flaminia 388, 00196 Rome, tel. 06/394641).

Tennis Tennis is one of Italy's most popular sports, and most towns and villages have public courts available for a booking fee. Many hotels have courts that are open to the public, and some private clubs offer temporary visitors' memberships to those traveling through the country. Contact local tourist offices for information.

Spectator Sports

Soccer *Calcio* (soccer) is the most popular spectator sport in Italy. All major cities, and most smaller ones, have teams playing in one league or another. Big-league games are played on Sunday afternoons from September to May. Inquire locally or write to **Federazione Italiana Giuoco Calcio** (Via G. Allegri 14, 00198 Rome, tel. 06/84911).

Horse Racing There are tracks in Milan, Rome, Palermo, and many other cities. Inquire locally for the best racing days.

Basketball Many Americans play on Italian pro teams, and basketball is gaining a big following around the country. For information, contact **Federazione Italiana Pallacanestro** (Via Fogliano 15 00199 Rome, tel. 06/816071).

Tennis A major international Grand Prix tennis tournament is held in Rome in May.

Dining

Dining in Italy is a pleasant aspect of the total Italian experience, a chance to enjoy authentic Italian specialties and ingredients. Visitors have a choice of eating places, ranging from a *ristorante* (restaurant) to a *trattoria, tavola calda,* or *rosticceria.* A trattoria is usually a family-run place, simpler in decor, menu, and service than a ristorante, and slightly less expensive. Some rustic-looking spots call themselves *osteria* but are really restaurants. (A true osteria is a wineshop, a very basic and down-to-earth tavern.) The countless fast-food places opening up everywhere are variations of the older Italian institutions of the tavola calda or rosticceria, which offer a selection of hot and cold dishes that you may take out or eat on the premises. (A tavola calda is more likely to have seating.) At a tavola calda or rosticceria, some items are priced by the portion, others by weight. You usually select your food, find out how much it costs, then pay the cashier and get a stub that you must give to the counterman when you pick up the food.

None of the above serves breakfast; in the morning you go to a coffee bar, which is where, later in the day, you will also find brioches and pastry and other snacks. In a bar you tell the cashier what you want, pay for it, and then take the stub to the counter, where you order. Remember that table service is extra, and you are expected not to occupy tables unless you are being served; on the other hand, you can linger as long as you like at a table without being pressed to move on.

In eating places of all kinds, the menu is always posted in the window or just inside the door so you can see what you're getting into (in a snack bar or tavola calda the price list is usually displayed near the cashier). In all but the simplest places there's a *coperto* (cover charge) and usually also a *servizio* (service charge) of 10%–15%, only part of which goes to the waiter. These extra charges will increase your check by 15%–20%. A *menu turistico* (tourist menu) includes taxes and service, but beverages are usually extra.

Beware of items on à la carte menus marked "SQ" (according to quantity), which means you will be charged according to the weight of the item you have ordered, or "L. 4,000 hg," which means the charge will be 4,000 lire per hectogram (3½ ounces). This type of price generally refers to items such as fresh fish or Florentine steaks and fillets.

Mealtimes Lunch is served in Rome from 1 to 3, dinner from 8 to 10, or later in some restaurants. Service begins and ends a half-hour earlier in Florence and Venice. Almost all eating places close one day a week and for vacations in summer and/or winter.

Precautions Tap water is safe almost everywhere unless labeled *"Non Potabile."* Most people order bottled *acqua minerale* (mineral water), either *gassata* (bubbles) or *naturale*, or *non gassata* (without). In a restaurant you order it by the *litro* (liter) or *mezzo litro* (half-liter), often the waiter will bring it without being asked, so if you don't like it, or want to keep your check down, make a point of ordering *acqua semplice* (tap water). You can also order *un bicchiere di acqua minerale* (a glass of mineral water) at any bar. If you are on a low-sodium diet, ask for everything (within reason) *senza sale* (without salt).

Ratings Restaurants in our listings are divided by price into four categories: Very Expensive, Expensive, Moderate, and Inexpensive. (*See* Dining in individual chapters for specific prices, which vary from region to region.) Prices quoted are for a three-course meal with house wine, including all service and taxes; particularly recommended establishments are indicated by a star ★.

Lodging

Italy offers a good choice of accommodations, especially in the main tourist capitals of Rome, Florence, and Venice. However, it's becoming more difficult to find satisfactory accommodations in the lower categories in these cities, where many hotels are being refurbished and upgraded. Throughout Italy you will find everything from deluxe five-star hotels to charming country inns, villas for rent, camping grounds, and hostels, in addition to well-equipped vacation villages in resort areas. In the major cities, room rates are on a par with other European capitals: Deluxe and superior first-class rates can be downright extravagant. In those categories, ask for one of the better rooms, since less desirable rooms—and there usually are some—don't give you what you're paying for. Otherwise, consider booking the better rooms in hotels that are one category lower than what you would ordinarily ask for. Hotels are justifying higher rates by refurbishing rooms and bathrooms and installing such accessories as hair dryers and personal safes. Such amenities as porters, room service, and in-house cleaning and laundering are disappearing in Moderate and Inexpensive hotels.

Taxes and service are included in the room rate, although a 19% IVA tax may be a separate item in deluxe hotels. Breakfast is an extra, optional, charge, but most hotels quote rates inclusive of breakfast. You are under no obligation to take breakfast at your hotel, but in practice most hotels expect you to do so.

Moderate and Inexpensive hotels may charge extra for optional air-conditioning. In older hotels the quality of rooms may be very uneven; if you don't like the room you're given, ask for another. This applies to noise, too. Front rooms may be larger and have a view, but they also may get a lot of noise. Specify if you care about having either a bath or shower, since not all rooms have both. In the Moderate and Inexpensive categories, showers may be the drain-in-the-floor type, guaranteed to flood the bathroom. Major cities have hotel-reservation service booths in train stations.

Hotels Italian hotels are officially classified from five-star (deluxe) to one-star (guest houses and small inns). Prices are established by local authorities and are listed in the *Annuari Alberghi* (hotel yearbooks), available at tourist information offices but rarely up to date. The rate quoted is for the room, unless otherwise stated. A rate card on the door of your room or inside the closet door tells you exactly what you will pay for that particular room. Any unforeseen variations are cause for complaint and should be reported to the local tourist office. **CIGA, Jolly, Space, Atahotels,** and **Italhotels** are among the reliable chains or groups operating in Italy. CIGA owns some of Italy's most luxurious properties, and Space hotels generally are well run, with a distinctive character. **Relais et Chateaux** hotels are small, quiet, and posh. Jolly hotels and the **AGIP** motels on main highways offer functional but anonymous accommodations that are the best choice in many out-of-the-way places.

Rentals Ideal for families and for extended vacations, rented villas offer fully equipped accommodations, often with maid service included. Make sure you see a photograph of the place you're intending to rent before you commit yourself. Also, make plans early because rentals are increasingly popular.

In the United States, **Villas International** (71 W. 23 St., New York, NY 10010, tel. 212/929–7585 or 800/221–2260) has villas and apartments in major cities, many in the Tuscany area. **At Home Abroad, Inc.** (405 E. 56 St., New York, NY 10022, tel. 212/421–9165) and **Hometours International, Inc.** (1170 Broadway, New York, NY 10001, tel. 212/689–0851 or 800/367–4668, fax 212/689–0679) have properties all over Europe, including a good selection in Italy.

Two London-based companies have a good selection of rentals on their books. **Villas Italia Ltd** (227 Shepherds Bush Rd., London W6, tel. 081/740–9988) has villas in Tuscany, Rome, and Positano. **CV Travel** (43 Cadogan St., London SW3 2PR, tel. 071/581–0851) has properties to rent in Tuscany and Porto Ercole: Choices include a palazzo in southern Italy and luxurious apartments on the sea.

Youth Hostels There are about 155 hostels in Italy, some in beautiful settings. Hostel rates are about 10,000 lire per person per night, including breakfast, but it's not easy to find accommodations, especially in tourist centers, unless you have reservations. Contact the **Associazione Italiana Alberghi per la Gioventù** (Piazza Civiltà del Lavoro, Quadrato della Concordia, 00144 Rome), a member of the International Youth Hostel Federation.

In the United States, contact **American Youth Hostels, Inc.** (Box 37613, Washington, DC 20013–7613, tel. 202/783–6161). In Canada contact the **Canadian Hostelling Association's** national office (1600 James Naismith Dr., Suite 608, Gloucester, Ontario K1B 5N4, tel. 613/784–5638). In the United Kingdom, contact the **International Youth Hostel Federation** (9 Guessens Rd., Welwyn City, Herts. AL8 6QW, tel. 707/332–487).

Ratings Hotels in our listings are divided by price into four categories: Very Expensive, Expensive, Moderate, and Inexpensive. (*See* Lodging sections in individual chapters for specific prices, which differ according to region.) Hotels in some regions, particularly the northern mountainous areas, offer attractive half- and full-board packages (in which some or all meals are included in the price) and usually require that you stay a number of days. These deals can often "lower" an establishment into a less expensive classification in real terms because the inclusive deal is a bargain. Particularly recommended places in each price category are indicated by a star ★.

Credit Cards

The following credit card abbreviations are used: AE, American Express; DC, Diners Club; MC, MasterCard; V, Visa.

2 Portrait of Italy

Italian Art
Through the Ages

by Sheila
Brownlee

A long-time
contributor to
Fodor's Guides,
Sheila Brownlee
is an art
historian who
writes regularly
on the arts for
many
publications.

Italy is the nursery of Western art. The discoveries that Italian artists made in the 14th and 15th centuries about how to render a realistic image of a person or an object determined the course of art in the Western world right up until the late 19th century, when, with the introduction of photography, representational art went out of fashion.

Art in the Middle Ages

The eastern half of the Roman Empire, based in Constantinople (Byzantium) remained powerful long after the fall of Rome in AD 476. Italy remained influenced—and at times ruled—by the Byzantines. The artistic revolution began when artists started to rebel against the Byzantine ethic, which dictated that art be exclusively Christian and that its aim be to arouse a sensation of mystical awe and reverence in the onlooker. This ethic forbade frivolous pagan portraits, bacchanalian orgy scenes, or delicate landscapes with maidens gathering flowers, as painted and sculpted by the Romans. Instead, biblical stories were depicted in richly colored mosaics—rows of figures against a gold background. (You can see some of the finest examples of this art at Ravenna, once the Western capital of the Empire, on the Adriatic coast.) Even altarpieces, painted on wood, followed the same model—stiff figures surrounded by gold, with no attempt made at an illusion of reality.

In the 13th century, the era of St. Francis and of a new humanitarian approach to Christianity, artists in Tuscany began to make an effort to portray real people in real settings. Cimabue was the first to feel his way in this direction, but it was Giotto who broke decisively with the Byzantine style. Even if his sense of perspective was nowhere near correct and his figures still had typically Byzantine slanting eyes, he was painting palpably solid people who you could tell were subject to real emotions.

By the end of the 14th century the International Gothic Style (which had arrived in Italy from France) had made further progress toward realism, but more with depictions of plants, animals, and clothes than with the human figure. And, as you can see from Gentile da Fabriano's *Adoration of the Magi,* in the Uffizi Gallery, in Florence, it was mainly a decorative art, still very much like a Byzantine mosaic.

Italian architecture during the Middle Ages followed a number of different trends. In the south, the solid Norman Romanesque style was predominant; towns such as Siena or Pisa in central Italy had their own individual Romanesque style, more graceful than its northern European counterparts. Like northern Romanesque, it was dominated by simple geometrical forms, but buildings were covered with decorative toylike patterns done in multicolored marble. In northern Italy building was in a more solemn red brick.

In Tuscany, the region around Florence, the 13th century was a time of great political and economic growth, and there was a desire to reflect the new wealth and power in the region's buildings. This is why civic centers such as the Palazzo Vecchio in Florence are so big and fortresslike. Florence's cathedral, the Duomo, was built on a colossal scale mainly in order to outdo the Pisans and the Sienese, Florence's rivals. All these Tuscan cathedrals are in the Italian version of Gothic, a style that originated in France and found its expression there in tall, soaring, light-and-airy verticality, intended to elevate the soul. The spiritual aspect of Gothic never really caught on in Italy, where the top priority for a church (as representative of a city) was to be grander and more imposing than the neighboring cities' churches.

Art in the Renaissance

The Renaissance, or "rebirth," did not evolve simply from a set of new-found artistic skills; the movement comprised a revolution in attitudes, in which each individual was thought to have a specific role to play in the divine scheme of things. By fulfilling this role, it was believed, the individual gained a new dignity. It was no coincidence that this revolution should have taken place in Florence, which in the 15th century was an influential, wealthy, highly evolved city-state. Artists here had the leisure, the prestige, and the self-confidence to develop their talent and produce works that would reflect this new dignity and strength, as well as their own prowess.

The sculptor Donatello, for instance, wanted to astound, rather than please, the spectator with his defiant warts-and-all likenesses and their intense, heroic gazes. In painting, Masaccio's figures have a similarly assured air.

Art had changed gears in the early Renaissance: The Classical Age was now the model for a noble, moving, and realistic art. Artists studied ancient Roman ruins for what they could learn about proportion and balance. They evolved the new science of perspective and took it to its limits with sometimes bizarre results, as in Uccello's dizzily receding *Deluge* (in Florence's church of Santa Maria Novella), or his carousellike *Battle of San Romano* (in the Uffizi in Florence). One of the most frequently used perspective techniques was that of foreshortening or making an object seem smaller and more contracted, to create the illusion of distance. From this technique emerged the *Sotto in Su* effect—literally, "from below upwards," meaning that the action in the picture takes place above you, with figures, buildings, and landscapes correspondingly foreshortened. It's a clever visual trick that must have delighted the visitors who walked into, for example, Mantegna's Camero degli Sposi, in Mantua, and saw what appeared to be people looking curiously down at them through a gap in the ceiling.

The concept of the universal man was epitomized by the artist who was at home with an array of disciplines, including the science of perspective, Greek, Latin, anatomy, sculpture, poetry, architecture, philosophy—even engineering, as in the case of Leonardo da Vinci, the universal man par excellence. Not surprisingly, there was a change in attitude toward artists: Whereas previously they had been considered merely anonymous workmen trained to carry out commissions, now they were seen as giant personalities, immensely skillful, with highly individual styles.

The new skills and realistic effects of Florentine painting rapidly found a sympathetic response among Venetian painters. Gentile Bellini and Antonio Carpaccio, just two of the many whose work fills the Accademia, took to covering their canvases with crowd scenes, buildings, canals, processions, dogs, ships, parrots, chimneys. These were generally narrative paintings, telling the story of a saint's life or simply everyday scenes recording a particular event.

It was its emphasis on color, though, that made Venetian art Venetian, and it was the 15th-century masters of color, preeminently Giovanni Bellini and Giorgione, who began to use it no longer as decoration but as a means to create a particular atmosphere. Imagine how different the effect of Giorgione's *Tempest* (in the Accademia) would be with a sunny blue sky instead of the ominous grays and dark greens that fill the background. For the first time, the atmosphere, not the figures, became the central focus of the painting.

In architecture the Gothic excesses of the 13th century were toned down in the 14th, while the 15th ushered in a completely new approach. The humanist ideal was expressed through classical Roman design. In Florence, Brunelleschi used Roman columns for the Basilica of San Lorenzo; Roman-style rustication (massive rough-surfaced blocks on the exteriors) for the Pitti Palace; and Roman round arches—as opposed to pointed Gothic ones—for his Spedale degli Innocenti (Foundling Hospital), which is generally considered the first truly classical building of the Renaissance. Leon Battista Alberti's treatise on ideal proportion was even more influential as a manifesto of the Renaissance movement. Suddenly, architects had become erudite scholars, and architecture correspondingly far more earnest.

High Renaissance and Mannerism

Florence in the late 15th century, and Rome in the early 16th, (following its sack in 1527) underwent a traumatic political and religious upheaval that naturally came to be reflected in art. Classical proportion and realism no longer seemed enough. Heroism suddenly looked hollow and out of date. Tuscan artists such as Pontormo and Rosso found expression for their unease in discordant colors, elongated forms, tortured looks in staring eyes. Giambologna carved his *Hercules and the Centaur* (in Florence's Museo del Bargello) at the most agonizing moment of their battle, when Hercules bends the Centaur's back to the point where it is about to snap. This is Mannerism, a style in which optimism and self-confidence are gone. What remains is a self-conscious, stylized show of virtuosity, the effect of which is neither to please (like Gothic) nor to impress (like Renaissance art), but to disquiet. Even Bronzino's portraits are cold and unsmiling and far removed from the relaxed mood of the Renaissance portrait. By the 1530s an artistic exodus from Florence had taken place; Michelangelo had left for Rome, and Florence's golden age was over.

Venice meanwhile was following its own path. Titian's painting was a more virtuoso version of Bellini's and Giorgione's poetic style, but Titian later shifted the emphasis back to the figures, rather than the atmosphere, as the central focus of his paintings. Titian's younger contemporaries in Venice—Veronese, Tintoretto, and Bassano—wanted to make names for themselves independently of Titian. They started working on huge canvases—which gave them more freedom of movement—playing all sorts of visual games, juggling with viewpoints and perspective and using dazzlingly bright colors. This visual trickery suggests a natural parallel with the self-conscious artifice of Florentine painting of the same period, but the exuberance of these Venetian painters, and the increasingly emotional quality of their work, chiefly their mysterious and subtle use of color, always remained significantly more vital than the arid and ever more sterile products of central Italy toward the end of the 16th century.

Mannerism found a fairly precise equivalent in architecture. In Florence the rebellious younger generation (Michelangelo, Ammanati, Vasari) used the same architectural vocabulary as the Renaissance architects, but distorted it deliberately and bizarrely in a way that would have made Alberti's hair stand on end. Michelangelo's staircase at the Biblioteca Laurenziana, in Florence, for instance, spreads out like a stone fan, filling almost the entire floor space of the vestibule. Likewise, the inside walls are treated as if they were facades, though with columns and niches disproportionately large for the size of the room.

Andrea del Palladio was one of the greatest architects of
the period, whose theories and elegant palaces were to be
immensely influential on architecture elsewhere in Europe
and as far north as England.

The 17th and 18th Centuries

In the second half of the 16th century, Italy was caught up
in the Counter-Reformation. This movement was a reaction
against the Protestant Reformation of the Christian church
that was sweeping through Europe. The Counter-Reformation enlisted art as a weapon: an instrument for the diffu-
sion of the Catholic faith. Artists were discouraged from
expressing themselves as freely as they had before and
from creating anything that was not of a religious nature.
But within this religious framework, they were able to
evolve a style that appealed to the senses.

The Baroque—an emotional and heroic style that lasted
through most of the 17th century—was propaganda art,
designed to overwhelm the masses through its visual illusion, dramatic lighting, strong colors, and violent movement. There was an element of seduction in this
propaganda: The repressive religiosity of the Counter-Reformation went hand in hand with a barely disguised eroti-
cism. The best-known example of this ambiguity is
Bernini's sculpture of the *Ecstasy of Santa Teresa*, in
Rome, in which the saint sinks back in what could be a
swoon, of either pain or pleasure, while a smiling angel
stands over her, holding an arrow in his hand. Both the
painting and architecture of this period make extensive use
of sensuous curves.

The cradle of the Baroque was Rome, where Pietro da Cortona and Bernini channeled their genius into spectacular,
theatrical frescoes; sculptures; palaces; and churches.
Rome had become the artistic center of Italy. Florence was
politically and artistically dead by this time, and Venice
was producing only hack imitations of Titian's and
Tintoretto's paintings.

In the 18th century Venice came back into its own, and
Rome was practically finished as an artistic center. Venetian artists adopted the new Rococo style, which had originated in France and was a softer, overripe version of the
Baroque—a style that celebrated sensuality for its own
sake, without the strength of Baroque. Although Venice
was nearing the last stages of its political decline, there was
still immense wealth in the city, mostly in the hands of families who wished to make the world know about it—and
what better way than through vast, dazzling Rococo canvases, reassuringly stylized and removed from reality? The
revival began with Sebastiano Ricci and was expertly elab-
orated on by Tiepolo. But it could never have taken place
had there not been a return to the city's great artistic tradi-

tions. Late-16th-century color technique and expertise were drawn on and fused with what had been learned from the Baroque to create the breathtaking, magical, decadent world of the Venetian Rococo.

This was the final flowering of Venetian painting. The death of Francesco Guardi in 1793, compounded by the fall of the Republic of Venice in 1797, marked the effective end of the city's artistic life. Neoclassicism found no champion here, except for the sculptor Canova, who, in any case, did his finest work once he had left Venice. Italy had made its contribution to the world of art, and went into an inexorable decline.

3 Rome

Introduction

From ancient times, Romans have been piling the present on top of the past, blithely building, layering, and overlapping their more than 2,500 years of history to create the haphazard fabric of modern Rome. The result is a city where antiquity is taken for granted, where you can have coffee in a square designed by Bernini and go home to a Renaissance palace. Normal life in Rome is carried on in the most extraordinary setting.

Don't be self-conscious in your wanderings about the city. Poke and pry under the surface of things. Walk boldly through gates that are just ajar to peek into the hidden world of Roman courtyards. But do it with a smile, to show the people you meet that you're truly interested in them. Warm and straightforward, the Romans are pleased to show you the nooks and crannies of their hometown.

The good-humored Romans have their problems, of course. The city is noisy, polluted, afflicted with hellish traffic, and exasperatingly inefficient. But at least the traffic problem is being tackled. Sizable areas of the city center have been designated for pedestrians only. The pollution problem is less easy to cure, and far too many of the monuments you will want to see are shielded in fine green netting, while work proceeds on cleaning and repairing them.

Keep your sightseeing flexible. You'll have to plan your day to take into account the wide diversity of opening times—which will mean mixing classical sites with Baroque, museums with parks, the center with the environs. However you do it, be sure to take plenty of time off for simply sitting and observing this kaleidoscopic city and the passing pageant of its teeming streets.

Inevitably, the environs of Rome are overshadowed by the five-star attractions of the Eternal City. However, the surrounding region, known as Lazio (Latium), has plenty to offer in its own right—ancient art and archaeology, medieval hill towns and abbeys, Renaissance pleasure gardens, lake and mountain scenery, and an easygoing pace, not to mention great local wines and homemade pasta. Intersperse city sightseeing with jaunts into the countryside. A breath of country air and a change of scenery can enhance your enjoyment of Rome and give you a new perspective on its many delights.

Essential Information

Arriving and Departing by Plane

Airports and Airlines Most international (there are nonstop flights from the United States with Alitalia, Pan Am, and TWA), and all domestic flights arrive at **Leonardo da Vinci** airport, also known as **Fiumicino,** 30 kilometers (18 miles) outside the city. Some international charter flights land at **Ciampino,** a military airport on the Via Appia Nuova, 15 kilometers (9 miles) from the center of Rome.

Between Leonardo da Vinci Airport and Downtown

By Train An express train (FS) service connects Fiumicino airport and the Air Terminal at Ostiense Station in Rome, with departures every 20 minutes. At Fiumicino, tickets can be purchased (5,000 lire) from ticket machines on the arrivals level or at a ticket window near the track. After intermediate stops (Muratella, Trastevere), the train arrives at the Ostiense Air Terminal. From here you can take a taxi (often easier to find at the Piazza Partigiani exit), a bus (there is a shuttle bus to Termini station), or walk the considerable distance (only partly served by moving sidewalks) to the Piramide Metro station, where you can take the metro (Line B) to the center of town. Centrally located hotels are a fairly short taxi ride from Ostiense air terminal.

By Taxi A taxi from the airport to the center of town costs about 60,000 lire, including supplements for airport service and luggage. Private limousines can be hired at booths in the arrivals hall; they charge a little more than taxis but can take more passengers. Ignore gypsy drivers; stick to yellow cabs. A booth inside the arrivals hall provides taxi information.

By Car Follow the signs for Rome on the expressway, which links with the Grande Raccordo Anulare (GRA), the beltway around Rome. The direction you take on the GRA depends on where your hotel is located, so get directions from the car-rental people at the airport.

Arriving and Departing by Car, Train, and Bus

By Car The main access routes from the north are Al (Autostrada del Sole) from Milan and Florence or the SS1 Aurelia highway from Genoa. The principal route to or from points south, including Naples, is the southern leg of A1. All highways connect with the GRA, which channels traffic into the center. Markings on the GRA are confusing: Take time to study the route you need.

By Train Termini Station is Rome's main train terminal; the Tiburtina and Ostiense stations serve a few long-distance trains. Some trains for Pisa and Genoa leave Rome from, or pass through, the Trastevere Station. For train information, call tel. 06/4775, 7–10:40 PM. You can find English-speaking staff at the information office at Termini Station, or ask for information at travel agencies. If you purchase tickets and book seat reservations in advance either at the main stations or at travel agencies bearing the FS (Ferrovie dello Stato) emblem, you'll avoid long lines at ticket windows. Tickets for train rides within a radius of 100 km of Rome can also be purchased at tobacco shops.

By Bus There is no central bus terminal in Rome. Long-distance and suburban buses terminate either near Termini Station or near Metro stops. For ACOTRAL bus information, call tel. 06/591–5551, Mon.–Fri. 7 AM–6, Sat. 7 AM–2 PM.

Getting Around

Although most of Rome's sights are in a relatively circumscribed area, the city is too large for you to be able to get around solely on foot. Take the Metro (subway), a bus, or a taxi to the area you plan to visit, and expect to do a lot of walking once you're there. Wear a pair of comfortable, sturdy shoes, preferably with rubber or crepe soles to cushion the impact of the cobblestones. Heed our advice on security and get away

Rome Metro

from the noise and polluted air of heavily trafficked streets by taking parallel streets whenever possible. You can buy transportation-route maps at newsstands and at ATAC (Rome's public transit authority) information and ticket booths. The free city map distributed by Rome EPT offices is good; it also shows Metro and bus routes, although bus routes are not always marked clearly.

By Metro This is the easiest and fastest way to get around, but it's limited in extent. The Metro opens at 5:30 AM, and the last trains leave the farthest station at 11:30 PM. The A line runs from the eastern part of the city to the Ottaviano stop, near the Vatican Museums. The fare is 700 lire. There are ticket booths at major stations, but elsewhere you must use complicated ticket machines. It's best to buy single tickets or books of five or 10 (the latter costs only 6,000 lire) at newsstands and tobacconists. The "BIG" daily tourist ticket, good on buses as well, costs 2,800 lire and is sold at Metro and ATAC ticket booths.

By Bus Orange ATAC city buses and two tram lines run from about 6 AM to midnight, with skeleton (*notturno*) services on main lines through the night. Remember to board at the back and exit at the middle. The fare is 800 lire and is valid on all ATAC bus lines for a total of 90 minutes. Time-stamp it in the machine on the first bus you board. Tickets are sold singly at tobacconists and newsstands. You must buy your ticket before boarding. A weekly tourist ticket costs 10,000 lire and is sold at ATAC booths. The BIG tourist ticket is also valid on the Metro for one day (*see* above).

By Taxi Taxis wait at stands and can also be called by phone, in which case you're charged a small supplement. The meter starts at 6,400 lire, a fixed rate for the first 3 km (1.8 mi); there are supplements for service after 10 PM and on Sundays or holidays, as well as for each piece of baggage. Use only metered yellow cabs. To call a cab, dial tel. 3875, 3570, 4994, or 8433. **Radio Taxi** (tel. 06/3875) accepts American Express and Diners Club credit cards, but you must specify when calling that you will pay that way.

By Bicycle Pedaling through Villa Borghese, along the Tiber, and through the center of the city when traffic is light is a pleasant way to see the sights, but remember: Rome is hilly. (For bicycle rentals, *see* Sports and Fitness in Exploring Rome, below.)

By Scooter You can rent a moped or scooter and mandatory helmet at **Scoot-a-Long** (Via Cavour 302, tel. 06/678–0206) or **Scooters For Rent** (Via della Purificazione 66, tel. 06/465485).

Important Addresses and Numbers

Tourist Information The main **EPT** (Rome Provincial Tourist Office) is at Via Parigi 5, tel. 06/488–3748. Open Mon.–Sat. 9–1:30, 2–7; closed Sun. There are also EPT booths at Termini Station and Leonardo da Vinci airport.

For information on places other than Rome, there is a booth at the **ENIT** (National Tourist Board), Via Marghera 2, tel. 06/497–1222.

Consulates **U.S. Consulate** (Via Veneto 121, tel. 06/46741). **Canadian Consulate** (Via Zara 30, tel. 06/440–3028). **U.K. Consulate** (Via Venti Settembre 80A, tel. 06/482–5441).

Emergencies **Police,** tel. 06/4686.

Ambulance (Red Cross), tel. 06/5100.

Doctors and Dentists: Call your consulate or the private Salvator Mundi Hospital (tel. 06/586041), which has English-speaking staff, for recommendations.

Late-Night Pharmacies You will find American and British products—or their equivalents—and English-speaking staff at **Farmacia Internazionale Capranica** (Piazza Capranica 96, tel. 056/679–4680), **Farmacia Internazionale Barberini,** (Piazza Barberini 49, tel. 06/462996), and **Farmacia Doricchi** (Via Venti Settembre 47, tel. 06/474–1471), among others. Most are open 8:30–1, 4–8; some are open all night. Pharmacies take turns opening on Sundays: A schedule is posted in each pharmacy.

English-Language Bookstores English-language paperback books and magazines are available at newsstands in the center of Rome, especially on Via Veneto. For all types of books in English, you should visit the **Economy Book and Video Center** (Via Torino 136, tel. 06/474–6877), the **Anglo-American Bookstore** (Via della Vite 27, tel. 06/679–5222), or the **Lion Bookshop** (Via del Babuino 181, tel. 06/322–5837).

Travel Agencies **American Express** (Piazza di Spagna 35, tel. 06/67641), **CIT** (Piazza della Repubblica 64, tel. 06/47941), **Wagons Lits/Cook** (Via Boncompagni 25, tel. 06/481–7545).

Opening and Closing Times

Rome's churches have erratic and unpredictable opening times; they are *not* open all the time. Most are open from about 7 to 12 and 3 to 7, but don't be surprised if the church you were especially keen on seeing is closed even during these times. Many churches that are shut during the week can, however, be visited on Sundays. Appropriate dress—no shorts—is required when visiting any church.

Banks are open weekdays from 8:30 to 1:30 and 3 or 3:30 to 4 or 4:30. Shops are open Monday to Saturday, 9:30 to 1 and 3:30 or 4 to 7 or 7:30. Many are closed Monday mornings from September to June and Saturday afternoons from July to August.

Guided Tours

Orientation   **American Express** (tel. 06/67641), **CIT** (tel. 06/47941), **Appian Line** (tel. 06/464151), and other operators offer three-hour tours in air-conditioned 60-passenger buses with English-speaking guides. There are four itineraries: "Ancient Rome" (including the Roman Forum and Colosseum), "Classic Rome" (including St. Peter's Basilica, Trevi Fountain, and the Janiculum Hill), "Christian Rome" (some major churches and the Catacombs), and "The Vatican Museums and Sistine Chapel." Most cost about 35,000 lire, but the Vatican Museums tour costs about 42,000 lire. American Express tours depart from Piazza di Spagna, and CIT from Piazza della Repubblica; Appian Line picks you up at your hotel.

American Express and other operators can provide a luxury car for up to three people, a limousine for up to seven, and a minibus for up to nine—all with English-speaking driver—but guide service is extra. A minibus costs about 300,000 lire for three hours. Almost all operators offer "Rome by Night" tours, with or without pizza or dinner and entertainment. You can book tours through travel agents.

The least-expensive organized sightseeing tour of Rome is that run by **ATAC,** the municipal bus company. Tours leave from Piazza dei Cinquecento, in front of Termini Station, last about two hours, and cost about 6,000 lire. There's no running commentary, but you're given an illustrated guide with which you can easily identify the sights. Buy tickets at the ATAC information booth in front of Termini Station. The least expensive sightseeing tours are the routes followed by bus no. 56, from Via Veneto to Trastevere, or the long, leisurely circle route of the No. 19 tram. For each, the cost is 800 lire one way.

Special-Interest   You can attend a public papal audience in the Vatican or at the Pope's summer residence at Castel Gandolfo through **CIT** (tel. 06/47941), **Appian Line** (Via Barberini 109, tel. 06/464151), or **Carrani** Tours (Via V. E. Orlando 95, tel. 06/460510). A bus tour of the sights, including a stop at the Vatican for a papal audience and returning you to or near your hotel, costs about 32,000 lire. An excursion to Castel Gandolfo costs about 37,000 lire.

Tourvisa Italia (Via Marghera 32, tel. 06/445–3224) organizes boat trips on the Tiber, leaving from Ripa Grande, at Ponte Sublicio. There are spring and September excursions to Ostia Antica, with a guided visit of the excavations, that return by bus. During the summer, boats equipped with telescopes head upstream on stargazing expeditions in the late evenings, with astronomers on hand to point out the planets.

Excursions Most operators offer half-day excursions to Tivoli to see the fountains and gardens of Villa d'Este. **Appian Line's** (tel. 06/464151) morning tour to Tivoli includes a visit to Hadrian's Villa, with its impressive Roman ruins. Most operators also have full-day excursions to Assisi, to Pompeii, to Capri, and to Florence. **CIT** (tel. 06/47941) also offers excursions to Anzio and Nettuno; its "Etruscan Tour" takes you to some interesting old towns in the countryside northwest of Rome.

Personal Guides You can arrange for a personal guide through **American Express** (tel. 06/67641); **CIT** (tel. 06/47941); or the main **EPT Tourist Information Office** (tel. 06/488–3748).

Walking If you have a reasonable knowledge of Italian, you can take advantage of the free guided visits and walking tours organized by Rome's cultural associations and the city council for museums and monuments. These usually take place on Sunday mornings. Programs are announced in the daily newspapers.

Exploring Rome

Orientation

Our exploration of Rome is divided into 10 small tours that highlight the city's major areas and attractions. We begin where Rome itself began, amid the ancient ruins, and follow with a look at the Vatican. From here, nine of the tours explore the sights and places of interest to be found in various sections of central Rome, while Tour 10 takes you on a short trip outside the city walls. With the exception of Tours 2 and 3, which concentrate on the Vatican, and Tour 9, which crosses the Tiber to the Trastevere district, the nine central-Rome tours begin in or around Piazza Venezia.

At the end of the chapter are three excursions into the surrounding countryside. Although all the places we suggest visiting could be seen on a day's trip from Rome, some itineraries combine several destinations and could be broken by an overnight stop somewhere along the way, to maintain the easy pace that makes rambling through the region a pleasure. If you're driving, you'll find good roads, but you may run into pockets of local traffic in the suburbs. Try not to schedule your excursions for Sundays, when the Romans make their weekly exodus and create traffic jams on their return.

Highlights for First-Time Visitors

Campidoglio (Tour 1: Ancient Rome).
Castel Sant'Angelo (Tour 2: The Vatican).
Colosseum (Tour 1: Ancient Rome).
Fountain of Trevi (Tour 5: The Spanish Steps and the Trevi Fountain).
Piazza Navona (Tour 4: Old Rome).
Roman Forum (Tour 1: Ancient Rome).
Saint Peter's (Tour 2: The Vatican).
Santa Maria Maggiore (Tour 6: Historic Churches).

Spanish Steps (Tour 5: The Spanish Steps and the Trevi Fountain).
Vatican Museums, including Sistine Chapel (Tour 3: Around the Vatican).

Tour 1: Ancient Rome

Numbers in the margin correspond with points of interest on the Rome map.

Rome, as is common knowledge, was built on seven hills. Its legendary founders, the twins Romulus and Remus, were abandoned as infants but were suckled by a she-wolf on the banks of the Tiber and adopted by a shepherd. Encouraged by the gods to build a city, the twins chose a site in 735 BC, fortifying it with a wall that has been identified by archaeologists digging on the Palatine, the first hill of Rome to be inhabited. During the building of the city, the brothers quarreled and in a fit of anger Romulus killed Remus. Excavations on the Palatine and in the Forum area have revealed hard evidence of at least some aspects of the city's legendary beginnings.

The monuments and ruins of the two most historic hills—the Capitoline and the Palatine—mark the center of ancient Rome, capital of the classical world and seat of a vast empire. The former hill held the seat of government, the Capitol, whose name is commemorated in every "capital" city in the world, as well as in government buildings, such as the Capitol in Washington, DC.

If you stand on the Capitoline and gaze out over the ruins of the Forum to the Palatine, with the Colosseum looming in the background, you can picture how Rome looked when it was the center of the known world. Imagine the Forum filled with immense, brightly painted temples. Picture the faint glow from the temple of Vesta, where the Vestal Virgins tended their sacred fire, and the glistening marble palace complex on the Palatine, its roof studded with statues, where the emperors and their retinues lived in incredible luxury. Then think of how the area looked in the Dark Ages, when Rome had sunk into malaria-ridden squalor.

The **Capitoline** hill is a good place to begin when exploring the city. Rome's first and most sacred temples stood here. The city's archives were kept in the Tabularium (hall of records), the tall, gray stone structure that forms the foundations of to-

❶ day's city hall, the **Palazzo Senatorio.** By the Middle Ages, the Campidoglio, as the hill was then known, had fallen into ruin. In 1537, Pope Paul III called on Michelangelo to restore it to grandeur, and the artist designed the ramp, the buildings on three sides of the **Campidoglio** Square, the slightly convex pavement and its decoration, and the pedestal for the bronze equestrian statue of Marcus Aurelius. A copy of the statue is due to go back on the pedestal, with the restored original on view indoors.

The palaces flanking Palazzo Senatorio contain two museums, the **Museo Capitolino** and the **Palazzo dei Conservatori,** whose collections were assembled in the 15th century by Pope Sixtus V, one of the earliest of the great papal patrons of the arts. Those with a taste for Roman and Greek sculpture will appreciate both museums; others may find the collections dull but the

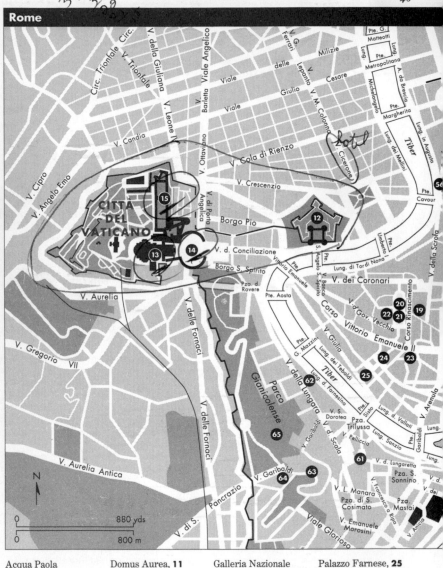

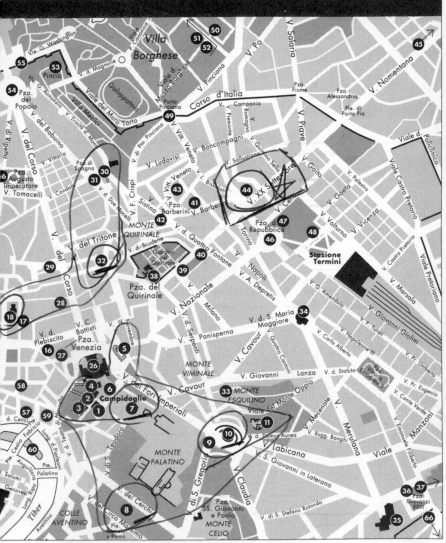

setting impressive. Many of the statues were restored by over-conscientious 18th- and 19th-century collectors who added heads and limbs with considerable abandon. Originally, almost all these works were brilliantly colored and gilded. Remember that many of the works here and in Rome's other museums are copies of Greek originals. For hundreds of years, craftsmen of ancient Rome prospered by producing copies of Greek statues on order; they used a process called "pointing," by which exact copies could be made.

Portraiture, however, was one area in which the Romans outstripped the Greeks. The hundreds of Roman portrait busts in ❷ the **Museo Capitolino** are the highlight of a visit here. In the courtyard, the reclining river god is one of the "talking statues" to which citizens of ancient Rome affixed anonymous political protests and satirical barbs. The most interesting pieces, on display upstairs, include the poignant *Dying Gaul* and the delicate *Marble Faun*, which inspired novelist Nathaniel Hawthorne's tale of the same name. Then you'll come upon the rows of portrait busts, a kind of ancient *Who's Who*, though rather haphazardly labeled. Look for cruel Caracalla, vicious Nero, and haughty Marcus Aurelius.

❸ Across the square is **Palazzo dei Conservatori** (Palace of Preserved Treasures), which contains similar treasures. The huge head and hand in the courtyard are fragments of a colossal statue of the emperor Constantine; these immense effigies were much in vogue in the later days of the Roman empire. The resplendent Salone dei Orazi and Curiazi upstairs is a ceremonial hall with a magnificent gilt ceiling, carved wooden doors, and 16th-century frescoes. Further on, you'll see the famous *Capitoline Wolf*, a 6th-century BC Etruscan bronze; the twins were

added during the Renaissance to adapt the statue to the legend of Romulus and Remus. *Museo Capitolino and Palazzo dei Conservatori, Piazza del Campidoglio, tel. 06/678-2862. Joint admission: 5,000 lire. Open Tues., Thurs. 9–1:30, 5–8; Wed., Fri., Sat. 9–1:30; Sat. (May–Sept.) also 8 PM–11 PM, Sun. 9–1.*

❹ The Capitoline's church of **Ara Coeli** was one of the first in the city built by the emerging Christians. It's known for Pinturicchio's 16th-century frescoes in the first chapel on the right and for a much-revered wooden figure of the Christ Child, kept in a small chapel in the sacristy.

The Campidoglio gardens offer the best view of the sprawling ruins of ancient Rome. **Caesar's Forum** lies below the garden, to the left of Palazzo Senatorio. It is the oldest of the Imperial Fora, those built by the emperors, as opposed to those built during the earlier, Republican period (6th–1st centuries BC), as part of the original Roman Forum.

Across Via dei Fori Imperiali, the broad avenue created by Premier Benito Mussolini for his triumphal parades, are, from ❺ the left, **Trajan's Column,** under which the emperor Trajan was buried, **Trajan's Forum,** with its huge semicircular market building, and the ruins of the **Forum of Augustus.**

Now turn your attention to the Roman Forum, in what was once a marshy valley between the Capitoline and Palatine hills. The shortest way down is Via San Pietro in Carcere—actually a flight of stairs descending to the church that stands over the ❻ **Mamertine Prison,** a series of gloomy, subterranean cells where Rome's vanquished enemies were finished off. Legend has it that St. Peter was held prisoner here and that he miraculously brought forth a spring of water in order to baptize his jailers. *Donations requested. Open daily 9–12:30, 2–7:30.*

From the main entrance on Via dei Fori Imperiali, descend into the extraordinary archaeological complex that is the **Roman Forum.** This was the civic heart of Republican Rome, the austere Rome that preceded the hedonistic society that grew up under the emperors in the 1st to the 4th century AD. Today it seems no more than a baffling series of ruins, marble fragments, isolated columns, a few worn arches, and occasional paving stones. Yet it once was filled with stately and extravagant buildings—temples, palaces, shops—and crowded with people from all corners of the world. What you see are the ruins not of one period, but of almost 900 years, from about 500 BC to AD 400. As the original buildings became too small or old-fashioned, they were pulled down and replaced by more lavish structures. Making sense of these scarred and pitted stones is not easy; you may want just to wander along, letting your imagination dwell on Julius Caesar, Cicero, and Mark Antony, who delivered the funeral address in Caesar's honor from the rostrum just left of the Arch of Septimius Severus. *Entrances on Via dei Fori Imperiali, Piazza Santa Maria Nova, and Via di San Gregorio, tel. 06/679–0333. Admission: 10,000 lire. Open Apr.–Sept., Mon., Wed.–Sat. 9–6, Tues. and Sun. 9–1; Oct.–Mar. Mon., Wed.–Sat, 9–3, Tues. and Sun. 9–1.*

Leave the Forum by the exit at Arco Tito (Arch of Titus), which is at the end of the Forum away from the Capitoline. From here, the Clivus Palatinus walkway leads up the Palatine hill, where the emperors built their palaces. From the belvedere you can see the **Circus Maximus,** where more than 300,000 spectators could watch chariot and horse races while the emperors looked on from this very spot. The Italian garden on the Palatine was laid out during the Renaissance. Leaving the Palatine by way of the Via di San Gregorio exit, you'll pass the imposing **Arch of Constantine,** erected in AD 315 to commemorate Constantine's victory over Maxentius at the Milvian bridge.

Just beyond is the **Colosseum,** the most famous monument of ancient Rome. Begun by the Flavian emperor Vespasian in AD 72, it was inaugurated by Titus eight years later with a program of games and shows lasting 100 days. On the opening day alone, 5,000 wild beasts perished in the arena. Its 573-yard circumference could contain more than 50,000 spectators. It was faced with marble and boasted an ingenious system of awnings to shade spectators from the sun. Originally known as the Flavian Amphitheater, in later centuries it came to be called the Colosseum, after a colossal gilded bronze statue of Nero that stood nearby. It served as a fortress during the 13th century and then as a quarry from which materials were filched to build sumptuous Renaissance churches and palaces. Finally it was declared sacred by the popes, in memory of the many Christians believed martyred there. If you pay admission to the upper levels, you can see a scale model of the Colosseum as it was in its heyday. *Piazza del Colosseo, tel. 06/735227. Admission free; admission to upper levels: 3,000 lire. Open Thurs.–Tues. 9–one hour before sunset, Wed. and Sun. 9–1.*

Behind the Colosseum at the Colle Oppio (Oppian Hill) on the Esquiline Hill, you can see what's left of Nero's fabulous

⑪ **Domus Aurea,** a sumptuous palace later buried under Trajan's Baths.

Time Out Facing the Colosseum, the appropriately named **Il Gladiatore** is a handy place for a moderately priced lunch. *Piazza del Colosseo. Closed Wed.*

If you head back toward Piazza Venezia on Via dei Fori Imperiale, you can get a good look at the Imperial Fora and Trajan's Market.

Tour 2: The Vatican

While the ancient Roman emperors presided over the decline of their empire, a vibrant new force emerged. Christianity came to Rome, the seat of the popes was established over the tomb of St. Peter, and the Vatican became the spiritual focus of the Roman Catholic Church. There are two principal reasons for seeing the Vatican. One is to visit St. Peter's, the largest church in the world and the most overwhelming architectural achievement of the Renaissance. The other is to visit the Vatican Museums—which contain collections of staggering richness and diversity—including, of course, the Sistine Chapel. There's little point in trying to take it all in on just one visit. See St. Peter's first, and come back later to see the Vatican Museums.

⑫ Start at **Castel Sant'Angelo,** the fortress that guarded the Vatican for hundreds of years. One of Rome's most beautiful bridges, **Ponte Sant'Angelo,** spans the Tiber in front of the fortress and is studded with graceful angels designed by Giovanni Lorenzo Bernini (1598–1680). The distinctive silhouette of Castel Sant'Angelo is a throwback to its original function; it was built as a mausoleum, or tomb, for the Emperor Hadrian in AD 135. By the 6th century, it had been transformed into a fortress, and it remained the military stronghold of Rome and a refuge for the popes for almost 1,000 years.

According to legend, the castle got its name during the plague of 590, when Pope Gregory the Great, passing by in a religious procession, had a vision of an angel sheathing its sword atop the stone ramparts. He interpreted this as a sign that the plague would end immediately, and, after it did, he had a chapel built on the highest level of the fortress, where he had seen the angel. Visit the lower levels, the base of Hadrian's mausoleum, and then climb ancient ramps and narrow staircases, to explore the castle's courtyards and frescoed halls; the collection of antique arms and armor; and the open loggia, where there's a café. Climb to the upper terraces for views of the city's rooftops and the lower bastions of the castle, as well as the Passetto, the fortified corridor connecting Castel Sant'Angelo with the Vatican. *Lungotevere Castello 50, tel. 06/687-5036. Admission: 8,000 lire. Open Apr.–Sept., Mon. 3–8; Tues., Wed., and Fri. 9–2; Thurs. and Sat. 9–7; Sun. 9–1; Oct.–Mar., Mon. 2–6, Tues.–Sat. 9–1; Sun. 9–noon.*

From Castel Sant'Angelo, turn right onto Via della Conciliazione, a broad, rather soulless avenue conceived by Mussolini in the 1930s to celebrate the "conciliation" between the Vatican and the Italian government under the Lateran Pact of 1929. The pact ended 60 years of papal protest against the state. (After Italian troops wrested control of Rome from the

pope in 1870 to make it the capital of a newly united Italy, the
popes refused to leave the Vatican or recognize the new state.)

13 The Via della Conciliazione approach to **St. Peter's** gives your
eye time to adjust to the enormous dimensions of the square
and the church, although the intent of Baroque artist Bernini,
who designed the square, was to surprise the visitor emerging
suddenly from shadowy alleys into the square's immense space
14 and full light. The **Piazza di San Pietro** (St. Peter's Square)
is one of Bernini's masterpieces, completed after 11 years'
work—a relatively short time in those days, considering the
vastness of the job. The square can hold as many as 400,000
people and is surrounded by a pair of quadruple colonnades,
topped by a balustrade and 140 statues of saints. Look for the
two stone disks set into the pavement on each side of the obelisk, between the obelisk and the fountains. If you stand on one
disk, a trick of perspective makes the colonnades seem to consist of a single row of columns.

The history of St. Peter's goes back to the year AD 319, when
the Emperor Constantine built a basilica here over the site of
the tomb of St. Peter. The original church stood for more than
1,000 years, undergoing a number of restorations, until it
threatened to collapse. Reconstruction began in 1452 but was
soon abandoned due to a lack of funds. In 1506 Pope Julius II
instructed the architect Donato Bramante (1444–1514) to raze
the existing structure and build a new and greater basilica, but
it wasn't until 1626 that the new church was completed and dedicated. Five of Italy's greatest Renaissance architects died
while working on it—Bramante, Raphael, Baldassare, Peruz-
zi, Antonio Sangallo the Younger, and Michelangelo. Bramante
outlined a basic plan for the church and built the massive pillars
that were to support the dome. After his death in 1514, his successors made little progress with the work and altered his master plan. In 1546 Pope Paul III more or less forced the aging
Michelangelo to take on the job of completing the building. Michelangelo returned to Bramante's ground plan and designed
the dome to cover the crossing, but his plans, too, were modi-
fied after his death. The result is nevertheless breathtaking.
As you approach the church, look at the people going in and out
of the portico, and note the contrast between their size and the
immense scale of the building. Persons wearing shorts, mini-
skirts, sleeveless T-shirts, or other revealing clothing are not
allowed entrance to St. Peter's or the Vatican Museums. Wom-
en should carry scarves to cover their bare upper arms.

Now climb the broad steps yourself and enter the portico. Notice Filarete's 15th-century bronze doors, salvaged from the
old basilica. Once inside, pause a moment to consider the size of
this immense temple. Look at the massive pillars, the holy-wa-
ter stoups borne by colossal cherubs, the distance to the main
altar. Look for the brass inscriptions in the marble pavement
along the center of the nave (the long central section), indicat-
ing the approximate length of the world's principal Christian
churches, all of which fall far short of St. Peter's. The chapel
immediately to your right holds Michelangelo's *Pieta*, one of
the world's most famous statues. It is now screened behind
shatterproof glass, after a serious incident of vandalism; it was
masterfully restored in the Vatican's workshops. This is the
only sculpture ever signed by Michelangelo. (Look for the signature on one of the left-arm folds of the Virgin's clothing.) The

story goes that he completed the work unsigned but stole back to sign it when he was told that others might take credit for it.

Four massive piers support the dome at the crossing, where the mighty Bernini *baldacchino* (canopy), made of bronze stripped from the Pantheon by order of the Barberini Pope Urban VIII, rises high above the papal altar. The pope celebrates mass here, over the crypt holding the tombs of many of his predecessors. Deep in the earth under the foundations of the original basilica is what is believed to be the tomb of St. Peter. A very old bronze statue of the saint stands at the last pillar on the right before the crossing, its foot worn and burnished by the kisses of the faithful over the centuries. Beautiful bronze vigil lights flicker around the ceremonial entrance to the crypt in front of the papal altar. In the niche below is an antique casket containing the *pallia* (bands of white wool conferred by the pope on archbishops as a sign of authority). The splendid gilt-bronze throne above the altar in the apse was designed by Bernini and contains a wooden-and-ivory chair that St. Peter was supposed to have used, though in fact it dates back no further than the Middle Ages. You can see a copy of the chair in the Treasury. Stroll up and down the aisles and transepts, noting the wealth of art works in mosaic, marble, bronze, and stucco.

Stop in to see the small collection of Vatican treasures in the little **museum** in the sacristy, among them priceless antique chalices and the massive 15th-century bronze tomb of Pope Sixtus V by Antonio Pollaiuolo (1429–98). *Admission: 2,000 lire. Open Apr.–Sept., daily 9–6:30; Oct.–Mar., daily 9–2:30.*

Take the elevator or climb the stairs from the entrance near the right crossing to the roof of the church, an interesting landscape of domes and towers. From here, climb a short interior staircase to the base of the dome for a dove's-eye view of the interior of the church. It's a taxing climb to the lantern—the architectural term for the delicate structure crowning the dome; the stairs are steep and narrow and one-way only, so there's no turning back. Those who make it are rewarded with views embracing the Vatican gardens and all Rome. *Entrance to roof and dome between Gregorian Chapel and right crossing. Admission: 4,000 lire if you use the elevator to the roof, 3,000 if you use the stairs. Open Apr.–Sept., daily 8–7; Oct.–Mar., daily 8–6.*

Finally, go from the heights to the depths and visit the **crypt** to see the tombs of the popes. The only exit from the crypt leads outside St. Peter's, so leave this for last. *Entrance at St. Longinus Pier but alternatively at one of the other piers. Admission free. Open Apr.–Sept., daily 7–6; Oct.–Mar., daily 7–5.*

For many, a **papal audience** is a highlight of a trip to Rome. The pope holds mass audiences on Wednesday mornings at about 11, and at 10 in the hottest months. During the winter audiences take place in a modern audience hall. From March to October they are held in St. Peter's Square and sometimes at the papal residence at Castel Gandolfo. You must apply for tickets in advance; you may find it easier to arrange for them through a travel agency. Of course, you can avoid the formalities by seeing the pope when he makes his weekly appearance at the window of the Vatican Palace, every Sunday at noon when he is in Rome. He addresses the crowd and gives a blessing. *For audience tickets, apply in writing well in advance, or go to the Pa-*

pal (Prefettura) Prefecture through the bronze door in the right-hand colonnade, tel. 06/6982. Open Mon.–Tues. 9–1, Wed. 9 until shortly before the audience commences, though last-minute tickets may not be available. You can also pick up free tickets from 4–6 PM at the office of the North American College, Via dell'Umiltà 30, tel. 06/678–9184, or you can arrange for tickets and transportation to and from the audience through a travel agent (see Guided Tours in Essential Information, above).

Tour 3: Around the Vatican

The Vatican Palace, which has been the residence of the popes on and off since 1377, is made up of several interlocking buildings containing 1,400 rooms, chapels, and galleries. The pope and his household occupy only a small part of the palace, most of which is given over to the Vatican Library and Museums. There is bus service between Piazza San Pietro and a secondary entrance to the museums; it takes a route through the Vatican gardens and costs 1,000 lire. The main entrance is a long walk from the Piazza. The bus service takes you to a side entrance and saves a lot of walking, while giving you the chance to see some of Vatican City that would be off-limits otherwise. *Service 9–12:30 on the half-hour, except Sun. and Wed.*

Time Out The street of Borgo Pio, a block or two from St. Peter's Square, has several trattorias offering tourist menus for about 13,000 lire. For about 15,000 lire you can have a simple à la carte meal at **La Casareccia,** which also serves pizza for lunch. *Borgo Pio 40. Closed Thurs.*

15 The collections of the **Vatican Museums** are immense, covering about 4½ miles of displays. Special posters at the entrance and throughout the museum plot a choice of four color-coded itineraries, the shortest taking approximately 90 minutes and the longest five hours. You can rent a taped commentary in English, explaining the Sistine Chapel and the Raphael Rooms. You're free to photograph what you like, although if you want to use a flash, tripod, or other special equipment, you have to get permission. The main entrance is on Viale Vaticano and can be reached by the No. 49 bus from Piazza Cavour, which stops right in front; on foot from the No. 81 bus or No. 19 tram, which stop at Piazza Risorgimento; or from the Ottaviano metro line A stop. Pick up a leaflet at the main entrance to the museums in order to see the overall layout. The Sistine Chapel, the main attraction for most visitors, is at the far end of the complex, and the leaflet charts two abbreviated itineraries through other collections to reach it. It would be a shame to miss the collections en route to the Sistine Chapel, and below we give some of the highlights, whether or not you follow the itineraries suggested by the curators. *Viale Vaticano, tel. 06/698–3333. Admission: 10,000 lire; free on last Sun. of month. Open Easter week and July–Sept. Mon.–Sat. 9–5 (no admission after 4); Oct.–June (except Easter) 9–2 (no admission after 1). Closed Sun. year-round, except last Sun. of month, and on religious holidays: Jan. 1, Jan. 6, Feb. 11, Mar. 10, Easter Sun. and Mon., May 1, Ascension Thurs., Corpus Christi, June 29, Aug. 14–15, Nov. 1, Dec. 8, Dec. 25–26.*

Among Vatican City's many riches, probably the single most important is the Sistine Chapel. However, unless you're following one of the two abbreviated itineraries, you'll begin your visit at the **Egyptian Museum** and go on to the **Chiaramonti** and **Pio Clementino Museums,** which are given over to classical sculptures (among them some of the best-known statues in the world—the *Laocoön*, the *Belvedere Torso*, and the *Apollo Belvedere*—works that, with their vibrant humanism, had a tremendous impact on Renaissance art. Next come the **Etruscan Museum** and three other sections of limited interest. All itineraries merge in the **Candelabra Gallery** and proceed through the **Tapestry Gallery,** which is hung with magnificent tapestries executed from Raphael's designs.

The Gallery of Maps is intriguing; the Apartment of Pius V, a little less so. After them you'll enter the Raphael Rooms, second only to the Sistine Chapel in artistic interest. In 1508, Pope Julius II employed Raffaelo Sanzio, on the recommendation of Bramante, to decorate the rooms with biblical scenes. The result was a Renaissance masterpiece. Of the four rooms, the second and third were decorated mainly by Raphael; the others, by Giulio Romano and other assistants of Raphael. The lovely Loggia (covered balcony) was designed and frescoed by the master himself. Next you pass through the Chiaroscuro Room to the tiny **Chapel of Nicholas V,** aglow with frescoes by Fra Angelico (1387–1455), the Florentine monk whose sensitive paintings were guiding lights for the Renaissance. If your itinerary takes you to the **Borgia Apartments,** you'll see their elaborately painted ceilings, designed and partially executed by Pinturicchio (1454–1513). The Borgia Apartments have been given over to the Vatican's large, but not particularly interesting, collection of modern religious art, which continues at a lower level. Once you've seen the Borgia Rooms, you can skip the rest in good conscience and get on to the Sistine Chapel.

In 1508, while Raphael was put to work on his series of rooms, Pope Julius II commissioned Michelangelo to fresco the more than 10,000 square feet of the **Sistine Chapel** ceiling singlehandedly. The task took four years of mental and physical anguish. It's said that for years afterward Michelangelo couldn't read anything without holding it up over his head. The result, however, was the masterpiece that you can now see, its colors cool and brilliant after recent restoration. Bring a pair of binoculars to get a better look at this incredible work, and if you want to have some leisure to study it, try to beat the tour groups by getting there early in the day. Some 20 years after completing the ceiling, Michelangelo was commissioned to paint the *Last Judgment* on the wall over the altar. The aged and embittered artist painted his own face on the wrinkled human skin in the hand of St. Bartholomew, below and to the right of the figure of Christ, which he clearly modeled on the *Apollo Belvedere*. The painting will remain hidden for at least two more years while being restored.

After this experience, which can be marred by the crowds of tourists, you pass through some of the exhibition halls of the **Vatican Library.** Look in on Room X, Room of the Aldobrandini Marriage, to see its beautiful Roman frescoes of a nuptial rite. You can see more classical statues in the new wing and then, perhaps after taking a break at the cafeteria, go on to the **Pinacoteca** (Picture Gallery). It displays mainly religious paintings by such artists as Giotto, Fra Angelico, and Filippo Lippi. The **Raphael Room** holds his exceptional *Transfiguration, Coronation,* and *Foligno Madonna.*

In the **Pagan Antiquities Museum,** modern display techniques enhance another collection of Greek and Roman sculptures. The **Christian Antiquities Museum** has early-Christian and medieval art, while the **Ethnological Museum** shows art and artifacts from exotic places throughout the world. The complete itinerary ends with the **Historical Museum**'s collection of carriages, uniforms, and arms.

In all, the Vatican Museums offer a staggering excursion into the realms of art and history. It's foolhardy to try to see all the collections in one day, and it's doubtful that anyone could be fervidly interested in everything on display. Simply aim for an overall impression of the artistic riches and cultural significance of the Vatican collections. If you want to delve deeper, you can come back another day.

Time Out Try the good neighborhood trattorias that are far better and far less popular with tourists than those opposite the Vatican Museum entrance. At **Hostaria Tonino** (Via Leone IV 60, closed Sun.), you can dine on typical Roman fare at moderate, even inexpensive, prices. On Piazza Risorgimento, look for the simple trattoria with the long name: **La Mejo Pastasciutta der Monno.** Great inexpensive pasta dishes. (Piazza Risorgimento 5, closed Mon.).

Tour 4: Old Rome

A district of narrow streets with curious names, airy Baroque piazzas, and picturesque courtyards, Old Rome *(Vecchia Roma)* occupies the horn of land that pushes the Tiber westward toward the Vatican. It has been an integral part of the city since ancient times, and its position between the Vatican and the Lateran palaces, both seats of papal rule, put it in the mainstream of Rome's development from the Middle Ages onward. Today it's full of old artisans' workshops, trendy cafés and eating places, and offbeat boutiques. On weekends and summer evenings Old Rome is a magnet for crowds of young people.

Start at Piazza Venezia and take Via del Plebiscito to the huge
16 Baroque **Il Gesù,** comparable only with St. Peter's for sheer grandeur. Inside it's encrusted with gold and precious marbles and topped by a fantastically painted ceiling that flows down over the pillars to become three-dimensional, merging with painted stucco figures in a swirling composition glorifying the Jesuit order. Then head for nearby Piazza della Minerva to see
17 the church of **Santa Maria Sopra Minerva,** a Gothic church with some beautiful frescoes by Filippo Lippi (1406–69), the monk who taught Botticelli. Bernini's charming elephant bearing an obelisk stands in the center of the piazza.

18 The huge brick building opposite is the Pantheon, one of the most harmonious and best-preserved monuments of antiquity. It was first erected in 27 BC by Augustus's general Agrippa and completely redesigned and rebuilt by Hadrian, who deserves the credit for this fantastic feat of construction. At its apex, the dome is exactly as tall as the walls, so that you could imagine it as the upper half of a sphere resting on the floor; this balance gives the building a serene majesty. The bronze doors are the original ones; most of the other decorations of gilt bronze and marble that covered the dome and walls were plundered by later Roman emperors and by the popes. The Pantheon gets light and air from the apex of the dome—another impressive feature of this remarkable edifice. *Piazza della Rotonda. Admission free. Oct.–June, Mon.–Sat. 9–5, Sun. 9–1; July–Sept., daily 9–6.*

Time Out The café scene in the square in front of the Pantheon rivals that of nearby Piazza Navona. The area is ice-cream heaven, with some of Rome's best *gelaterie* (ice-cream parlors) within a few steps of one another. Romans consider **Giolitti** superlative and take the counter by storm. Remember to pay the cashier first and hand the stub to the man at the counter when you order your cone. Giolitti has a good snack counter, too. *Via Uffizi del Vicario 40. Closed Mon.*

(19) From Piazza della Rotonda in front of the Pantheon, take Via Giustiniani onto Via della Dogana Vecchia to the church of **San Luigi dei Francesi.** In the last chapel on the left are three stunning works by Caravaggio (1571–1610), the master of the heightened approach to light and dark. A light machine (operated with a couple of 100-lire coins) provides illumination to view the paintings. *Open Fri.–Wed. 7:30–12:30, 3:30–7; Thurs. 7:30–12:30.*

(20) In the church of **Sant' Agostino,** close by, there is another Caravaggio over the first altar on the left. Just beyond these churches is **Piazza Navona,** a beautiful Baroque piazza that stands over the oval of Emperor Domitian's stadium. It still has the carefree air of the days when it was the scene of Roman circus games, medieval jousts, and 17th-century carnivals. (21) Bernini's splashing **Fountain of the Four Rivers,** with an enormous rock squared off by statues representing the four corners of the world, makes a fitting centerpiece. Behind it stands the church (22) of **Sant' Agnese in Agone.** Its Baroque facade is by Francesco Borromini (1599–1667), a contemporary and sometime rival of Bernini. One story has it that the Bernini statue nearest the church is hiding its head because it can't bear to look upon the inferior Borromini facade.

Time Out The sidewalk tables of the **Tre Scalini** café offer a grandstand view of the piazza. This is the place that invented the *tartufo*, a luscious chocolate ice-cream specialty. *Piazza Navona 30. Closed Wed.*

(23) If you leave Piazza Navona by way of the Corsia Agonalis, midway along, you'll see the 17th-century **Palazzo Madama,** now the Senate, and the church of **Sant' Andrea della Valle** at the end of Corso Rinascimento. Gray with grime, the church looms mightily over a busy intersection. Puccini set the first act of his opera *Tosca* here.

(24) Now make your way through side streets to **Campo dei Fiori.** Once the scene of public executions (including that of philosopher-monk Giordano Bruno, whose statue broods in the center), it now holds one of Rome's busiest, most colorful morning markets.

Continue on to Piazza Farnese, where Michelangelo had a hand
(25) in building **Palazzo Farnese,** now the French Embassy and perhaps the most beautiful of the Renaissance palaces in Rome.
The twin fountains in the piazza are made with basins of Egyptian granite from the Baths of Caracalla. Behind Palazzo Farnese, turn onto Via Giulia, where you'll see some elegant
palaces (step inside the portals to take a look at the courtyards), old churches, and a number of antiques shops.

Tour 5: The Spanish Steps and the Trevi Fountain

The walk up the Corso from Piazza Venezia takes you to Rome's
classiest shopping streets and to two visual extravaganzas: the
Spanish Steps and the Fountain of Trevi.

(26) Start at the **Vittorio Emanuele Monument** in Piazza Venezia.
Rome's most flamboyant landmark, it was erected in the late
19th century to honor Italy's first king, Vittorio Emanuele II,
and the unification of Italy. This vast marble monument, said to
resemble a wedding cake or a Victorian typewriter, houses the
Tomb of the Unknown Soldier, with its eternal flame. Although
the monument has been closed to the public for many years,
plans are in the works to reopen it; the views from the top are
among Rome's best.

(27) On the left, as you look up Via del Corso, is **Palazzo Venezia,** a
blend of medieval solidity and Renaissance grace. It contains a
good collection of paintings, sculptures, and *objets d'art* in
handsome salons, some of which Mussolini used as his offices.
Notice the balcony over the main portal, from which Il Duce addressed huge crowds in the square below. *Via del Plebiscito
118, tel. 06/679–8865. Admission: 8,000 lire. Open Mon.–Sat.
9–2, Sun. 9–1.*

Along the Corso you'll pass some fine old palaces and a church
(28) or two. Make a detour to the left to see the church of **Sant'
Ignazio,** where what seems to be the dome is really an illusion-
ist canvas. Put some coins in the light machine to illuminate the
dazzling frescoes on the vault of the nave. Next you'll come to
(29) Piazza Colonna, named for the ancient **Column of Marcus Aurelius,** with its extraordinarily detailed reliefs spiraling up to the
top.

Time Out **Alfio,** on the corner of Via Bergamaschi, is popular for a stand-
up lunch of sandwiches at the counter or a more relaxing meal
in the upstairs dining room. *Via Della Colonna Antonina 33.
Closed Sun.*

From Largo Goldoni, on Via del Corso, you get a head-on view
of the Spanish Steps and the church of Trinità dei Monti as you
start up Via Condotti, an elegant and expensive shopping
street. Look for the historic **Caffè Greco** on the left. More than
200 years old, it was the haunt of Goethe, Byron, and Liszt; now
it's a hangout for well-dressed ladies carrying Gucci shopping
bags.

(30) Piazza di Spagna and the **Spanish Steps** get their names from
the Spanish Embassy to the Holy See (the Vatican), opposite
the American Express office, though they were built with
French funds. This was once the core of Rome's bohemian quarter, especially favored by American and British artists and
writers in the 18th and 19th centuries. At the center of the

square is Bernini's **Fountain of the Barcaccia** (the Old Boat), and just to the right of the steps is the house where Keats and Shelley lived. Sloping upward in broad curves, the Spanish Steps are perfect for socializing, and they draw huge crowds on weekend and holiday afternoons. From mid-April to early May, the steps are blanketed with azaleas in bloom.

Time Out **La Rampa,** in a corner of Piazza Mignanelli, behind the American Express office, is a picturesque place for lunch, with an extensive menu of moderately priced dishes. *Piazza Mignanelli 18. Closed Sun.*

From the narrow end of the piazza, take Via Propaganda Fide to Sant'Andrea delle Fratte, swerving left on Via del Nazareno, then crossing busy Via del Tritone to Via della Stamperia. This street leads to the **Fountain of Trevi,** one of Rome's most spectacular fountains when it's gushing. It was featured in the 1954 film *Three Coins in the Fountain.* And legend has it that you can ensure your return to Rome by tossing a coin in the fountain. Unfortunately, legend doesn't tell you how to cope with the souvenir vendors and aggressive beggars who are looking for a share of your change.

Tour 6: Historic Churches

Three churches are the highlights of this walk, two of them major basilicas with roots in the early centuries of Christianity. Not far from Piazza Venezia and the Roman Forum off Via Cavour is the church of **San Pietro in Vincoli.** Look for Via San Francesco da Paola, a street staircase that passes under the old Borgia palace and leads to the square in front of the church. Inside the church are St. Peter's chains (under the altar) and Michelangelo's *Moses,* a powerful statue almost as famed as his frescoes in the Sistine Chapel. The *Moses* was destined for the tomb of Julius II, but Michelangelo was driven to distraction by the interference of Pope Julius and his successors, and the tomb was never finished. The statue of Moses, intended as part of the tomb, is a remarkable sculpture and a big tourist attraction. Crass commercialism has ruined the starkly majestic effect of this memorial: The church is usually jammed with tour groups, and the monument itself is a front for a large and ugly souvenir shop.

Continue along Via Cavour to **Santa Maria Maggiore,** one of the oldest and most beautiful churches in Rome. Built on the spot where a 3rd-century pope witnessed a miraculous midsummer snowfall, it is resplendent with gleaming mosaics—those on the arch in front of the main altar date back to the 5th century; the apse mosaic dates to the 13th century—and an opulent carved wood ceiling supposed to have been gilded with the first gold brought from the New World. Urgently needed restoration may be under way in 1992, hiding some of the interior from view.

Via Merulana runs straight as an arrow from Santa Maria Maggiore to the immense cathedral of Rome, **San Giovanni in Laterano,** where the early popes once lived and where the present pope still officiates in his capacity as Rome's bishop. The towering facade and Borromini's cool Baroque interior emphasize the majesty of its proportions.

㊱ Across the street, opposite the Lateran Palace, a small building houses the **Scala Santa** (Holy Stairs), claimed to be the staircase from Pilate's palace in Jerusalem. Circle the palace to see the 6th-century octagonal **Baptistery of San Giovanni,** forerunner of many similar buildings throughout Italy, and Rome's oldest and tallest obelisk, brought from Thebes and dating to the 15th century BC.

㊲ One more church awaits you just down Via Carlo Felice. **Santa Croce in Gerusalemme,** with a pretty Rococo facade and Baroque interior, shelters what are believed to be relics of the True Cross found by St. Helena, mother of the Emperor Constantine and a tireless collector of holy objects.

Tour 7: The Quirinale and Piazza della Repubblica

Although this tour takes you from ancient Roman sculptures to Early Christian churches, it's mainly an excursion into the 16th and 17th centuries, when Baroque art—and Bernini—triumphed in Rome. The **Quirinale** is the highest of Rome's seven original hills (the others are the Capitoline, Palatine, Esquiline, Viminal, Celian, and Aventine) and the one where ancient Romans and later the popes built their residences in order to escape the deadly miasmas and the malaria of the low-lying **㊳** area around the Forum. **Palazzo del Quirinale,** the largest on the square, belonged first to the popes, then to Italy's kings, and is now the official residence of the nation's president. The fountain in the square boasts ancient statues of Castor and Pollux reining in their unruly steeds and a basin salvaged from the Roman Forum.

Along Via Venti Settembre are two interesting little churches, **㊴** each an architectural gem. The first you'll come upon is **Sant' Andrea,** a small but imposing Baroque church designed and decorated by Bernini, who considered it one of his finest works and liked to come here occasionally just to sit and enjoy it. The **㊵** second is the church of **San Carlo alle Quattro Fontane** (Four Fountains) at the intersection. It was designed by Bernini's rival, Borromini, who created a building that is an intricate exercise in geometric perfection, all curves and movement.

㊶ Turn left down Via delle Quattro Fontane to a splendid 17th-century palace, **Palazzo Barberini.** Inside, the **Galleria Nazionale** offers some fine works by Raphael (the *Fornarina*) and Caravaggio and a salon with gorgeous ceiling frescoes by Pietro da Cortona. Upstairs, don't miss the charming suite of rooms decorated in 18th-century fashion. *Via delle Quattro Fontane 13, tel. 06/481–4591. Admission: 6,000 lire. Open Mon.–Sat. 9–2, Sun. 9–1:30.*

㊷ Down the hill, Piazza Barberini has Bernini's graceful **Tritone Fountain,** designed in 1637 for the sculptor's munificent patron, Pope Urban VIII, whose Barberini coat of arms, featuring bees, is at the base of the large shell.

Time Out Located on Via Barberini, next to a movie house, **Italy Italy** offers the Italian version of fast food, tasty and inexpensive. *Via Barberini 19. Closed Sun.*

Via Veneto winds its way upward from Piazza Barberini past **㊸** **Santa Maria della Concezione,** a Capuchin church famous for its crypt, where the skeletons and assorted bones of 4,000 dead

monks are artistically arranged in four macabre chapels. *Via
Veneto 27, tel. 06/462850. Donations (monetary) requested.
Open daily 9–noon, 3–6.*

The avenue curves past the American Embassy and Consulate;
the luxurious Excelsior Hotel; and Doney's and the Café de
Paris, famous from the days of *la dolce vita* in the 1950s. At the
U.S. Embassy, take Via Bissolati to Piazza San Bernardo. The
church of **Santa Maria della Vittoria,** on the corner, is known for
Bernini's sumptuous Baroque decoration of the Cornaro Chapel, an exceptional fusion of architecture, painting, and sculpture, in which the *Ecstasy of St. Theresa* is the focal point. The
statue represents a mystical experience in what some regard as
very earthly terms. This could be a good point at which to inter-
rupt this tour and pick it up again after a rest.

An interesting side trip from Piazza San Bernardo takes you to
the Early Christian churches of **Sant'Agnese** and **Santa
Costanza,** about a mile beyond the old city walls. Take bus
No. 36, 37, 60, or 136 along Via Nomentana to get there. Santa
Costanza, a church-in-the-round, has vaults decorated with
bright 4th-century mosaics. The custodian of the catacomb of
Sant'Agnese accompanies you up the hill to see it. Art buffs
should make this side trip; others may find it unrewarding.
*Via di Sant'Agnese, tel. 06/832–0743. Admission to Santa
Costanza is free, but a tip is in order if you do not buy a ticket to
see the catacomb of Sant'Agnese. Open Mon.–Sat. 9–noon,
4–6, Sun. 4–6.*

From Piazza San Bernardo, it's not far to Piazza della Repubblica, where the pretty **Fountain of the Naiadi** (nymphs), a
turn-of-the-century addition, features voluptuous bronze ladies wrestling happily with marine monsters. On one side of
the square is an ancient Roman brick facade, which marks the
church of **Santa Maria degli Angeli,** adapted by Michelangelo
from the vast central chamber of the colossal Baths of Diocleti-
an, built in the 4th century AD, the largest and most impressive
of the ancient baths. The baths were on such a grandiose scale
that the church and the former monastery, which now houses
the Museo Nazionale around the corner to the right, account
for only part of the area occupied by them. Inside the church,
take a good look at the eight enormous columns of red granite
that support the beams; these are the original columns of the
baths' central chamber and are 45 feet high and more than 5
feet in diameter.

After years of delay and restorations, the **Museo Nazionale** is
once again able to display the famous Ludovisi collection of ancient sculptures and has just opened another section in Palazzo
Massimo, across the square on the other side of the gardens. In
an upstairs gallery of the former monastery, frescoes from Empress Livia's villa outside Rome are delightful depictions of a
garden in bloom. *Via delle Terme di Diocleziano, tel. 06/475–
0181. Admission: 4,000 lire. Open Tues.–Sat. 9–2, Sun. 9–1.*

Tour 8: The Villa Borghese to the Ara Pacis

A half-mile walk northwest from Piazza della Repubblica up
Via Orlando and Via Vittorio Veneto leads you to **Porta Pin-
ciana** (Pincian Gate), one of the historic city gates in the Au-
relian Walls surrounding Rome. The Porta itself was built in
the 6th century AD, about three centuries after the walls were

built to keep out the Barbarians. These days it is one of the entrances to the **Villa Borghese,** which is in fact the name of Rome's large 17th-century park, built as the pleasure gardens of the powerful Borghese family.

Once inside the park, turn right up Viale del Museo Borghese **50** and make for the **Galleria Borghese,** in what was once the summer house and casino. Despite its size, the building was never lived in. At the time of this writing, it was undergoing extensive renovations, so parts of the gallery may be closed. The second floor contains the picture collection. There is a sculpture collection on the first floor, where you can see Canova's famous statue of Pauline Borghese, wife of Camillo Borghese and sister of Napoleon. Officially known as *Venus Vincitrix*, it is really a depiction of a haughty (and very seductive) Pauline, lying provocatively on a Roman sofa. The next two rooms hold two important Baroque sculptures by Bernini: *David* and *Apollo and Daphne*. In each you can see the vibrant attention to movement that marked the first departure from the Renaissance preoccupation with the idealized human form. Daphne is being transformed into a laurel tree while fleeing from a lecherous Apollo: Twigs sprout from her fingertips while her pursuer recoils in amazement. *Piazzale Museo Borghese, tel. 06/858577. Admission free for the duration of the renovations. Open Mon.–Sat. 9–1:30, Sun. 9–1.*

A right, then a left turn from the museum lead across the park **51** to the **Galleria Nazionale d'Arte Moderna** (the National Gallery of Modern Art), a large white building boasting the leading collection of 20th-century works in Italy. A large new wing was opened in 1988. *Via delle Belle Arti 131, tel. 06/322–4151. Admission: 4,000 lire. Open Tues.–Sat. 9–2, Sun. 9–1.*

52 Close by is the **Museo di Villa Giulia,** housing one of the world's great Etruscan collections. The villa is a former papal summer palace set in lovely gardens. This is the place to study the strange, half-understood Etruscan civilization, for here are magnificent terra-cotta statues, figurines, jewelry, household implements, sarcophagi—a whole way of life on display. Among the most precious gems are the *Apollo of Veio* and the *Sarcophagus of the Sposi*. When you have had your fill of these treasures, step out into the nymphaeum (the architectural term for this place of cool recesses and fern-softened fountains) and take a close look at the full-scale reconstruction of an Etruscan temple in the garden. *Piazza di Villa Giulia 9, tel. 06/320–1951. Admission: 8,000 lire. Open Tues.–Sat. 9–7, Sun. 9–1.*

53 The **Pincio** is an extension of Villa Borghese, with gardens on a terrace overlooking much of Rome. It was laid out by the early-19th-century architect Valadier as part of his overall plan for Piazza del Popolo. The Pincio offers a superb view, absolutely spectacular when there is a fine sunset, and it's also a vantage **54** point from which you can study Valadier's arrangement of **Piazza del Popolo.**

This is one of Rome's largest squares and a traditional place for mass meetings and rallies. At the center, four dignified stone lions guard an obelisk relating the life and times of Ramses II in the 13th century BC. Next to the 400-year-old **Porta del Popolo, 55** Rome's northern city gate, stop in at the church of **Santa Maria**

del Popolo to see a pair of Caravaggios and some Bernini sculptures in a rich Baroque setting.

From here, it's a short walk down Via Ripetta to the large **Augusteum,** the mausoleum built by Augustus for himself and his family. It gives you an idea of what Hadrian's Mausoleum must have looked like before it became Castel Sant'Angelo.

⑤⑥ Next to it is an unattractive modern edifice that shelters the **Ara Pacis** (Altar of Augustan Peace), erected in 13 BC to celebrate the era of peace ushered in by Augustus's military victories. The reliefs on the marble enclosure are magnificent. *Via Ripetta, tel. 06/671–0271. Admission: 4,500 lire. Open Wed.–Fri. 9–1:30, Tues. and Sat. 9–1:30, 3:30–7:30, Sun. 9–1.*

Tour 9: The Jewish Ghetto and Trastevere

For the authentic atmosphere of Old Rome, explore the old Jewish ghetto and the narrow streets of Trastevere, two tightly knit communities whose inhabitants proudly claim descent—whether real or imagined—from the ancient Romans. Then climb the Janiculum, a hill with views over the whole city, a vantage point beloved of all Romans. Wander into the shadowy area bounded by Piazza Campitelli and Lungotevere Cenci, the ancient Jewish ghetto. Within this cramped quarter, until 1847, all Rome's Jews (and they were many, tracing their presence in the city to ancient Roman times) were confined under a rigid all-night curfew. At the little church opposite Quattro Capi bridge, they were forced to attend sermons that aimed to convert them to Catholicism, and to pay for the privilege.

⑤⑦ Many Jews have remained here, close to the bronze-roofed **synagogue** on Lungotevere Cenci and to the roots of their community. Among the most interesting sights in the ghetto are
⑤⑧ the pretty **Fontana delle Tartarughe** (Turtle Fountain) on Piazza Mattei; the old houses on Via Portico d'Ottavia, where medieval inscriptions and ancient friezes testify to the venerable
⑤⑨ age of these buildings; and the **Teatro di Marcello,** hardly recognizable as a theater now, but built at the end of the 1st century BC by Julius Caesar to hold 20,000 spectators.

Time Out Stop to indulge in American and Austrian baked goods at **Dolceroma,** *Via Portico d'Ottavia 20/b. Closed Sun. afternoon and Mon.*

⑥⓪ Cross the Tiber over the ancient Ponte Fabricio to the **Tiberina Island,** where a city hospital stands on a site that has been dedicated to healing ever since a temple to Aesculapius was erected here in 291 BC. If you have time, and if the river's not too high, go down the stairs for a different perspective on the island and the Tiber.

Then continue across Ponte Cestio into **Trastevere,** a maze of narrow streets that, despite creeping gentrification, is still one of the city's most authentically Roman neighborhoods (for another, explore the jumble of streets between the Roman Forum, Santa Maria Maggiore, and the Colosseum). Among self-consciously picturesque trattorias and trendy tearooms, old shops, in alleys festooned with washing hung out to dry,
⑥① and in dusty artisans' workshops. Be sure to see **Piazza Santa Maria in Trastevere,** the heart of the quarter, with one of

Rome's oldest churches, decorated inside and out with 12th- and 13th-century mosaics.

Follow Via della Scala to Via della Lungara, where Raphael **62** decorated the garden loggia of **Villa Farnesina** for extravagant host Agostino Chigi, who delighted in impressing guests by having his servants clear the table by casting precious gold and silver dinnerware into the Tiber. Naturally, the guests did not know of the nets he had stretched under the water line to catch everything. *Via della Lungara 230, tel. 06/654–0565. Admission free. Open Mon.–Sat. 9–1.*

Trastevere's population has become increasingly diverse, and it has acquired a reputation for purse-snatching and petty thievery, much to the chagrin of the authentic Trasteverini, so keep a close eye on your belongings as you stroll these byways.

From Porta Settimiana you can follow Via Garibaldi as it curves **63** up to the Janiculum, past the church of **San Pietro in Montorio,** known for its views and for the Tempietto, Bramante's little **64** temple in the cloister. Beyond the impressive **Acqua Paola 65 Fountain,** you'll come upon the **Janiculum Park,** which offers splendid views of Rome.

Tour 10: The Catacombs and the Appian Way

This tour gives you a respite from museums, though it's no easier on the feet. Do it on a sunny day and either take along a picnic or plan to have lunch at one of the pleasant restaurants near the catacombs. Take the No. 118 bus from San Giovanni in **66** Laterano to the **Via Appia Antica** (the Queen of Roads), completed in 312 BC by Appius Claudius, who also built Rome's first aqueduct. You pass Porta San Sebastiano, which gives you a good idea of what the city's 5th-century fortifications looked like, and farther along you'll see the little church of **Domine Quo Vadis,** where tradition says that Christ appeared to St. Peter, inspiring him to return to Rome to face martyrdom.

There are two important catacombs on the Via Appia Antica. The first you come upon is that of San Callisto, one of the best preserved of these underground cemeteries. A friar will guide you through its crypts and galleries. *Via Appia Antica 110, tel. 06/513–6725. Admission: 4,000 lire. Open Apr.–Sept., Thurs.– Tues. 8:30–noon, 2:30–6; Oct.–Mar., Thurs.–Tues. 8:30– noon, 2:30–5.*

The 4th-century catacomb of San Sebastiano, a little farther on, which was named for the saint who was buried here, burrows underground on four levels. The only one of the catacombs to remain accessible during the Middle Ages, it is the origin of the term "catacomb," for it was located in a spot where the road dips into a hollow, a place the Romans called *catacumbas* (near the hollow). Eventually, the Christian cemetery that had existed here since the 2nd century came to be known by the same name, which was applied to all underground cemeteries discovered in Rome in later centuries. *Via Appia Antica 136, tel. 06/ 788–7035. Admission: 4,000 lire. Open Fri.–Wed. 9–noon and 2:30–5.*

On the other side of Via Appia Antica are the ruins of the **Circus of Maxentius,** where the obelisk now in Piazza Navona once stood. Farther along the ancient road is the circular **Tomb of Cecilia Metella,** mausoleum of a Roman noblewoman who lived at the time of Julius Caesar. It was transformed into a fortress in the 14th century.

Time Out There are several trattorias along the Via Appia Antica, most of which are moderately priced (*see* Dining, below). For a sandwich or a snack, the bar on the corner of Via Appia Antica and Via Cecilia Metella, just beyond the tomb, can provide sustenance and a relaxing pause in the adjoining garden.

The Tomb of Cecilia Metella marks the beginning of the most interesting and evocative stretch of the Via Appia Antica, lined with tombs and fragments of statuary. Cypresses and umbrella pines stand guard over the ruined sepulchers, and the occasional tracts of ancient paving stones are the same ones trod by triumphant Roman legions.

Rome for Free

Sightseeing in many capital cities can often lead to a steady draining of your resources, leaving your budget blown by day one. Rome is an exception because most of its sights are either inexpensive or, more commonly, free of charge. You could construct several memorable itineraries devoted exclusively to architecture and religious art—taking in dozens of piazzas, churches, streets, and fountains—and not part with a single lira. Museums and galleries, of course, usually do charge admission, but it's rarely steep, and there are some surprising exceptions, such as the following:

The Colosseum—Lower Level (Tour 1: Ancient Rome).
The Tombs of the Popes (Tour 2: The Vatican).
The Vatican Museums on the Last Sunday of the Month (Tour 3: Around the Vatican).
The Pantheon (Tour 4: Old Rome).
Galleria Borghese (Tour 8: The Villa Borghese to the Ara Pacis).
Villa Farnesina (Tour 9: The Jewish Ghetto and Trastevere).

What to See and Do with Children

There's a lot to do in Rome that children—and their parents—will enjoy. Take the children to a **pizzeria** with a wood-burning oven, where they can see the chef work with the dough. Take a ride in a **horse and carriage**—it's fun and feels a lot less silly than it looks. Visit the **Zoo** in Villa Borghese, or climb to **the top of St. Peter's**—arduous but worth it for the incomparable views inside and outside the church. Spend some time in the **Villa Borghese,** perhaps taking in a **Punch and Judy show** on the Pincio. There's another Punch and Judy show on the **Janiculum** hill, where there is also a colorful stand selling puppets.

In December and early January, visit the big **Christmas bazaar** at Piazza Navona, then stop at the huge toy store at the north end of the square. For an almost comical display of orchestration, pause awhile to watch the policeman directing traffic from his little podium in the middle of **Piazza Venezia.** An even greater spectacle, but completely serious, is the daily **changing of the guard** at the Quirinale Palace, the residence of the president of Italy. Every day at 4 PM there's a military band and parade as the guards change shifts.

Rome's residential suburb EUR is the home of the well-run **Luna Park** amusement center. The park's big Ferris wheel is an attraction, as are the roller coaster and other rides and games. It can be reached by bus No. 707 from San Paolo fuori le Mura. *Via delle Tre Fontane, tel. 06/592–5933. Admission free, but you pay for each ride. Closed Tues.*

There's usually a **circus** somewhere in town: Check billboards and newspaper listings. Also check listings for cartoon films at the movies and for puppet shows and other children's programs at theaters.

Explore **Castel Sant'Angelo** (*see* Tour 2: The Vatican, above). It's got dungeons, battlements, cannons, and cannonballs, and a collection of antique weapons and armor.

Rent **bicycles** and ride around Villa Borghese and the center of town on Sunday, when the traffic is lighter.

In spring or summer, take a boat ride to **Ostia Antica** (*see* Excursion 1: Ostia Antica, below).

Off the Beaten Track

Stroll through the quiet, green neighborhood of the **Aventine Hill,** one of the seven hills of ancient Rome that most tourists don't see. It has several of the city's oldest and least-visited churches, as well as a delightful surprise: the view from the keyhole in the gate to the garden of the Knights of Malta.

Visit the excavations under St. Peter's for a fascinating glimpse of the underpinnings of the great basilica, which was built over the cemetery where archaeologists say they have found **St. Peter's tomb.** *Apply several days in advance to the Ufficio Scavi (Excavations Office), to the right beyond the Arco delle Campane entrance to the Vatican, which is left of the basilica. Just tell the Swiss guard you want the Ufficio Scavi, and he will let you enter the confines of the Vatican City. Tel. 06/698–5318. Admission: 5,000 lire with guide, 3,000 lire with taped guide.*

See the **Protestant Cemetery** behind the Piramide, a stone pyramid built in 12 BC at the order of the Roman praetor (senior magistrate) who was buried there. The cemetery is reminiscent of a country churchyard. Among the headstones you'll find Keats's tomb and the place where Shelley's heart was buried. *Via Caio Cestio 6, tel. 06/574–1141. Ring for the custodian. An offering of 500–1,000 lire is customary. Open daily 8–11:30, 3:20–5:30.*

Explore the subterranean dwellings under the church of **San Clemente.** *Via San Giovanni in Laterano, tel. 06/731–5723. Donation requested. Open Mon.–Sat. 9–noon, 3:30–6; Sun. 10–noon.*

Have an inexpensive lunch at **L'Eau Vive,** run by lay Catholic missionary workers, whose mission in this case is running a restaurant. Though it's elegant and fairly expensive for an evening meal, the good fixed-price lunch is a bargain. *Via Monterone 85 (off Piazza Sant'Eustachio), tel. 06/654–1095. AE, DC, V. Closed Sun.*

Shopping

Shopping in Rome is part of the fun, no matter what your budget. You're sure to find something that suits your fancy *and* your pocketbook, but don't expect to get bargains on Italian brands, such as Benetton, that are exported to the United States; prices are about the same on both sides of the Atlantic.

Shops are open from 9 or 9:30 to 1 and from 3:30 or 4 to 7 or 7:30. There's a tendency in Rome for shops in central districts to stay open all day, but for many this is still in the experimental stage. Department stores and centrally located UPIM and Standa stores are open all day. Remember that most stores are closed Sunday and, with the exception of food and technical-supply stores, are also closed Monday mornings from September to June and Saturday afternoons in July and August. Most Italian sizes are not uniform, so always try on clothing before you buy or measure gift items. Glove sizes are universal. In any case, remember that Italian stores generally will *not* refund your purchases and that they often cannot exchange goods because of limited stock. *Always* take your purchases with you; having them shipped home from the shop can cause hassles. If circumstances are such that you can't take your goods with you and if the shop seems reliable about shipping, get a firm statement of *when* and *how* your purchase will be sent.

Prezzi fissi means that prices are fixed and it's a waste of time bargaining unless you're buying a sizable quantity of goods or a particularly costly object. Most stores have a fixed-price policy, and most honor a variety of credit cards. They will also accept foreign money at the current exchange rate, give or take a few lire. Ask for a receipt for your purchases; you may need it at customs on your return home. Bargaining is still an art at Porta Portese flea market and is routine when purchasing anything from a street vendor.

It's theoretically possible to obtain a refund on the VAT tax, which is included in the selling price. In practice, however, the mechanism is so complex that it is hardly worthwhile worrying about it. To be eligible for a refund, you must spend more than 605,000 lire on one item in a store and then endure considerable rigmarole at the airport when you leave. The Europe Tax-free Shopping system streamlines the process somewhat. Look for the "Tax-free for Tourists" sign in shops if you plan to purchase anything for that amount.

Shopping Districts The most elegant and expensive shops are concentrated in the **Piazza di Spagna** area. That's where you'll find the big-name boutiques, too: Versace, Ferre, and Laura Biagiotti on **Via Borgognona;** Valentino on **Via Bocca di Leone;** Armani and Missoni on **Via del Babuino. Via Margutta** is known for art galleries and **Via del Babuino** for antiques. There are several high-fashion outlets on **Via Gregoriana** and **Via Sistina.** Bordering this top-price shopping district is **Via del Corso,** which—along with **Via Frattina** and **Via del Gambero**—is lined with shops and boutiques of all kinds where prices and goods are competitive.

Via del Tritone, leading up from Piazza Colonna off Via del Corso, has some medium-priced, and a few expensive, shops selling everything from fashion fabrics to trendy furniture. Still farther up, on **Via Veneto,** you'll find more high-priced boutiques and shoe stores, as well as newsstands selling En-

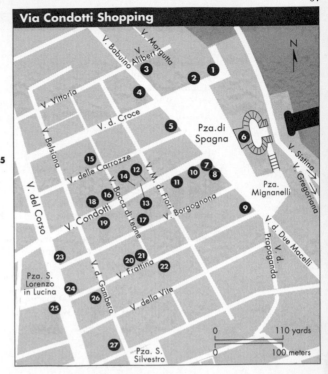

glish-language newspapers, magazines, and paperback books. **Via Nazionale** features shoe stores, moderately priced boutiques, and shops selling men's and women's fashions. **Via Cola di Rienzo** offers high-quality goods of all types; it's a good alternative to the Piazza di Spagna area.

In Old Rome, **Via dei Coronari** is lined with antique shops and some new stores selling designer home accessories. **Via Giulia** and **Via Monserrato** also feature antiques dealers galore, plus a few art galleries. In the **Pantheon** area there are many shops selling liturgical objects and vestments. But the place to go for religious souvenirs is, obviously, the area around St. Peter's, especially **Via della Conciliazione** and **Via di Porta Angelica**.

Department Stores   Rome has only a handful of department stores. **Rinascente,** at Piazza Colonna, sells clothing and accessories only. Another Rinascente, at Piazza Fiume, has the same stock. **Coin,** on Piazzale Appio, near San Giovanni in Laterano, has fashions for men and women. There is another Coin store in the U.S.-style shopping mall at Cinecittà Due (Subaugusta Metro stop). The **UPIM** and **Standa** chains offer low to moderately priced medium-quality goods. They're the place to go if you need a pair of slippers, a sweater, a bathing suit, or such to see you through until you get home. In addition, they carry all kinds of toiletries and first-aid needs. Most Standa and UPIM stores have invaluable while-you-wait shoe-repair service counters.

Food and Flea   Rome's biggest and most colorful outdoor food markets are at
Markets   **Campo dei Fiori** (just south of Piazza Navona), **Via Andrea Doria** (Trionfale, about a quarter mile north of the entrance to

Rome Shopping

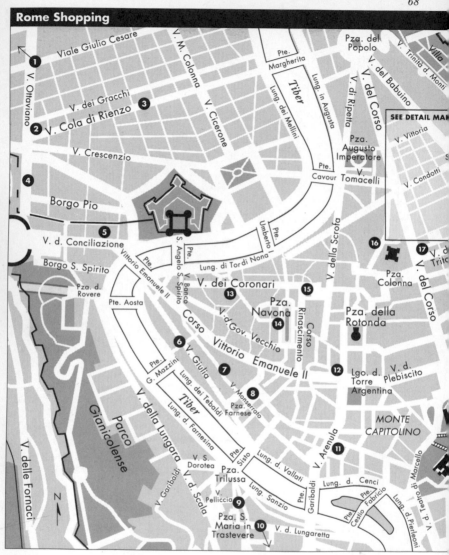

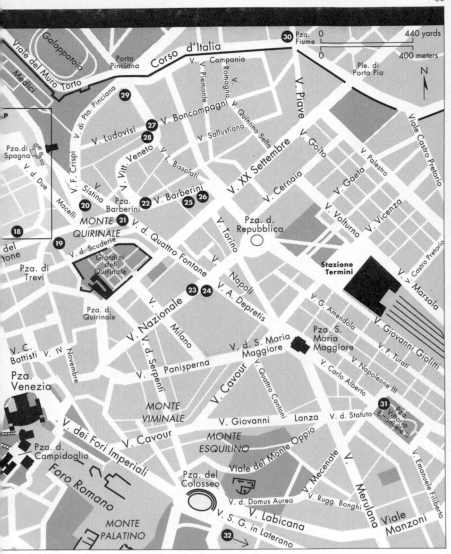

the Vatican museums), and **Piazza Vittorio** (just down Via Carlo Alberto from the church of Santa Maria Maggiore). There's a flea market on Sunday morning at **Porta Portese;** it now offers mainly new or secondhand clothing, but there are still a few dealers in old furniture and sundry objects, much of it intriguing junk. Bargaining is the rule here, as are pickpockets; beware. To reach Porta Portese, take Via di San Francesco south for about half a mile from Santa Maria in Trastevere. All outdoor markets are open from early morning to about 2, except Saturdays, when they may stay open all day.

Clothing Boutiques All the big names in Italian fashion are represented in the Piazza di Spagna area. **Sorelle Fontane** (Salita San Sebastianello 6), one of the first houses to put Italy on the fashion map, has a large boutique with an extensive line of ready-to-wear clothing and accessories. **Carlo Palazzi** (Via Borgognona 7) has elegant men's fashions and accessories. **Mariselaine** (Via Condotti 70) is a top-quality women's fashion boutique. **Camomilla** (Piazza di Spagna 85), has trendy styles for women.

Specialty Stores *Antiques and Prints* For old prints and antiques, the **Perera** shop (Via del Babuino 92b) is a good hunting ground. Early photographs of Rome and views of Italy from the archives of **Alinari** (Via Aliberti 16/a) make interesting souvenirs. **Nardecchia** (Piazza Navona 25) is reliable for prints. **Le Bateleur** (71 Via S. Simone, tel. 06/654–4676), in a tiny 11th-century sacristy under a flight of stone steps, shows changing exhibits and a bit of everything from the 17th to the 20th century.

Handicrafts For pottery, handwoven textiles, and other handicrafts, **Myricae** (Via Frattina 36, with another store at Piazza del Parlamento 38) has a good selection. **Galleria del Batik** (Via della Pelliccia 29) in Trastevere is off the beaten track but well worth a visit; it has a wealth of handicrafts, beautifully displayed in a rustic setting. A bottle of liqueur, jar of marmalade, or bar of chocolate handmade by Cistercian monks in several monasteries in Italy makes an unusual gift to take home; they are all on sale at **Ai Monasteri** (Piazza Cinque Luna 2).

Household Linens and Embroidery **Frette** (Piazza di Spagna 10) is a Roman institution for fabulous trousseaux. **Cesari** (Via Barberini 1) is another; it also has less-expensive gift items, such as aprons, beach towels, and place mats. **Lavori Artigianali Femminili** (Via Capo le Case 6) offers exquisitely embroidered household linens, infants' and children's clothing, and blouses.

Jewelry **Bulgari** (Via Condotti 10) is to Rome what Cartier is to Paris; the shop's elegant display windows hint at what's beyond the guard at the door. **Buccellati** (Via Condotti 31) is a tradition-rich Florentine jewelry house famous for its silverwork; it ranks with Bulgari for quality and reliability. **Fornari** (Via Frattina 71) and **Frugoni** (Via Arenula 83) have tempting selections of small silver objects. **Bozart** (Via Bocca di Leone 4) features dazzling costume jewelry geared to the latest fashions.

Knitwear **Luisa Spagnoli** (Via del Corso 382, with other shops at Via Frattina 116 and Via Veneto 130) is always reliable for good quality at the right price and styles to suit American tastes. **Miranda** (Via Bocca di Leone 28) is a treasure trove of warm jackets, skirts, and shawls, handwoven in gorgeous colors of wool or mohair, or in lighter yarns for summer.

Leather Goods **Gucci** (Via Condotti 8 and 77) is the most famous of Rome's leather shops. It has a full assortment of accessories on the first floor; a fashion boutique for men and women and a scarf department on the second floor; and a full complement of Japanese customers, who line up to get in on busy days. **Roland's** (Piazza di Spagna 74) has an extensive stock of good-quality leather fashions and accessories, as well as stylish casual wear in wool and silk. **Ceresa** (Via del Tritone 118) has more reasonably priced fine-leather goods, including many handbags and leather fashions. **Volterra** (Via Barberini 102) is well stocked and offers a wide selection of handbags at moderate prices. **Sermoneta** (Piazza di Spagna 61) shows a varied range of gloves in its windows, and there are many more inside. **Di Cori**, a few steps away, also has a good selection of gloves; there's another Di Cori store at Via Nazionale 183. **Merola** (Via del Corso 143) carries a line of expensive top-quality gloves and scarves.

Nichol's (Via Barberini 94) is in the moderate price range and is one of the few stores in Rome that stocks shoes in American widths. **Ferragamo** (Via Condotti 73) is one of Rome's best stores for fine shoes and leather accessories, and its silk scarves are splendid; you pay for quality here, but you can get great buys during the periodic sales. **Mario Valentino** (Via Frattina 58) is a top name for stylish shoes and leather fashions. **Magli** (Via del Gambero 1 and Via Veneto 70) is known for well-made shoes and matching handbags at high to moderate prices. **Campanile** (Via Condotti 58) has four floors of shoes in the latest, as well as classic styles, and other leather goods.

Silks and Fabrics **Galtrucco** (Via del Tritone 18), **Bises** (Via del Gesù 56), and **Meconi** (Via Cola di Rienzo 305) have the best selections of world-famous Italian silks and fashion fabrics. You can find some real bargains when remnants *(scampoli)* are on sale.

Sports

Biking You can rent a bike at Via del Pellegrino 82 (tel. 06/654–1084), near Campo dei Fiori, and at Piazza Navona 82. There are rental concessions at Piazza di Spagna, Piazza del Popolo, Largo San Silvestro, Largo Argentina, Viale della Pineta in Villa Borghese, and at Viale del Bambino on the Pincio.

Bowling There's a large American-style bowling center, **Bowling Brunswick** (Lungotevere Acqua Acetosa, tel. 06/808–6147) and a smaller one, **Bowling Roma** (Viale Regina Margherita 181, tel. 06/855–1184).

Fitness Facilities **The Cavalieri Hilton** (Via Cadlolo 101, tel. 06/31511) offers a 600-meter jogging path on the hotel grounds in the elegant Monte Mario area, as well as an outdoor pool, two clay tennis courts, an exercise area, a sauna, and a steam room. **The Sheraton Roma** (Viale del Pattinaggio, tel. 06/14223) has a heated outdoor pool, a tennis court, two squash courts, and a sauna, but no gym. **The St. Peter's Holiday Inn** (Via Aurelia Antica 415, tel. 06/5872) has two tennis courts on the hotel grounds, plus two more nearby. It also has a 25-meter outdoor pool.

The **Roman Sport Center** (Via del Galoppatoio 33, tel. 06/360–1667) is a full-fledged sports center occupying vast premises next to the underground parking lot in Villa Borghese; it has two swimming pools, a gym, aerobic workout areas, squash courts, and saunas. It is affiliated with the **American Health Club** (Largo Somalia 60, tel. 06/839–4488).

Golf The oldest and most prestigious golf club in Rome is the **Circolo del Golf Roma** (Via Acqua Santa 3, tel. 06/780–3407). The newest is the **Country Club Castel Gandolfo** (Via Santo Spirito 13, Castel Gandolfo, tel. 06/931–3084), with a course designed by Robert Trent Jones and a 17th-century villa as a clubhouse. The **Golf Club Fioranello** (Viale della Repubblica, tel. 06/713–8291) is at Santa Maria delle Mole, off the Via Appia Antica. There is a 18-hole course at the **Olgiata Golf Club** (Largo Olgiata 15, on the Via Cassia, tel. 06/378–9141). Nonmembers are welcome in these clubs but must show membership cards of their home golf or country clubs.

Horseback Riding There are several riding clubs in Rome. The most central is the **Associazione Sportiva Villa Borghese** (Via del Galoppatoio 23, tel. 06/360–6797). You can also ride at the **Società Ippica Romana** (Via Monti della Farnesina 18, tel. 06/396–6214) and at the **Circolo Ippico Olgiata** (Largo Olgiata 15, tel. 06/378–8792), outside the city on the Via Cassia.

Jogging The best bet for jogging in the inner city is at the **Villa Borghese**. A circuit of the Pincio, among the marble statuary, measures half a mile. A longer run in the park of Villa Borghese itself might include a loop around **Piazza di Siena**, a grass horse track measuring a quarter of a mile. Although most traffic is barred from Villa Borghese, government and police cars sometimes speed through. Be careful to stick to the sides of the roads. For a long run away from all traffic, try **Villa Ada** and **Villa Doria Pamphili** on the Janiculum. On the other hand, if you really love history, you can jog at the old **Circus Maximus**, now reduced to a large traffic island surrounded by honking vehicles, or along Via delle Terme di Caracalla, which is flanked by a park inside of the Circus, where footing is easiest. (Also, *see* **The Cavalieri Hilton** in Fitness Facilities, above.)

Swimming The large Olympic swimming pool at the **Foro Italico** is open to the public June–September (Lungotevere Maresciallo Cadorna, tel. 06/360–8591). The outdoor pools of the **Cavalieri Hilton** (Via Cadlolo 101, tel. 06/31511) and the **Hotel Aldovrandi** (Via Ulisse Aldovrandi 15, tel. 06/322–3993) are lush summer oases open to nonguests. The **Roman Sport Center** (Via del Galoppatoio 33, tel. 06/360–1667) has two swimming pools, and there's another one at the **American Health Club** (Largo Somalia 60, tel. 06/839–4488).

Tennis Increasingly popular with Italians, tennis is played in private clubs and on many public courts that can be rented by the hour. Your hotel *portiere* will direct you to the nearest courts and can book for you. A prestigious Roman club is the **Tennis Club Parioli** (Largo de Morpurgo 2, Via Salaria, tel. 06/839–0392).

Spectator Sports

Basketball Basketball continues to grow in popularity (in Italy) with many American pros now playing on Italian teams. In Rome, games are played at the **Palazzo dello Sport** in the EUR district (Piazzale dello Sport, tel. 06/592–5107).

Horseback Riding The **International Riding Show,** held the last few days of April and the first week in May, draws a stylish crowd to the amphitheater of Piazza di Siena in Villa Borghese. The competition is stiff, and the program features a cavalry charge staged by the dashing mounted corps of the *carabinieri*. For information, call the **Italian Federation of Equestrian Sports** (Viale Tiziano 70, tel. 06/36851).

Horse Racing There's flat racing at the lovely century-old **Capanelle** track (Via Appia Nuova 1255, tel. 06/799–0551), frequented by a chic crowd on big race days. The trotters meet at the **Tor di Valle** track (Via del Mare, tel. 06/592–4205).

Soccer Italy's favorite spectator sport stirs passionate enthusiasm among partisans. Games are usually held on Sunday afternoons throughout the fall–spring season. Two teams—Roma and Lazio—play their home games in the Olympic Stadium at **Foro Italico.** Tickets are on sale at the box office before the games; your hotel *portiere* may be able to help you get tickets in advance. The Olympic Stadium is on Viale dei Gladiatori, in the extensive Foro Italico sports complex built by Mussolini on the banks of the Tiber (tel. 06/396–4661).

Foro Italico will host the 1990 **World Cup Soccer Championships,** June 8–July 9. The official ticket agent for the event is **Novanta Tours** (Via Silvio di Amico 40, 00145 Rome, tel. 06/54701).

Tennis A top-level international tournament is held at the Tennis Stadium at **Foro Italico** in May. For information, call the **Italian Tennis Federation** (Viale Tiziano 70, tel. 06/368–58213).

Beaches

The beaches nearest Rome are at **Ostia,** a busy urban center in its own right; **Castelfusano,** nearby; **Fregene,** a villa colony; and **Castelporziano,** a public beach area maintained by the city. At Ostia and Fregene, you pay for changing cabins, cabanas, umbrellas, and such, and for the fact that the sand is kept clean and combed. Some establishments, such as **Kursaal** (Lungomare Catullo 36 at Castelfusano, tel. 06/562–1303) have swimming pools, strongly recommended as alternatives to the murky waters of the Mediterranean, which are notoriously polluted. You can reach Ostia by Metro from Termini or Ostiense Station, Castelfusano and Castelporziano by bus from Ostia, and Fregene by ACOTRAL bus from the Via Lepanto stop of Metro Line A in Rome. All beaches are crowded during July and August.

For cleaner water and more of a resort atmosphere, you have to go farther afield. To the north of Rome, **Santa Marinella** and **Santa Severa** offer shoals, sand, and attractive surroundings. To the south, **Sabaudia** is known for miles of sandy beaches, **San Felice Circeo** is a classy resort, and **Sperlonga** is a picturesque old town flanked by beaches and pretty coves.

Dining

Our recommendations were made under the direction of Eliana Cosimini, noted Italian food and travel writer.

There was a time when you could predict the clientele and prices of a Roman eating establishment by whether it was called a *ristorante,* a *trattoria,* or an *osteria* (tavern). Now these names are interchangeable. A rustic-looking spot that calls itself an osteria or hostaria may turn out to be chic and expensive. Generally speaking, however, a trattoria is a family-run place, simpler in decor, menu, and service—and slightly less expensive—than a ristorante. A true osteria is a wine shop, very basic and down to earth, where the only function of the food is to keep the customers sober.

As the pace of Roman life quickens, more fast-food outlets are opening, offering tourists a wider choice of light meals. They are variations on the older Italian institutions of *tavola calda* (literally, "hot table") and *rosticceria* (roast meats), both of which offer a selection of hot and cold dishes to be taken out or eaten on the premises. A tavola calda is more likely to have seating. At both, some dishes are priced by portion; others by weight. You usually select your food, find out how much it costs, and pay the cashier, who'll give you a stub to give to the counter person when you pick up the food. Snack bars cater to the new demand for fast food with cold or toasted sandwiches. If you want to picnic, buy your provisions in any *alimentari* (grocery) store. *Pizza Rustica* outlets sell slices of various kinds of pizza; there's one on every other block in Rome, or so it seems.

Despite these changes, many Romans stick to the tradition of having their main meal at lunch, from 1 to 3, although you won't be turned away if hunger strikes shortly after noon. Dinner is served from 8 or 8:30 until about 10:30 or 11. Some restaurants stay open much later, especially in summer, when patrons linger at sidewalk tables to enjoy the cool breeze *(ponentino)*. Almost all restaurants close one day a week (it's usually safest to call ahead to reserve) and for at least two weeks in August, when it can sometimes seem impossible to find sustenance in the deserted city.

Tap water is safe everywhere in Rome. Most Romans order bottled mineral water *(acqua minerale)*, either with bubbles *(gassata)* or without *(naturale* or *non gassata)*. It comes by the liter *(litro)* or the half-liter *(mezzo litro)*. If you're on a budget, keep your check down by ordering tap water *(acqua semplice)*. If you are on a low-sodium diet, ask for everything *senza sale* (without salt).

Always check the menu that's on display in the window of a restaurant or just inside the door. In all but the simplest places, there will be a cover charge *(pane e coperto)* and usually a service charge *(servizio)* of 10%–15%. A *menu turistico* (fixed-price tourist menu) includes taxes and service, but usually not drinks. Beware dishes on à la carte menus, such as fish, Florentine steaks, or fillets: For those marked "SQ," you will be charged according to the weight of the item; for those marked "L. 4,000 hg," you'll be charged 4,000 lire for a hectogram (about 3½ ounces).

Highly recommended restaurants in each price category are indicated by a star ★.

Category	Cost*
Very Expensive	over 110,000 lire
Expensive	65,000–110,000 lire
Moderate	30,000–65,000 lire
Inexpensive	under 30,000 lire

*per person, for a three-course meal, including house wine and taxes

Central Rome

Very Expensive **La Cupola.** The elegant restaurant of the Hotel Excelsior serves classic regional Italian and international cuisine with flair. The empire decor is luxurious; service is courteous and highly professional. Perfect pasta dishes, such as *bucatini all'amatriciana* (an earthy Roman specialty) and *gnocchetti di ricotta all' Excelsior* (small ricotta dumplings with tomato-and-basil sauce), are reason enough to eat here. *Hotel Excelsior, Via Veneto 125, tel. 06/4708. Reservations not required. Jacket and tie preferred. AE, DC, MC, V.*

Le Jardin. Located in the Parioli residential district, this restaurant is one of Rome's classiest establishments. It's in the exclusive Lord Byron Hotel, itself a triumph of studied interior decoration. The imaginative menu is a tempting compendium of seasonal specialties served with style. If they are on the menu, try the risotto with seafood and vegetable sauce or the fillet of beef with morels. *Hotel Lord Byron, Via Giuseppe De Notaris 5, tel. 06/322-0404. Reservations required. Jacket and tie preferred. AE, DC, MC, V. Closed Sun.*

★ **Le Restaurant.** The restaurant of the luxurious Grand hotel (*see* Lodging, below) is the ultimate in elegance and the discreet haunt of Rome's chicest crowd. The resplendent dining room is a model of 19th-century opulence, lavished with crystal chandeliers, fine oil paintings, and damasks and velvets in pale golden tones. The menu varies with the season; there are always daily recommendations. Among the specialties are *carpaccio tiepido di pescatrice* (brill—a flatfish—with thin slices of raw beef) and *medaglioni di vitello al marsala con tartufo* (veal medallions with marsala wine and truffles). The wine list offers some choice vintages. *Via Vittorio Emanuele Orlando 3, tel. 06/482931. Reservations advised. Jacket and tie required. AE, DC, MC, V.*

★ **El Toulà.** Take a byway off Piazza Nicosia in Old Rome to find this prestigious restaurant, one of a number in Italy of the same name; all are spin-offs of a renowned restaurant in Treviso in northern Italy (*see* Dining and Lodging in Chapter 7). Rome's El Toulà has the warm, welcoming atmosphere of a 19th-century country house, with white walls, antique furniture in dark wood, heavy silver serving dishes, and spectacular arrangements of fruits and flowers. There's a cozy bar off the entrance, where you can sip a *prosecco* (Venetian semi-sparkling white wine), the aperitif best suited to the chef's Venetian specialties, which include the classic *pasta e fagioli* (pasta and bean soup), risotto with artichokes, and *fegato alla veneziana* (liver with onions). *Via della Lupa 29/b, tel. 06/687-3750. Reservations required. Jacket and tie required. AE, DC, MC, V. Closed Sat. lunch, Sun., all of Aug., Dec. 24-26.*

Expensive **Alberto Ciarla.** Located on a large square in Trastevere, scene
★ of a busy morning food market, Alberto Ciarla is thought by many to be the best seafood restaurant in Rome. In contrast with its workaday location, the interior is polished with red-and-black decor. Bubbling aquariums—a sure sign that the food is superfresh—are set along the wall. Seafood salads are a specialty. Meat eaters will find succor in the house pâté and the lamb. Order carefully, or the check will soar. *Piazza San Cosimato 40, tel. 06/581-8668. Reservations required. Jacket and tie suggested. AE, DC, MC, V. Dinner only. Closed Sun., Aug. 5-25, Christmas.*

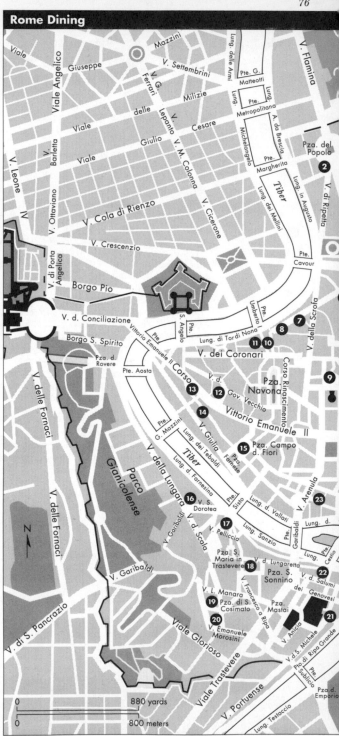

Rome Dining

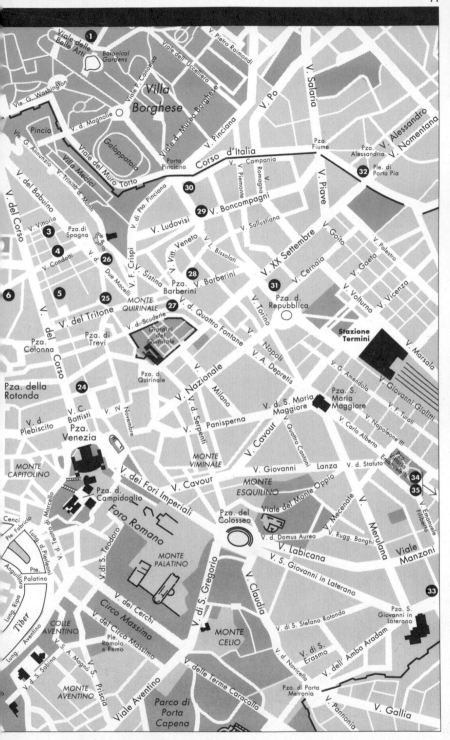

★ **Andrea.** Ernest Hemingway and King Farouk used to eat here; Nowadays, you're more likely to hear the murmured conversation of Italian powerbrokers. Half a block from Via Veneto, this restaurant offers classic Italian cooking in an intimate, clubby setting, in which snowy table linens gleam against a discreet background of dark-green paneling. The menu features delicacies such as homemade *tagliolini* (thin noodles) with shrimp and spinach sauce, spaghetti with seafood and truffles, and mouth-watering *carciofi all'Andrea* (artichokes simmered in olive oil). *Via Sardegna 26, tel. 06/482–1891. Reservations advised. Dress: casual but neat. AE, DC, MC, V. Closed Sun. and most of Aug.*

Coriolano. The only tourists who find their way to this classic restaurant near Porta Pia are likely to be gourmets looking for quintessential Italian food, and that means light homemade pastas, choice olive oil, and market-fresh ingredients, especially seafood. The small dining room is decorated with antiques, and tables are set with immaculate white linen, sparkling crystal, and silver. Although seafood dishes vary, *tagliolini all'aragosta* (thin noodles with lobster sauce) is usually on the menu, as are *porcini* mushrooms in season (cooked to a secret recipe). The wine list is predominantly Italian, but includes some French and California wines, too. *Via Ancona 14, tel. 06/855–1122. Jacket and tie preferred. Reservations advised. AE, DC, MC, V. Closed Sun. and Aug. 1–25.*

Passetto. Benefiting from a choice location near Piazza Navona, Passetto has been a favorite with Italians and tourists for many years: It's a place you can rely on for classic Italian food and courteous service. If you can, eat on the terrace—it's especially memorable at night; the mirrored dining room is more staid. Roman specialties, such as *cannelloni* (stuffed pasta tubes) and *abbacchio* (baby lamb), are featured. *Via Zanardelli 14, tel. 06/687–9937. Reservations advised. Jacket and tie preferred. AE, DC, MC, V. Closed all day Sun., Mon. lunch.*

Piperno. A favorite, located in the old Jewish Ghetto next to historic Palazzo Cenci, Piperno has been in business for more than a century. It is *the* place to go for Rome's extraordinary *carciofi alla giudia* (crispy-fried artichokes, Jewish-style). You eat in three small wood-paneled dining rooms or at one of a handful of tables outdoors. Try *filetti di baccalà* (cod fillet fried in batter), *pasta e ceci* (a thick soup of pasta tubes and chickpeas), *fiori di zucca* (stuffed zucchini flowers), and *carciofi* (artichokes). *Monte dei Cenci 9, tel. 06/654–2772. Reservations advised. Dress: casual. AE, DC, MC, V. Closed Sun. dinner, Mon., Christmas, Easter, Aug.*

★ **Ranieri.** Walk down a quiet street off fashionable Via Condotti, near the Spanish Steps, to find this historic restaurant, founded by a one-time chef of Queen Victoria. Ranieri remains a favorite with tourists for its traditional atmosphere and decor, with damask-covered walls, velvet banquettes, crystal chandeliers, and old paintings. The Italian-French cuisine is excellent: Portions are abundant and checks remain comfortably within the lower range in this category. Among the many specialties on the vast menu are *gnocchi alla parigina* (souffléd dumplings with tomato and cheese sauce) and *mignonettes alla Regina Vittoria* (veal with pâté and cream). *Via Mario de' Fiori 26, tel. 06/679–1592. Reservations advised. Dress: casual but neat. AE, DC, MC, V. Closed Sun.*

Il Tentativo. Food critics regularly lavish praise on this sophisticated spot in Trastevere, typical of the restaurants in Rome that are serving the new Italian cuisine. The decor is subdued but elegant, with small modern lamps over the tables creating pools of warm light and discreetly focusing attention on the real reason for coming here: the food—always presented with flair—and the carefully selected wines. The menu changes seasonally, but you can usually find *ravioli di branzino bianco e nero* (freshly made pasta colored with squid ink and stuffed with bass) and veal fillet with a variety of sauces. *Via della Luce 5, tel. 06/589–5234. Reservations required. Jacket and tie preferred. AE, DC, MC. Dinner only. Closed Sun. and Aug.*

Moderate **Dal Bolognese.** Long a favorite with the art crowd, this classic restaurant on Piazza del Popolo is a handy place for a leisurely lunch between sightseeing and shopping. While dining, feast your eyes on an extensive array of contemporary paintings, many of them by customers, both illustrious and unknown. As the name of the restaurant promises, the cooking here adheres to the hearty tradition of Bologna, with homemade pastas in creamy sauces and steaming trays of boiled meats. For dessert, there's *dolce della mamma*, a concoction of ice cream, zabaglione, and chocolate sauce. *Piazza del Popolo 1, tel. 06/361–1426. Reservations advised. Dress: casual. DC, V. Closed Mon. and Aug. 7–22.*

La Campana. This inconspicuous trattoria off Via della Scrofa has a centuries-old tradition: There has been an inn on this spot since the 15th century, and the two plain dining rooms occupy what were once stables. It's a homey place, with friendly waiters, a vigil light in front of a painted Madonna over the kitchen entrance, and good Roman food at reasonable prices. The menu offers specialties like *vignarola* (sautéed fava beans, peas, and artichokes), rigatoni with *prosciutto* (ham) and tomato sauce, and *olivette di vitello con puré* (tiny veal rolls with mashed potatoes). *Vicolo della Campana 18, tel. 06/686–7820. Reservations advised for dinner. Dress: casual. AE, V. Closed Mon. and Aug.*

Cannavota. Located on the square next to San Giovanni Laterano, Cannavota has a large and faithful following and has fed generations of neighborhood families over the years. Seafood dominates, but carnivores are catered to, also. Try one of the pastas with seafood sauce—fettuccine with shrimp and scampi is a good choice—and then go on to grilled fish or meat. The cheerful atmosphere and rustic decor make for an authentically Roman experience. *Piazza San Giovanni in Laterano 20, tel. 06/775007. Reservations advised. Dress: casual. AE, DC, MC, V. Closed Wed. and Aug. 1–20.*

Da Checcho er Carrettiere. You'll find Da Checcho tucked away behind Piazza Trilussa in Trastevere. It has the look of a country inn, with braids of garlic hung from the roof and an antipasto table that features some unusual specialties, such as a well-seasoned mashed potato-and-tomato mixture. Among the hearty pasta offerings are *spaghetti alla carrettiera*, with black pepper, sharp cheese, and olive oil, and linguine with scampi. Seafood (which can be expensive) is the main feature on the menu, but traditional Roman meat dishes are offered, too. This is a great place to soak up genuine Trastevere color and hospitality. *Via Benedetta 10, tel. 06/581–7018. Reservations advised. Dress: casual. AE, DC, V. Closed Sun. evening and Mon.*

Colline Emiliane. Not far from Piazza Barberini, this unassuming trattoria offers exceptionally good food. Behind an opaque glass facade are a couple of plain dining rooms, where you are served light homemade pastas, a special chicken broth, and meats ranging from boiled beef to *giambonetto di vitella* (roast veal) and *cotoletta alla bolognese* (veal cutlet with cheese and tomato sauce). Family run, it's quiet and soothing, a good place to rest after a sightseeing stint. Service is cordial and discreet. *Via degli Avignonesi 22, tel. 06/481–7538. Reservations advised. Dress: casual. No credit cards. Closed Fri.*

Fortunato al Pantheon. Just a block away from the House of Representatives, Fortunato is a favorite of politicos. (It's also a couple of paces from Piazza della Rotonda by the Pantheon.) With politicians around, there is, of course, a back room, but you can happily settle for the largest of the three dining rooms or even a table outside in good weather. For his faithful and demanding clientele, Fortunato varies his specialties, offering several pastas—such as *penne all'arrabbiata*, with piquant tomato sauce—and *risotto alla milanese*, with saffron or with *porcini* mushrooms. He also serves many types of fish and meat dishes, some with expensive truffles. *Via del Pantheon 55, tel. 06/679–2788. Reservations advised. Dress: casual but neat. AE. Closed Sun.*

★ **Mario.** Mario has been running this restaurant in the heart of Rome's shopping district for 30 years. Even when crowded, the restaurant has an intimate and relaxed feeling. The walls are full of paintings and photographs of celebrity customers who come for hearty Tuscan food. *Papardelle alla lepre* (noodles with hare sauce) and *coniglio* (rabbit) are specialties, but be sure to try *panzanella* (Tuscan bread salad), perhaps as an antipasto. The house Chianti can be recommended. *Via della Vite 55, tel. 06/678–3818. Dress: casual. Dinner reservations advised. AE, DC, MC, V. Closed Sun. and Aug.*

Da Meo Patacca. A picturesque square in Trastevere is the setting for an entertaining evening of live music in an endearingly bogus Old Rome atmosphere. Strolling musicians in folk costumes sing and play your requests, and everybody joins in. The food is surprisingly good, and you can't go wrong with the pasta and meat specialties "alla Meo." The ground-floor and downstairs dining rooms are strewn with an array of garlic, peppers, and antique junk. In the summer, you can dine outside. *Piazza del Mercanti, in Trastevere, tel. 06/581–6198. Reservations advised. Dress: casual. AE, DC, V. Dinner only.*

Orso 80. This bright and bustling trattoria, recently redecorated and air-conditioned, is located in Old Rome, on a street famed for artisans' workshops. It has both a Roman and an international following, and is known, above all, for a fabulous antipasto table. If you have room for more, try the homemade egg pasta or the *bucatini all'amatriciana* (thin, hollow pasta with a tomato, bacon, and pecorino cheese sauce); there's plenty of seafood on the menu, too. For dessert, the ricotta cake, a genuine Roman specialty, is always good. *Via dell'Orso 33, tel. 06/686–4904. Reservations advised. Dress: casual. AE, DC, MC, V. Closed Mon. and Aug. 10–20.*

Paris. On a small square just off Piazza Santa Maria in Trastevere, Paris (named after a former owner, not the city) has a reassuring, understated ambience, without the hoky, folky flamboyance of so many eating places in this gentrified neighborhood. It also has a menu featuring the best of classic Roman cuisine: homemade *fettuccine*, delicate *fritto misto* (zucchini flowers and artichokes, among other things, fried in batter) and, of course, *baccalà* (fried cod fillets). In fair weather you eat at tables on the little piazza. *Piazza San Callisto 7/a, tel. 06/585378. Reservations advised for dinner. Dress: casual. AE, DC, MC, V. Closed Sun. eve. and Mon., and three weeks in Aug.*

Pierluigi. Pierluigi, in the heart of Old Rome, is a longtime favorite with foreign residents of Rome and Italians in the entertainment field. On busy evenings it's almost impossible to find a table, so make sure you reserve well in advance. Seafood dominates (if you're in the mood to splurge, try the lobster), but traditional Roman dishes are offered, too, including *orecchiette con broccoli* (ear-shaped pasta with greens) and simple spaghetti. Eat in the pretty piazza in summer. *Piazza dei Ricci 144, tel. 06/686–1302. Reservations advised. Dress: casual. AE, V. Closed Mon. and 2 weeks in Aug.*

★ **La Rampa.** A haven for exhausted shoppers and sightseers, La Rampa is right behind the American Express office on Piazza Mignanelli, off Piazza di Spagna. The attractive decor evokes a colorful old Roman marketplace, and there are a few tables for outdoor dining on the piazza. The specialties of the house are a lavish antipasto, *bombolotti alla vodka* (pasta with a tomato-and-vodka sauce), *pinturicchio* (veal scallops with creamy sauce in a pastry shell), and *frittura alla Rampa* (deep-fried vegetables and mozzarella). La Rampa is popular and busy, and you may have to wait for a table. Get there early (or late). *Piazza Mignanelli 18, tel. 06/678–2621. No reservations. Dress: casual. No credit cards. Closed Sun., Mon. lunch, and all Aug.*

★ **Romolo.** Generations of Romans and tourists have enjoyed the romantic garden courtyard and historic dining room of this charming Trastevere haunt, reputedly the one-time home of Raphael's lady love, the Fornarina. In the evening, strolling musicians serenade diners. The cuisine is appropriately Roman; specialties include *mozzarella alla fornarina* (deep-fried mozzarella with ham and anchovies) and *braciolette d'abbacchio scottadito* (grilled baby lamb chops). Alternatively, try one of the new vegetarian pastas featuring *carciofi* (artichokes) or *radicchio*. Meats are charcoal-grilled; there's also a wood-burning oven. *Via di Porta Settimiana 8, tel. 06/581–8284. Reservations advised. Dress: casual. AE, DC, V. Closed Mon. and Aug. 2–23.*

Tullio. This Tuscan trattoria opened in the 1950s between Via Veneto and Piazza Barberini, in the Dolce Vita days when this area was the center of Roman chic and bohème. It soon acquired a faithful clientele of politicians, journalists, and creative people, and it has changed little over the years. Decor and menu are simple. The latter offers typically Tuscan *pasta e fagioli*, grilled steaks and chops, and *fagioli all 'uccelletto* (beans with tomato and sage). *Via San Nicolò da Tolentino 26, tel. 06/475–8564. Reservations advised. Dress: casual but neat. AE, DC, MC, V. Closed Sun. and Aug.*

Inexpensive **Baffetto.** The emphasis here is on good old-fashioned value: The food is much more important than the surroundings. Baffetto is Rome's best-known inexpensive pizza restaurant, plainly decorated and very popular. You'll probably have to wait in line outside on the *sampietrini* (cobblestones) and then share your table once inside. The interior is mostly given over to the ovens, the tiny cash desk, and the simple, paper-covered tables. *Bruschetta* (toast) and *crostini* (mozzarella toast) are the only variations on the pizza theme. Turnover is fast: This is not the place to linger over your meal. *Via del Governo Vecchio 114, tel. 06/686–1617. No reservations. Dress: casual. No credit cards. Open evenings only. Closed Sun. and Aug.*

★ **Birreria Tempera.** This old-fashioned beer hall is very busy at lunchtime, when it's invaded by businessmen and students from the Piazza Venezia area. There's a good selection of salads and cold cuts, as well as pasta and daily specials. Bavarian-style specialties such as goulash and wurst and sauerkraut prevail in the evening, when light or dark Italian beer flows freely. *Via San Marcello 19, tel. 06/678–6203. No reservations. Dress: casual. No credit cards. Closed Sun. and Aug.*

Fiammetta. For an inexpensive meal at the Fiammetta, you have to order pizza and, perhaps, a vegetable dish or a salad; other dishes will send your check into the Moderate range. Although boasting a central Rome location, near Piazza Navona, Fiammetta betrays its Tuscan origins in the frescoed views of Florence. In fair weather you sit outdoors under an arbor. *Piazza Fiammetta 8, tel. 06/687–5777. No reservations. Dress: casual. No credit cards. Closed Tues.*

Hostaria Farnese. This is a tiny trattoria between Campo dei Fiori and Piazza Farnese, in the heart of Old Rome. Mamma cooks; Papa serves; and, depending on what they've picked up at the Campo dei Fiori market, you may find rigatoni with tuna and basil, spaghetti with vegetable sauce, *spezzatino* (stew), and other homey specialties. *Via dei Baullari 109, tel. 06/654–1595. Reservations advised. Dress: casual. AE, V. Closed Thurs.*

Otello alla Concordia. The clientele in this popular spot—it's located off a shopping street near Piazza di Spagna—is about evenly divided between tourists and workers from shops and offices in the area. The former like to sit outdoors in the courtyard in any weather; the latter have their regular tables in one of the inside dining rooms. The menu offers classic Roman and Italian dishes, and service is friendly and efficient. Since every tourist in Rome knows about it and since the regulars won't relinquish their niches, you may have to wait for a table; go early. *Via della Croce 81, tel. 06/679–1178. No reservations. Dress: casual. No credit cards. Closed Sun. and Christmas.*

Polese. It's best to come here in good weather, when you can sit outdoors under trees and look out on the charming square off Corso Vittorio Emanuele in Old Rome. Like most centrally located, inexpensive eateries in Rome, it is crowded on weekends and weekday evenings in the summer. Straightforward Roman dishes are featured; specialties include *fettuccine alla Polese* (with cream and mushrooms) and *vitello alla fornara* (roast brisket of veal with potatoes). *Piazza Sforza Cesarini 40, tel. 06/686–1709. Reservations advised on weekends. Dress: casual. No credit cards. Closed Tues., 15 days in Aug., 15 days in Dec.*

Tavernetta. The central location—between the Trevi Fountain and the Spanish Steps—and the good-value tourist menu make this a reliable bet for a simple but filling meal. The menu features Sicilian and Abruzzi specialties; try the pasta with eggplant or the *porchetta* (roast suckling pig). Both the red and the white house wines are good. *Via del Nazareno 3, tel. 06/679–3124. Reservations required for dinner. Dress: casual. AE, DC, MC, V. Closed Mon. and Aug.*

Tulipano Nero. This bright and noisy Trastevere pizzeria is very much a place for the under-25s. Unusual pasta dishes—rigatoni with a walnut and cheese sauce—and a U.S.-style salad bar are featured. *Via Roma Libera 15 (Piazza San Cosimato), tel. 06/581-8309. Reservations advised for groups. Dress: casual. No credit cards. Closed Wed.*

Along Via Appia Antica

Moderate **L'Archeologia.** In this farmhouse just beyond the catacombs, you dine indoors beside the fireplace in cool weather or in the garden under age-old vines in the summer. The atmosphere is friendly and intimate, and specialties include homemade pastas, *abbacchio scottadito* (grilled baby lamb chops), and seafood. *Via Appia Antica 139, tel. 06/788-0494. Reservations advised for dinner and weekends. Dress: casual. No credit cards. Closed Thurs.*

Cecilia Metella. From the entrance on the Via Appia Antica, practically opposite the catacombs, you walk uphill to a low-lying but sprawling construction designed for weddings feasts and banquets. There's a large terrace shaded by vines for outdoor dining. Although obviously geared to larger groups, Cecilia Metella also gives couples and small groups full attention, good service, and fine Roman-style cuisine. The specialties are the searing-hot *crespelle* (crepes), served in individual casseroles, and *pollo alla Nerone* (chicken à la Nero; *flambéed*, of course). *Via Appia Antica 125, tel. 06/513-6743. Reservations advised on weekends. Dress: casual. AE. Closed Mon.*

Lodging

The wide range of Roman accommodations are graded officially from five stars down to one. You can be sure of palatial comfort and service in a five-star establishment, but some of the three-star hotels are, in reality, more modest affairs, superficially spruced up to capitalize on a central location. You'll find less charm, perhaps, but more standard facilities in newer hotels in the moderate or expensive category. The old-fashioned Roman pension no longer exists as an official governmental category, but, while now graded as inexpensive hotels, some preserve the homey atmosphere that makes visitors prefer them, especially for longer stays.

There are distinct advantages to staying in a hotel within easy walking distance of the main sights, particularly now that so much of downtown Rome is closed to daytime traffic. You can leave your car at a garage and explore by foot. One disadvantage, however, can be noise, because the Romans are a voluble people—with or without cars to add to the racket. Ask for an inside room if you are a light sleeper, but don't be disappointed if it faces a dark courtyard.

Because Rome's religious importance makes it a year-round tourist destination, there is never a period when hotels are predictably empty, so you should always try to make reservations. If you do arrive without reservations, try one of the following **EPT** information offices: Via Parigi 5 (tel. 06/463748), Termini Station (tel. 06/487-1270), Leonardo da Vinci Airport (tel. 06/601-1255). All can help with accommodations, and there is no charge. Students can try the **Protezione Giovanni** office at Termini Station; it specializes in finding low-cost accommodations for girls, but will help all students if it is not too busy. **CTS** (Via Genova 16, tel. 06/46791) is a student travel agency by Termini

Station. Avoid official-looking men who approach tourists at Termini Station: They tout for the less desirable hotels around the train station.

Room rates in Rome are on a par with those in most other European capitals. Some hotels quote separate rates for breakfasts—an extra charge of between 7,000 and 27,000 lire, depending on the hotel category. If you object to paying extra for breakfast, remember that you're not obliged to pay, but make it clear when you check in that you will not be having breakfast. Air-conditioning in lower-priced hotels may cost extra; in more expensive hotels it will be included in the price. All hotels have rate cards on the room doors or inside the closet. These specify exactly what you have to pay and detail any extras.

Highly recommended lodgings in each price category are indicated by a star ★.

Category	Cost*
Very Expensive	over 400,000 lire
Expensive	250,000–400,000 lire
Moderate	120,000–250,000 lire
Inexpensive	under 120,000 lire

All prices are for a standard double room for two, including tax and service.

Very Expensive

★ **Eden.** Now a member of the Trusthouse Forte chain, the Eden celebrated its centennial in 1989 by renovating three of its four floors. Just off Via Veneto, it combines a convenient location with discreet comfort and polished service. From the cozy wood-paneled lounge to the individually decorated rooms and suites, the hotel exudes a sense of well-appointed luxury, and further renovations promise to make it even more luxurious. There's a touch of romance and fun in the uncluttered decor: a mixture of antique, art deco, and streamlined modern, with lots of mirrors and marble. Rooms on the upper floors have terrific views (the best view is from the penthouse bar and restaurant). *Via Ludovisi 49, tel. 06/474–3551. 93 rooms and suites with bath. Facilities: bar, restaurant. AE, DC, MC, V.*

Grand. A 100-year-old establishment of class and style, this CIGA-owned hotel caters to an elite international clientele. It's located only a few minutes from Via Veneto. Off the richly decorated, split-level main bar—where afternoon tea is served every day—there are a smaller, intimate bar and a buffet restaurant. The spacious bedrooms are decorated in gracious empire style, with smooth fabrics and thick carpets in tones of blue and pale gold. Crystal chandeliers and marble baths add a luxurious note. The Grand also offers one of Italy's most beautiful dining rooms, called simply Le Restaurant (*see* Dining, above). *Via Vittorio Emanuele Orlando 3, tel. 06/4709, fax 06/474–7307. 170 rooms and suites with bath. Facilities: bar, 2 restaurants. AE, DC, MC, V.*

★ **Hassler.** Located at the top of the Spanish Steps, the Hassler boasts what is probably the most scenic location of any hotel in the city. The front rooms and penthouse restaurant have sweeping views of Rome; other rooms overlook the gardens of

Villa Medici. The hotel is run by the distinguished Wirth family of hoteliers. They assure a cordial atmosphere and magnificent service from the well-trained staff. The public rooms are memorable—especially the first-floor bar, a chic rendezvous, and the glass-roofed lounge, with gold marble walls and a hand-painted tile floor. The elegant and comfortable guest rooms are decorated in a variety of classic styles; some feature frescoed walls. The penthouse suite has a mirrored ceiling in the bedroom and a huge terrace. *Piazza Trinità dei Monti 6, tel. 06/ 678–2651, fax 06/678–9991. 101 rooms and suites with bath. Facilities: bar, restaurant. AE, MC, V.*

Expensive **Borgognoni.** Centrally located off Via del Tritone, in the heart of the shopping district, is this small but discreetly elegant hotel. The rooms, some with terraces, are decorated in soft beiges and blues and have tasteful art deco motifs. There's no restaurant, but room service provides cold snacks. Though it has only been open since 1989, the staff offers superior service because the management aims to make Borgognoni one of the city's premier small hotels. *Via del Bufalo 126, tel. 06/678– 0041, fax 06/684–1501. 50 rooms with bath. Facilities: garage, bar, cable TV, safes in rooms. AE, DC, MC, V.*

Flora. With its Old-World decor and style, now largely refurbished with entirely new bathrooms, the Flora has a solid position among Via Veneto hotels. The rooms are ample and comfortable, and many have fine views of Villa Borghese. Potted plants are featured in the public rooms and marble-lined hallways. Period furniture, Oriental rugs, and old paintings add character to the rooms. Service is attentive, with a personal touch; this, together with the unostentatious comfort, is what keeps its regular clientele coming back year after year. The management is especially proud of the lavish breakfasts, served either in your room or in the old-fashioned dining room, which is complete with crystal chandelier, oil paintings, and red-velvet chairs. *Via Veneto 191, tel. 06/497821, fax 06/482– 0359. 172 rooms with bath. AE, DC, MC, V.*

★ **Forum.** A centuries-old palace converted into a fine hotel, the Forum is on a quiet street within shouting distance of the Roman Forum and Piazza Venezia. Although it seems tucked away out of the mainstream, it's actually handily located for all the main sights. The wood-paneled lobby and street-level bar are warm and welcoming. The smallish bedrooms are furnished in rich pink and beige fabrics; the bathrooms are ample, with either tub or shower. What's really special about the Forum, though, is the rooftop restaurant: The view toward the Colosseum is superb. Breakfast on the roof or a nightcap at the roof bar can be memorable. *Via Tor dei Conti 25, tel. 06/679–2446, fax 06/678–6479. 76 rooms with bath. Facilities: bar, restaurant. AE, DC, MC, V.*

Giulio Cesare. An aristocratic townhouse in the residential, but central, Prati district, the Giulio Cesare is a 10-minute walk across the Tiber from Piazza del Popolo. It's beautifully run, with a friendly staff and a quietly luxurious air. The rooms are elegantly furnished, with thick rugs, floor-length drapes, rich damasks in soft colors, and crystal chandeliers. Public rooms have Oriental carpets, old prints and paintings, and marble fireplaces. *Via degli Scipioni 287, tel. 06/321–0751, fax 06/321– 1736. 90 rooms with bath. Facilities: bar, garden, and terrace. AE, DC, MC, V.*

Jolly Via Veneto. If you're looking for contemporary efficiency

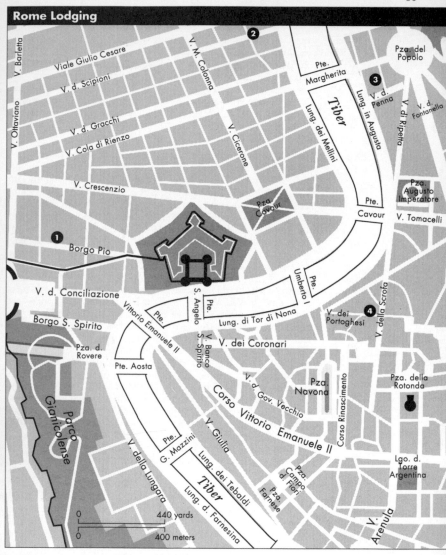

Rome Lodging

Ausonia, **8**

Borgognoni, **7**

Britannia, **18**

Carriage, **6**

Eden, **12**

Flora, **14**

Forum, **19**

Giulio Cesare, **2**

Grand, **17**

Hassler, **9**

Internazionale, **11**

Jolly Via Veneto, **15**

Locarno, **3**

Margutta, **5**

Portoghesi, **4**

La Residenza, **13**

Sant'Anna, **1**

Suisse, **10**

Victoria, **16**

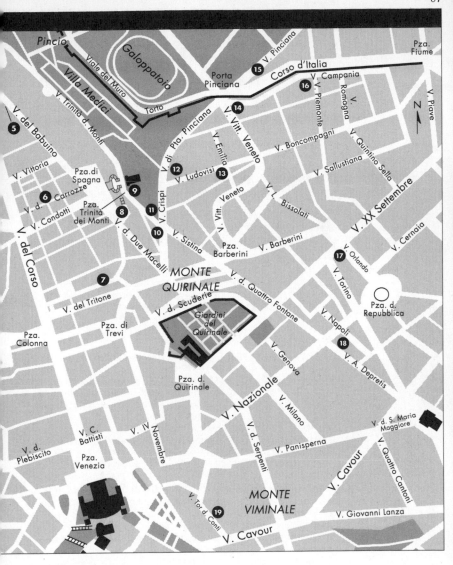

and a classy location, the Jolly will fill the bill. It's at the top of Via Veneto, on the edge of Villa Borghese, in a striking steel-and-glass building. Chocolate-brown carpeting and functional built-in white fittings are keynotes throughout. Try for a room overlooking Villa Borghese; it's worth the extra charge. *Corso d'Italia 1, tel. 06/8495, fax 06/862445. 200 rooms with bath. Facilities: bar, restaurant, garage. AE, DC, MC, V.*

★ **Victoria.** Considerable luxury in the public rooms, solid comfort throughout, and impeccable management are the main features of this hotel near Via Veneto. Oriental rugs, oil paintings, welcoming armchairs, and fresh flowers add charm to the public spaces, and the homey rooms are decorated in soothing combinations of peach, blue, and green. American businessmen, who prize the hotel's personalized service and restful atmosphere, are frequent guests. Some upper rooms and the roof terrace overlook the majestic pines of Villa Borghese. The restaurant offers à la carte meals and a good-value fixed-price menu featuring Roman specialties. *Via Campania 41, tel. 06/473931, fax 06/462343. 110 rooms with bath. Facilities: bar, restaurant. AE, DC, MC, V.*

Moderate **Britannia.** Located close to Termini Station and next to St. Paul's Episcopal Church, the Britannia is a bright, quiet, and compact hotel. The rooms are small but well planned; 401 and 402 both have terraces. Rooms are decorated in blue-gray or beige, and all have luxurious marble bathrooms. *Via Napoli 64, tel. 06/465785. 32 rooms with bath. Facilities: lounge, bar. AE, DC, MC, V.*

★ **Carriage.** Stay here for the location (by the Spanish Steps), the Old World elegance, and the reasonable rates. Totally renovated over the past few years, the hotel is decorated in soothing tones of blue and pale gold, with subdued Baroque accents adding a touch of luxury. The rooms have antique-looking closets and porcelain telephones. Double room 402 and single room 305 have small balconies; elegant room 302 is spacious, with an oversize bathroom. Alternatively, try for one of the two rooms adjoining the roof terrace. *Via delle Carrozze 36, tel. 06/679-4106, fax 06/678-8279. 27 rooms and suites with bath. AE, DC, MC, V.*

★ **Internazionale.** With an excellent location near the top of the Spanish Steps, the Internazionale has long been known as one of the city's best mid-size hotels. It's in a totally renovated building on desirable Via Sistina and is within easy walking distance of many downtown sights. Doubly thick windows ensure peace and quiet in the compact rooms. Rooms on the fourth floor have terraces; the fourth-floor suite has a private terrace and a frescoed ceiling. The decor throughout is in soothing pastel tones, with some antique pieces, mirrors, and chandeliers heightening the English country-house look. Guests relax in small, homey lounges downstairs and begin the day in the pretty breakfast room. *Via Sistina 79, tel. 06/679-3047, fax 06/678-4764. 40 rooms with bath. AE, DC, MC, V.*

Locarno. The central location off Piazza del Popolo helps keep the Locarno a favorite among the art crowd, which also goes for its intimate mood, though some of Locarno's fine *fin de siècle* character has been lost in renovations. An attempt has been made to retain the hotel's original charm, however, while modernizing the rooms. The latest additions are electronic safes and air-conditioning. The decor features coordinated prints in wallpaper and fabrics, lacquered wrought-iron beds, and some antiques. *Via della Penna 22, tel. 06/361–0841, fax 06/321–5249. 38 rooms with bath. Facilities: bar/lounge. AE, V.*

★ **La Residenza.** In a converted town house near Via Veneto, this hotel is a good value, offering first-class comfort and atmosphere at reasonable rates. The canopied entrance, spacious well-furnished lounges, and the bar and terrace are of the type you would expect to find in a deluxe category. Rooms have large closets, color TV, fridge-bar, and air-conditioning; bathrooms have heated towel racks. The decor includes a color scheme of aquamarine and beige, combined with bentwood furniture. The clientele is mostly American. Rates include a generous American-style buffet breakfast. *Via Emilia 22, tel. 06/460789, fax 06/485721. 27 rooms with bath or shower. Facilities: bar, rooftop terrace, parking. No credit cards.*

Sant'Anna. If there were any doubts that the picturesque Borgo neighborhood in the shadow of St. Peter's was becoming fashionable, this stylish hotel goes some way toward dispelling them. Decorated with a flair that at times seems overdone, especially in the ample art deco bedrooms, the mood here is nonetheless soothing and welcoming. There is a frescoed breakfast room; the courtyard terrace boasts a fountain. There's no elevator to take you up the four floors, but it's worth the climb to the top floor to stay in one of the spacious blue-and-white attic rooms, each with a little terrace. *Borgo Pio 134, tel. 06/654–1882, fax 06/654–8717. 19 rooms with bath. AE, DC, MC, V.*

Inexpensive **Ausonia.** This small pension's big advantages are its location on Piazza di Spagna and its helpful management and family atmosphere. Six rooms face the famous square (quieter now that most through-traffic has been banned); all others face the inner courtyard. Furnishings are simple, but standards of cleanliness are high and rates are low. The hotel has many American guests; make sure you reserve well in advance. *Piazza di Spagna 35, tel. 06/679–5745. 10 rooms without bath. No credit cards.*

★ **Margutta.** This small hotel is centrally located on a quiet side street between the Spanish Steps and Piazza del Popolo. Lobby and halls are unassuming, but rooms are a pleasant surprise, with light walls, a clean and airy look, attractive wrought-iron bedsteads and modern baths. Ongoing redecoration is bringing all rooms up to this standard. Three rooms on the roof terrace are much in demand for their views of the city's domes, bell towers, and the pines of the Pincian hill. Though it's in an old building, there is an elevator. *Via Laurina 34, tel. 06/322–3674. 24 rooms with bath or shower. AE, DC, MC, V.*

★ **Portoghesi.** In the heart of Old Rome, facing the so-called Monkey Tower, the Portoghesi is a fine small hotel with considerable atmosphere and low rates for the level of comfort offered. From a tiny lobby, an equally tiny elevator takes you to the quiet bedrooms, all decorated with floral prints and handsome pieces of old furniture. There's a breakfast room, but no restaurant. *Via dei Portoghesi 1, tel. 06/686–4231, fax 06/687–6976. 27 rooms, most with bath. MC, V.*

★ **Suisse.** This homey and simple hotel has an unbeatable location—five minutes' walk from the Spanish Steps. Clean and comfortable rooms and reasonable rates make the Suisse an excellent value. The mood in the public rooms is old-fashioned—the check-in desk is distinctly drab—but the rooms, though small, are cheerful, with bright bedspreads, framed prints, and old furniture. The lounge has large windows and well-upholstered armchairs. Some rooms face the fairly quiet court-yard. There's an upstairs breakfast room, but no restaurant. *Via Gregoriana 56, tel. 06/678–3649. 28 rooms, half with bath. No credit cards.*

The Arts and Nightlife

The Arts

Rome offers a vast selection of music, dance, opera, and film. Schedules of events are published in daily newspapers; in the "Trovaroma" Thursday supplement of *La Reppubblica;* in the *Guest in Rome* booklet distributed free at hotel desks; and in the monthly *Carnet,* available free from EPT offices.

Concerts   Rome has long been a center for a wide variety of classical mu-sic concerts, although it is a common complaint that the city does not have adequate concert halls or a suitable auditorium. Depending on the location, concert tickets can cost from 5,000 to 35,000 lire. The principal concert series are those of the **Ac-cademia di Santa Cecilia** (offices at Via dei Greci, box office tel. 06/654–1044), the **Accademia Filarmonica Romana** (Teatro Olimpico, Via Gentile da Fabriano 17, tel. 06/396–2635), the **Instituzione Universitaria dei Concerti** (San Leone Magno audi-torium, Via Bolzano 38, tel. 06/361–0051), and the **RAI** Italian Radio-TV series at Foro Italico (tel. 06/368–6625). There is also the internationally respected **Gonfalone** series, which concen-trates on Baroque music (Via del Gonfalone 32, tel. 06/687–5952). The **Associazione Musicale Romana** (tel. 06/656–8441) and **Il Tempietto** (tel. 06/513–6148) organize music festivals and concerts throughout the year. There are also many small con-cert groups. Many concerts are free, including all those per-formed in Catholic churches, where a special ruling permits only concerts of religious music. Look for posters outside churches announcing free concerts.

Rock, pop, and jazz concerts are frequent, especially in sum-mer, although even performances by big-name stars may not be well advertised. Tickets for these performances are usually handled by **Orbis** (Piazza Esquilino 37, tel. 06/481–4721).

Opera   The opera season runs from November to May, and perfor-mances are staged in the **Teatro dell'Opera** (Via del Viminale, information in English: tel. 06/675–95725; ticket reservations in English: tel. 06/675–95721). Tickets go on sale two days be-fore a performance, and the box office is open 10–1 and 5–7. Prices range from 8,000 to 44,000 lire for regular perfor-mances; they can go up to 64,000 lire for special performances, like an opening night or an appearance by an internationally ac-claimed guest singer. Standards may not always measure up to those set by Milan's fabled La Scala, but, despite strikes and shortages of funds, most performances are respectable.

As interesting for its spectacular location as for the music is the summer opera season in the ruins of the ancient **Baths of Cara-calla.** Tickets go on sale in advance at the Teatro dell'Opera box office, or at the box office at the Baths of Caracalla, 8–9 PM on the evening of the performance. Take a jacket or sweater and something to cover bare legs: Despite the daytime heat of a Ro-man summer, nights at Caracalla can be cool and damp.

Dance The **Rome Opera Ballet** gives regular performances at the Teatro dell'Opera (*see* above), often with leading international guest stars. Rome is regularly visited by classical ballet companies from the Soviet Union, the United States, and Europe; performances are at Teatro dell'Opera, Teatro Olimpico, or at one of the open-air venues in summer. Small classical and modern dance companies from Italy and abroad give performances in various places; check concert listings for information.

Film Rome has dozens of movie houses, but the only one to show exclusively English-language films is the **Pasquino** (Vicolo del Piede, just off Piazza Santa Maria in Trastevere, tel. 06/580–3622). Films shown here have subtitles and are not dubbed. Programs change frequently, so pick up a weekly schedule at the theater or consult the daily papers. Occasionally, certain film clubs and movie theaters also show English-language films in English; consult the newspapers.

Nightlife

Although Rome is not one of the world's most exciting cities for nightlife (despite the popular image of the city as the birthplace of *La Dolce Vita*), discos, live-music spots, and quiet late-night bars have proliferated in recent years. This has been true in the streets of the old city and in far-flung parts of town. The "flavor of the month" factor works here, too, and many places fade into oblivion after a brief moment of popularity. The best source for an up-to-date list of late-night spots is the weekly entertainment guide "Trovaroma," published every Thursday in the Italian daily newspaper *La Repubblica*.

Bars Rome has a range of bars offering drinks and background music. Jacket and tie are in order in the elegant **Blue Bar** of the Hostaria dell'Orso (Via dei Soldati 25, tel. 06/686–4221) and in **Le Bar** of the Grand hotel (Via Vittorio Emanuele Orlando 3, tel. 06/482931). **Harry's Bar** (Via Veneto 150, tel. 06/474–5832) is popular with American businessmen and Rome-based journalists. **Little Bar** (Via Gregoriana 54a, tel. 06/679–6386) is open from 9 PM until very late; it's in the Piazza di Spagna area.

Young Romans favor **Calisé** (Piazza Mastai 7, tel. 06/580–9404) in Trastevere, where sandwiches and salads, as well as drinks, are available until 3 AM. **Enoteca dell'Orologio** (Via del Governo Vecchio 23, tel. 06/656–1904) is a popular wine bar; it's closed Sunday. The informal and cheerful **Bue Toscano** (Via Tor Margana 3, tel. 06/679–8158), near Piazza Venezia, offers wine, cocktails, a cold buffet, and music from 8:30 PM until the small hours; it's also open for lunch but is closed Monday.

"In" places around the Pantheon, a hub of after-dark activity, include **La Palma** (Via della Maddalena 22, tel. 06/654–0752) and **Hemingway** (Piazza delle Coppelle 10, tel. 06/654–4135), which attracts a crowd from the movies, TV, and fashion worlds. Both are open evenings only, until very late.

Beer halls and pubs are popular with young Italians. **Fiddler's Elbow** (Via dell'Olmata 43, no phone) is open 5 PM–midnight but is closed Monday. **Four Green Fields** (Via Costantino Morin 42, off Via della Giuliana, tel. 06/359–5091) features live music and is open daily from 8:30 PM to 1 AM.

Music Clubs Jazz, folk, pop, and Latin music clubs are flourishing in Rome, particularly in the picturesque Trastevere neighborhood. Jazz clubs are especially popular, and talented local groups may be joined by visiting musicians from other countries. As admission, many clubs require that you buy a membership card for about 10–20,000 lire. The Rome EPT sponsors a Rome By Music pass that costs about 30,000 lire and will admit you to several of the best clubs. It is sold at major hotels. For information call 06/0578–3309.

In the Trionfale district near the Vatican, **Alexanderplatz** (Via Ostia 9, tel. 06/359–9398) has both a bar and a restaurant, and features nightly live programs of jazz and blues played by Italian and foreign musicians. For the best live music, including jazz, blues, rhythm and blues, African, and rock, go to **Big Mama** (Vicolo San Francesco a Ripa 18, tel. 06/582551). There is also a bar and snack food. Latin rhythms are the specialty at **Clarabella** (Piazza San Cosimato 39, tel. 06/581–7654), a live music club in the heart of Trastevere. There are usually two shows nightly. It's closed Monday.

In the trendy Testaccio neighborhood, **Caffè Latino** (Via di Monte Testaccio 96, tel. 06/574–4020) attracts a thirtysomething crowd with concerts (mainly jazz) in one room and a separate video room and bar for socializing. **Music Inn** (Largo dei Fiorentini 3, tel. 06/654–4934) is Rome's top jazz club and features some of the biggest names on the international scene. Open Thursday through Sunday evenings.

Live performances of jazz, soul, and funk by leading musicians draw celebrities to **St. Louis Music City** (Via del Cardello 13a, tel. 06/474–5076). There is also a restaurant. Closed Thursday.

Discos and Nightclubs Most discos open about 10:30 PM and charge an entrance fee of around 25,000–30,000 lire, which sometimes includes the first drink. Subsequent drinks cost about 10,000–15,000 lire. Some discos also open on Saturday and Sunday afternoons for under-16s.

There's deafening disco music at **The Krypton** (Via Schiaparelli 29–30, tel. 06/322–1360) for the under-30 crowd, which sometimes includes young actors. Special events, such as beauty pageants, fashion shows, and theme parties, are featured, and there is a restaurant. Despite the address, the entrance is actually on Via Luciani 52. It's closed Monday.

Casanova (Piazza Rondanini 36, tel. 06/654–7314), is a disco for the under-25 crowd. Located near the Pantheon, there's live music and a cabaret to entertain before the deejay takes over. Roman yuppies mingle with a sophisticated show biz crowd while dancing to disco music at **Fabula** (Via Arco dei Ginnasi 14, Largo Argentina, tel. 06/679–7075). **Fonclea** (Via Crescenzio 82a, tel. 06/689–6302), near Castel Sant'Angelo, has a pub atmosphere and live music ranging from jazz to Latin American to rhythm-and-blues, depending on who's in town. The kitchen serves Mexican and Italian food.

Gilda (Via Mario dei Fiori, near Piazza di Spagna, tel. 06/678–4838) is the place to spot famous Italian actors and politicians. Formerly the Paradise supper club, this hot nightspot now has two restaurants, as well as live disco music. It's closed Monday. **Hysteria** (Via Giovanelli 12, tel. 06/864587) attracts a very young crowd who come to enjoy the variety of music: disco, funk, soul, and hard rock. It's located off Via Salaria by the Galleria Borghese. It's closed Monday, also. A glittering disco, piano bar, and restaurant attracts over-25s to the **Open Gate** (Via San Nicolo di Tolentino 4, tel. 06/475–0464). Dancing starts at midnight.

One of Rome's first discos, **The Piper** (Via Tagliamento 9, tel. 06/854459) is an "in" spot for teenagers. It has disco music, live groups, and pop videos. Occasionally, there's ballroom dancing for an older crowd. It opens weekends at 4 PM and is closed Monday and Tuesday. Funky music and huge video screens make **Scarabocchio** (Piazza Ponziani 8, tel. 06/580–0495) another popular spot. It's closed Monday.

Veleno (Via Sardegna 27, tel. 06/493583) is one of the few places in Rome to offer black dance music, including disco, rap, funk, and soul. It attracts sports personalities and other celebrities.

For singles Locals and foreigners of all nations and ages gather at Rome's cafés on **Piazza della Rotonda** in front of the Pantheon, at **Piazza Navona,** or **Piazza Santa Maria** in Trastevere. The cafés on **Via Veneto** and the bars of the big hotels draw mainly tourists and are good places to meet other travelers in the over-30 age group. In fair weather, under-30s will find crowds of contemporaries on the **Spanish Steps,** where it's easy to strike up a conversation.

Excursion 1: Ostia Antica

One of the easiest excursions from the capital takes you west to the sea, where tall pines stand among the well-preserved ruins of Ostia Antica, the main port of ancient Rome. Founded around the 4th century BC, it gives you an idea of what Rome itself must have been like then. Ostia Antica conveys the same impression as Pompeii, but on a smaller scale and in a prettier, parklike setting. The city was inhabited by a cosmopolitan population of rich businessmen, wily merchants, sailors, and slaves. The great *horrea* (warehouses), were built in the 2nd century AD to handle huge shipments of grain from Africa; the *insulae*, forerunners of the modern apartment building, provided housing for the growing population. Under the combined assaults of the barbarians and the anopheles mosquito, the port was eventually abandoned, and it silted up. Tidal mud and windblown sand covered the city, and it lay buried until the beginning of this century. Now extensively excavated and excellently maintained, it makes for a fascinating visit on a sunny day.

Tourist Information

There is an overall charge for entrance to the excavation complex, and it includes entrance to the Ostiense Museum, which is on the grounds and observes the same opening hours. *Scavi di Ostia Antica. Admission: 8,000 lire. Open daily 9–one hour before sunset.*

Escorted Tours

Tourvisa (Via Marghera 32, tel. 06/495–0284) offers daily bus excursions in spring and in September to Ostia Antica, with a guided visit to the excavations.

Getting Around

By Car The Via del Mare leads directly from Rome to Ostia Antica; the ride takes about 35 minutes.

By Train There is a Metro service from Termini Station to Ostia Antica. You can choose from several morning departures and three afternoon returns to Rome. The ride takes about 25 minutes. There is also a regular train service from Ostiense train station, near Porta San Paolo. Trains leave every half-hour, and the ride takes about 30 minutes.

Exploring

Numbers in the margin correspond with points of interest on the Rome Environs map.

Near the entrance to the *Scavi* (excavations) is a fortress built in the 15th century for Pope Julius II. The hamlet that grew up around it is charming. However, your visit to **Ostia Antica** itself starts at **Via delle Tombe,** lined with sepulchers from various periods. From here, you enter the **Porta Romana,** one of the city's three gates. This is the beginning of the **Decumanus Maximus,** the main thoroughfare crossing the city from end to end.

About 300 yards up on the right are the **Terme di Nettuno** (Baths of Neptune), decorated with black-and-white mosaics representing Neptune and Amphitrite. Directly behind the baths is the barracks of the fire department, which played an important role in a town with warehouses full of valuable goods and foodstuffs.

Just ahead, and also on the right side of Decumanus Maximus, is the beautiful **Theater,** built by Augustus and completely restored by Septimus Severus in the 2nd century AD. Behind it, in the vast Piazzale delle Corporazioni, where trade organizations similar to guilds had their offices, is the **Temple of Ceres:** This is appropriate for a town dealing in grain imports, since Ceres, who gave her name to cereal, was the goddess of agriculture. Next to the theater, where there is a coffee bar, you can visit the **House of Apuleius,** built in Pompeiian style—containing fewer windows, and built lower, than those in Ostia. Next to it is the **Mithraeum,** with balconies and a hall decorated with symbols of the cult of Mithras. This men-only religion, imported from Persia, was especially popular with legionnaires.

On the Via dei Molini, 200 yards beyond the theater, there is a mill, where grain for the warehouses next door was ground with the stones you see there. Along Via di Diana, a left turn 50 yards up Via dei Molini, you'll come upon a **thermopolium** (bar) with a marble counter and a fresco depicting the fruit and foodstuffs that were sold here. Turn right at the end of Via di Diana onto Via dei Dipinti; at the end is the **Museo Ostiense,** which displays some of the ancient sculptures and mosaics found among the ruins.

Retrace your steps along Via dei Dipinti and turn right just before Via di Diana for the **Forum,** with monumental remains of the city's most important temple, dedicated to Jupiter, Juno, and Minerva; other ruins of baths; a basilica (in Roman times a basilica served the secular purpose of a hall of justice); and smaller temples.

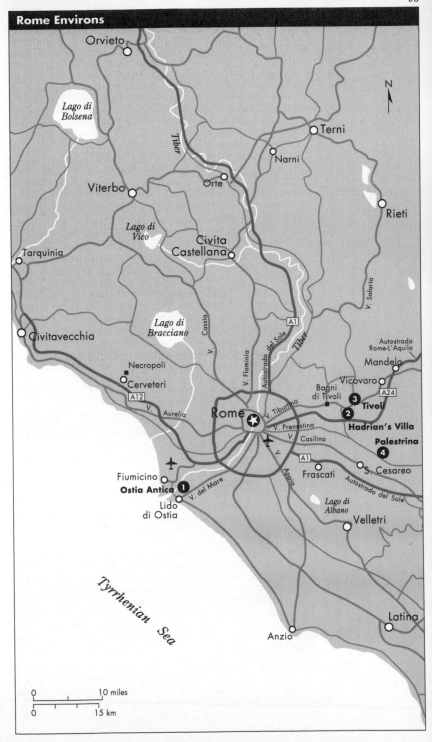

Rome Environs

A continuation of Decumanus Maximus leads from the Forum. From the crossroads, about 100 yards on, Via Epagathiana, on the right, leads down toward the Tiber, where there are large warehouses, erected in the 2nd century AD to deal with enormous amounts of grain imported into Rome during that period, the height of the Empire.

Take the street opposite the entrance to the warehouses to the **House of Cupid and Psyche,** a residential house named for a statue found there; you can see what remains of a large pool in an enclosed garden decorated with marble and mosaic motifs. It takes little imagination to notice that house building even then put a premium on water views: The house faces the shore, which would have been only about a quarter-mile away. Take Via del Tempio di Ercole left and then go right on Via della Foce to see (on the left) the **House of Serapis,** a 2nd-century multi-level dwelling, and the **Baths of the Seven Wise Men,** named for a fresco found there.

Take Via del Tempio di Serapide away from Via della Foce and then the Cardo Degli Aurighi, where you'll pass—just up on the left—another apartment building. The road leads back to the Decumanus Maximus, which continues to the **Porta Marina.** Off to the left, on what used to be the seashore, are the ruins of the **Synagogue,** one of the oldest in the Western world. This is where you begin your return; Porta Marina is the farthest point in the tour. Go right at the **Bivio del Castrum,** past the slaughterhouse and the large round temple. You'll come to the **Cardine Massimo,** a road lined with ruined buildings. From here, turn left onto Via Semita dei Cippi to see the **House of Fortuna Annonaria,** the richly decorated house of a wealthy Ostian. This is another place to marvel at the skill of the mosaic artists and, at the same time, to realize that this really was someone's home. One of the rooms opens onto a secluded garden.

Continue on Via Semita dei Cippi for about 150 yards until you turn right on Decumanus Maximus to retrace your last leg of the tour back to the entrance.

Dining

Monumento. Handily located near the entrance to the excavations, this attractive trattoria serves Roman specialties and seafood. *Piazza Umberto I, tel. 5650021. Reservations advised in the evening. Dress: casual. AE, DC, MC, V. Closed Mon. and Aug. 20–Sept. 7. Moderate.*

Sbarco di Enea. Also near the excavations, this restaurant is heavy on ancient-Roman atmosphere, with Pompeiian-style frescoes and chariots in the garden. On summer evenings you dine outdoors by torchlight, served by waiters in Roman costume. You'll probably come for lunch, when you can enjoy *farfalle con granchio* (pasta with crab sauce) or *linguine con aragosta* (with lobster sauce) and other seafood specialties, without all the hoopla. *Via dei Romagnoli 675, tel. 06/565–0034. Reservations advised in the evening. Dress: casual. AE, MC. Closed Mon. and Feb. Moderate.*

Excursion 2: Tivoli, Palestrina, and Subiaco

East of Rome lie some of the region's star attractions, which could be combined along a route that loops through the hills where ancient Romans built their summer resorts. The biggest attraction is Tivoli, which could be seen on a half-day excursion from Rome. But if you continue eastward to Palestrina, you can see a vast sanctuary famous in ancient times. And you could also fit in a visit to the site on which St. Benedict founded the hermitage that gave rise to Western monasticism. The monastery of St. Benedict is in Subiaco—not easy to get to unless you have a car, but you may want to make the effort to gain an insight into medieval mysticism.

Tourist Information

Tivoli (Giardino Garibaldi, tel. 0774/293522).
Subiaco (Via Cadorna 59, tel. 0774/85397).

Escorted Tours

American Express (tel. 06/67641) and **CIT** (tel. 06/479–4372) have half-day excursions to Villa d'Este in Tivoli. **Appian Line** (tel. 06/464151) and **Carrani Tours** (tel. 06/482–4194) have morning tours that include Hadrian's Villa.

Getting Around

By Car   For Tivoli, take the Via Tiburtina or the Rome–L'Aquila autostrada (A24). From Tivoli to Palestrina, follow signs for the Via Prenestina and Palestrina. To get to Palestrina directly from Rome, take either the Via Prenestina or Via Casilina or take the Autostrada del Sole (A2) to the San Cesareo exit and follow signs for Palestrina; this trip takes about one hour. To get to Subiaco from either Tivoli or Palestrina or directly from Rome, take the autostrada for L'Aquila (A24) to the Vicovaro-Mandela exit, then follow the local road to Subiaco; from Rome, the ride takes about one hour.

By Train   The FS train from Termini station to Palestrina takes about 40 minutes; you can then board a bus from the train station to the center of town.

By Bus   ACOTRAL buses leave every 15 minutes from Via Gaeta, near Termini Station, for Tivoli, but not all take the route that passes near Hadrian's Villa. Inquire which bus passes closest to Villa Adriana and tell the driver to let you off there. The ride takes about 75 minutes. For Palestrina, take the ACOTRAL bus from Piazza dei Cinquecento (Termini Station) at the corner of Via Cavour. There is local bus service between Tivoli and Palestrina, but check schedules locally. From Rome to Subiaco, take the ACOTRAL bus from Viale Castro Pretorio; buses leave every 40 minutes and those that take the autostrada make the trip in 70 minutes, as opposed to an hour and 45 minutes by another route.

Exploring

Numbers correspond with points of interest on the Rome Environs map.

The road east from Rome to Tivoli passes through some unattractive industrial areas and burgeoning suburbs. You'll know you're close when you see vast quarries of travertine marble and smell the sulphurous vapors of the little spa, Bagni di Tivoli. This was once green countryside; now it's ugly and overbuilt. But don't despair because this tour takes you to two of the Rome area's most attractive sights: Hadrian's Villa and Villa d'Este. Villa d'Este is a popular destination; fewer people go to Hadrian's Villa. Both are outdoor sights, which entail a lot of walking, and in the case of Villa D'Este, stair climbing. That also means that good weather is a virtual prerequisite for enjoying the itinerary.

❷ Visit **Hadrian's Villa** first, especially in the summer, to take advantage of the cooler morning sun: There's little shade. Hadrian, who succeeded Trajan as emperor in AD 117, was a man of genius and intellectual curiosity. Fascinated by the accomplishments of the Hellenistic world, he decided to re-create it for his own enjoyment by building this villa over a vast tract of land below the ancient settlement of Tibur. From AD 118 to 130, architects, laborers, and artists worked on the villa, periodically spurred on by the emperor himself, as he returned from another voyage full of ideas for even more daring constructions. After Hadrian's death in AD 138, the fortunes of his villa declined. The villa was sacked by barbarians and Romans alike; by the Renaissance, many of his statues and decorations had ended up in Villa d'Este. Still, it is an impressive complex.

Study the exhibits in the visitor center at the entrance and the scale model in the building adjacent to the bar, close by. They will increase your enjoyment of the villa itself by helping you make sense out of what can otherwise be a maze of ruins. It's not the single elements, but the peaceful and harmonious effects of the whole, that make Hadrian's Villa such a treat. Oleanders, pines, and cypresses growing among the ruins heighten the visual impact. *Villa Adriana. Admission: 8,000 lire. Open daily 9–90 minutes before sunset.*

Time Out   The **Adriano** restaurant, at the entrance to Hadrian's Villa, is a handy place to have lunch and to rest before heading up the hill to Villa d'Este. The food is good, and the atmosphere is relaxing. *AE, DC, MC, V. Closed Mon. Moderate.*

❸ From Hadrian's Villa, catch the local bus up to **Tivoli's** main square, Largo Garibaldi. Take a left onto Via Boselli and cross Piazza Trento, with the church of Santa Maria Maggiore on your left, to reach the entrance to **Villa d'Este.** Ippolito d'Este was an active figure in the political intrigues of mid-16th-century Italy. He was also a cardinal, thanks to his grandfather, Alexander VI, the infamous Borgia pope. To console himself at a time when he saw his political star in decline, Ippolito tore down part of a Franciscan monastery that occupied the site he had chosen for his villa. Then the determined prelate diverted the Aniene River into a channel to run under the town and provide water for Villa d'Este's fountains. Big, small, noisy, quiet, rushing, and running, the fountains create a late-Renaissance playground where sunlight, shade, water, gardens, and carved stone make a magical setting. *Villa d'Este. Admission: 10,000 lire. Open daily 9–90 minutes before sunset.*

Only 27 kilometers (17 miles) south of Tivoli on S636 and 37 kilometers (23 miles) outside Rome along Via Prenestina, **Palestrina** is set on the slopes of Mount Ginestro, from which it commands a sweeping view of the green plain and distant mountains. It is surprisingly little known outside Italy, except to students of ancient history and music lovers. Its most famous native son, Giovanni Pierluigi da Palestrina, born here in 1525, was the renowned composer of 105 masses, as well as madrigals, magnificats, and motets. But the town was celebrated long before the composer's lifetime.

Ancient Praeneste, modern Palestrina, was founded much earlier than Rome. It was the site of the Temple of Fortuna Primigenia, which dates from the beginning of the 2nd century BC. This was one of the biggest, richest, and most frequented temple complexes in all antiquity. People came from far and wide to consult its famous oracle, yet in modern times, no one had any idea of the extent of the complex until World War II bombings exposed ancient foundations that stretched way out into the plain below the town. It's since become clear that the temple area was larger than the town of Palestrina is today. Now you can make out the four superimposed terraces that formed the main part of the temple; they were built up on great arches and were linked by broad flights of stairs. The whole town sits on top of what was once the main part of the temple.

Large arches and terraces scale the hillside up to **Palazzo Barberini,** built in the 17th century along the semicircular lines of the original temple. It's now a museum containing a wealth of material found on the site, some dating back to the 4th century BC. The collection of engraved bronze urns is splendid, but the chief attraction is a 1st century BC mosaic representing the Nile in flood. This delightful work is a large-scale composition in which form, color, and innumerable details captivate the eye. It's worth making the trip to Palestrina just for this. But there's more: a perfect scale model of the temple as it was in ancient times, which will help you appreciate the immensity of the original construction. *Museo Nazionale Archeologico, Palazzo Barberini. Admission: 6,000 lire. Open Tues.–Sun., spring and fall 9–6, summer 9–7:30, winter 9–4.*

If you are driving or if you don't mind setting out on a roundabout route by local bus, you could continue on to **Subiaco,** tucked away in the mountains above Tivoli and Palestrina. Take S155 east for about 40 kilometers (25 miles) before turning left on S411 for 25 kilometers (15 miles) to Subiaco. Its inaccessibility was undoubtedly a point in its favor for St. Benedict: The 6th-century monastery that he founded here became a landmark of Western monasticism.

This excursion is best made by car because it's nearly a 3-kilometer (2-mile) walk from Subiaco to Santa Scholastica, and another half-hour by footpath up to San Benedetto. If you don't have a car, inquire in Subiaco about a local bus to get you at least part of the way.

The first monastery you come upon is that of **Santa Scholastica,** actually a convent, and the only one of the hermitages founded by St. Benedict and his sister Scholastica to have survived the

Lombard invasion of Italy in the 9th century. It has three cloisters, the oldest dating back to the 13th century. The library, which is not open to visitors, contains some precious volumes; this was the site of the first print shop in Italy, set up in 1474. *Admission free. Open daily 9–12:30, 4–6.*

Drive up to the **monastery of St. Benedict,** or take the footpath that climbs the hill. The monastery was built over the grotto where St. Benedict lived and meditated. Clinging to the cliff on nine great arches, the monastery has resisted the assaults of man and nature for almost 800 years. You climb a broad, sloping avenue and enter through a little wooden veranda, where a Latin inscription augers "peace to those who enter." You find yourself in the colorful world of the upper church, every inch of it covered with frescoes by Umbrian and Sienese artists of the 14th century. In front of the main altar, a stairway leads down to the lower church, carved out of the rock, with yet another stairway down to the grotto, or cave, where Benedict lived as a hermit for three years. The frescoes here are even earlier than those above; look for the portrait of St. Francis of Assisi, painted from life in 1210, in the Chapel of St. Gregory and for the oldest fresco in the monastery, in the Shepherd's Grotto. Back in town, if you've got the time, stop at the 14th-century **church of San Francesco** to see the frescoes by Il Sodoma. *Admission free. Open daily 9–12:30, 3–6.*

Dining

Palestrina
★ **Coccia.** In this dining room of a small, centrally located hotel in Palestrina's public garden, you'll find scenic views, a cordial welcome, and local dishes with a few interesting variations. The fettucine is light and freshly made, served with a choice of sauces. A more unusual item on the menu is the *pasta e fagioli con frutti di mare* (thick bean and pasta soup with shellfish). *Piazzale Liberazione, tel. 06/955–8172. Reservations not needed. Dress: casual. AE, DC, V. Moderate.*

Subiaco
Belvedere. This small hotel on the road between the town and the monasteries is equipped to serve crowds of skiers from the slopes of nearby Mount Livata, as well as pilgrims on their way to St. Benedict's hermitage. The atmosphere is homey and cordial. Specialties include homemade fettuccine with a tasty *ragú* sauce and grilled meats and sausages. *Via dei Monasteri 33, tel. 0774/85531. No reservations. Dress: casual. No credit cards. Inexpensive.*

Mariuccia. This modern barnlike restaurant, located close to the monasteries, caters to weddings and other functions, but is calm enough on weekdays. There's a large garden and a good view from the picture windows. House specialties are homemade fettuccine with *porcini* mushrooms and *scaloppe al tartufo* (truffled veal scallops). In the summer you dine outdoors under bright umbrellas. *Via Sublacense, tel. 0774/84851. Reservations advised for lunch. Dress: casual. No credit cards. Closed Mon. and Nov. Inexpensive.*

Tivoli
Del Falcone. A central location—on the main street leading off Largo Garibaldi—means that this restaurant is popular and often crowded. In the ample and rustic dining rooms, you can try homemade fettuccine and cannelloni. Country-style grilled meats are excellent. *Via Trevio 34, tel. 0774/22358. Reservations advised. Dress: casual. No credit cards. Inexpensive.*

4 Florence

Introduction

by George Sullivan Florence is one of the preeminent treasures of Europe, and it is a time-honored Mecca for sightseers from all over the world. But as a city, it can be surprisingly forbidding to the first-time visitor. Its architecture is predominantly Early Renaissance and retains many of the harsh, implacable, fortresslike features of pre-Renaissance palazzi, whose facades were mostly meant to keep intruders out rather than to invite sightseers in. With the exception of a very few buildings, the stately dignity of the High Renaissance and the exuberant invention of the Baroque are not to be found here. The typical Florentine exterior gives nothing away, as if obsessively guarding secret treasures within.

The treasures, of course, are very real. And far from being a secret, they are famous the world over. The city is an artistic treasure house of unique and incomparable proportions. A single historical fact explains the phenomenon: Florence gave birth to the Renaissance. In the early 15th century the study of antiquity—of the glory that was Greece and the grandeur that was Rome—became a Florentine passion, and with it came a new respect for learning and a new creativity in art and architecture. In Florence, that remarkable creativity is everywhere in evidence.

Prior to the 15th century, Florence was a medieval city not much different from its Tuscan neighbors. It began as a Roman settlement, laid out in the first century BC, and served as a provincial capital when the Roman Empire was at its height. Its rise to real power, however, did not begin until the era of the medieval Italian city-states, beginning in the 11th century.

From the 11th to the 14th centuries, northern Italy was ruled by feudal lords, and by the 13th century Florence was a leading contender in the complicated struggle between the Guelphs and the Ghibellines. Florence was mostly Guelph, and its Ghibelline contingent ruled the city only sporadically (which did not, however, keep the Florentine Guelphs from squabbling among themselves). In those bloody days Florence was filled with tall defensive towers built by the city's leading families on a competitive anything-you-can-build-I-can-build-bigger basis; the towers (and the houses below them) were connected by overhead bridges and catwalks, constructed to allow the members of allied families access to each other's houses without venturing into the dangerous streets below. The era gave rise, possibly for the first time in history, to the concept of turf, and its urban conflicts were at times just as vicious and irrational as the gang warfare within cities today.

The Guelph-Ghibelline conflict ended, finally, with the victory of the Guelphs and the rise of the Medici in the 15th century. The famous dynasty (which ruled Florence, and later all Tuscany, for more than three centuries) began with Giovanni di Bicci de' Medici and his son Cosimo, who transformed themselves from bankers into rulers. The dynasty reached its zenith with Cosimo's grandson Lorenzo the Magnificent (1449–92), patron and friend of some of Florence's most famous Renaissance artists. The towers were torn down, and the city assumed a slightly softer aspect. It still looks today much as it did then.

The history of modern Florence was shaped by its six years as the capital of the Kingdom of Italy. In 1861 Tuscany united with most of the other states on the Italian peninsula, and in 1865 Florence became the new nation's capital. In 1871 Florence relinquished the honor, when the final unification of Italy was effected by the capitulation of Rome.

But the city's history was equally influenced by the flood of November 4, 1966. The citizens of Florence went to bed the night before in a heavy downpour after three days of rain and a particularly wet autumn; they awoke the next morning to confront the worst disaster in the city's history. Florence was entirely under water. The Piazza del Duomo became a rushing river; the church of Santa Croce was battered by a torrent more than 20 feet deep; the Ponte Vecchio disappeared completely as the Arno broke into the walls of its shops and flowed through. Only toward midnight did the flood begin to recede.

The Ponte Vecchio—amazingly—survived. But the damage to the rest of the city, including some of its greatest artistic treasures, was horrific. Technologically and financially ill-equipped to cope with such a disaster, Florence asked for, and received, advice and help from an army of international experts. Today, most of the damage to the city has been repaired. But little has been done to keep this kind of ruin from happening again.

Essential Information

Arriving and Departing by Plane

Airports and Airlines The local airport, called **Peretola** (tel. 055/373498) is 10 kilometers (6 miles) northwest of Florence. Although expanding to accommodate flights from Milan, Rome, and some European cities, it is still a relatively minor airport. **Galileo Galilei** airport in Pisa (tel. 050/28088) is 80 kilometers (50 miles) west of Florence and is used by most international carriers.

Between the Airports and Downtown **By Car:** From Peretola take Autostrada A11 directly into the city. Driving from Pisa airport, take S67, a direct route to Florence.

By Train: A scheduled service operates on the one- hour connection between the station at Pisa airport and Santa Maria Novella train station in Florence. Trains start running about 7 AM from the airport, 6 AM from Florence, and continue service every hour until about 11:30 PM from the airport, 8 PM from Florence. You can check in for departing flights at the air terminal at Track 5 of the train station (tel. 055/216973).

By Bus: Don't think you can make the connection from **Pisa** airport because there is no direct service to Florence. Buses do go to Pisa itself, but then you have to change to a slow train service. There is a local bus service from Peretola to Florence (*see* Getting Around By Bus, below).

Arriving and Departing by Car, Train, and Bus

By Car Florence is connected to the north and south of Italy by Autostrada A1. It takes about an hour's scenic drive to reach Bologna and about three hours to get to Rome. The Tyrrhenian coast is an hour away on A11 west. Upon entering the city, abandon all hope of using a car, since most of the downtown area is a pedestrian zone. For traffic information in Florence, call 055/577777.

By Train Florence is on the principal Italian train route between most European capitals and Rome and within Italy is served quite frequently from Milan, Venice, and Rome by the new nonstops called Intercity (IC). The **Santa Maria Novella** station is near the downtown area; avoid trains that stop only at the Campo di Marte station in an inconvenient location on the east side of the city. For train information in Florence, call 055/278–785.

By Bus Long-distance buses run by **SITA** (Via Santa Caterina da Siena 15r, tel. 055/211487) and **Lazzi Eurolines** (Via Mercadante 2, tel. 055/215154) offer inexpensive if somewhat claustrophobic service between Florence and other cities in Italy and Europe.

Getting Around

By Bus ATAF, the local city bus company, operates an efficient, extensive network of buses within the city and the outlying area. Maps and timetables are available for a small fee at the ATAF booth in the station or at the office at Piazza Duomo 57r, or for free at the main tourist office (*see* Important Addresses and Numbers, below). There are two types of tickets valid for one or more rides on all lines. One costs 800 lire and is valid for 70 minutes; the other costs 1,000 lire for 120 minutes. A 24-hour tourist ticket costs 4,000 lire. They must be purchased in advance at tobacco stores, newsstands, or ATAF booths next to the train station or near the cathedral. You have to cancel them on the small validation machines immediately on boarding the bus. Buses displaying a sign of a hand holding a coin have ticket-dispensing machines that accept exact change. Long-term visitors or frequent users of the bus should look into the monthly passes sold at the ATAF office.

By Taxi Taxis usually wait at stands throughout the city (such as in front of the train station and in Piazza della Repubblica), or they can be called by dialing 055/4390 or 055/4798.

By Moped Those who want to go native and rent a noisy Vespa (Italian for wasp) or other make of motorcycle or moped may do so at **Motorent** (Via San Zanobi 9r, tel. 055/490113) or **Program** (Borgo Ognissanti 135/r, tel. 055/282916). Helmets are mandatory and can be rented here.

By Bicycle Brave souls many also rent bicycles at easy-to-spot locations at Fortezza da Basso, Santa Maria Novella train station, and Piazza Pitti, or from an organization called **Ciao e Basta** (Via Alamanni, next to the station, tel. 055/213307).

By Foot This is definitely the best way to see the major sights of Florence, since practically everything of interest is within walking distance along the city's crowded, narrow streets or is otherwise accessible by bus.

Important Addresses and Numbers

Tourist Information The city information office is at Via Cavour 1r (next to Palazzo Medici Riccardi), tel. 055/276–0382. Open 8:30–7.

The **APT** (tourist office) is just off Piazza Beccaria, at Via Manzoni 16, tel. 055/247–8141. Open Mon.–Fri. 8:30–1:30, 4–6:30; Sat. 8:30–1:30.

Consulates **U.S.** Lungarno Vespucci 38, tel. 055/298276. Open Mon.–Fri. 8:30–12, 2–4.
British. Lungarno Corsini 2, tel. 055/284133. Open Mon.–Fri. 9:30–12:30, 2:30–4:30.
Canadians should contact their embassy in Rome.

Emergencies **Police.** Tel. 113. The main police station is located at Via Zara 2, near Piazza della Liberta.

Doctors and For English-speaking doctors and dentists, get a list from the
Dentists U.S. consulate, or contact **Tourist Medical Service** (Viale Lorenzo Il Magnifico, tel. 055/475411). **Ambulance.** Misericordia (Piazza del Duomo 20, tel. 055/212222).

Late-Night Pharmacies. The following are open 24 hours a day, seven days a week. For others, call 055/110.

Comunale No. 13 (train station, tel. 055/263435).

Molteni (Via Calzaiuoli 7r, tel. 055/263490).

Taverna (Piazza San Giovanni 20r, tel. 055/284013).

English-Language **Paperback Exchange** (Via Fiesolana 31r, tel. 055/2478154) will
Bookstores do just that, besides selling books outright. **BM Bookshop** (Borgo Ognissanti 4r, tel. 055/294575) has a fine selection of books on Florence. **Seeber** (Via Tornabuoni 68, tel. 055/215697) has English-language books alongside the other titles. *All are open 9–1, 3:30–7:30. Closed Mon. mornings, Sun.*

Travel Agencies **American Express** (Via Guicciardini 49r, near Piazza Pitti, tel. 055/278751) is also represented by **Universalturismo** (Via Speziali 7r, off Piazza della Repubblica, tel. 055/217241). **CIT** has a main office (Via Cavour 56 tel. 055/294306) and also a branch near the train station (Piazza Stazione 51, tel. 055/284-145). **Wagon-Lits Turismo/Thomas Cook** (Via del Giglio 27r, tel. 055/218851). *All agencies are open Mon.–Fri. 9–12:30, 3:30–7:30; Sat. 9–noon.*

Guided Tours

Orientation Visitors who have a limited amount of time in Florence may find guided tours an efficient way of covering the city's major sights. The major bus operators (*see* Arriving and Departing by Car, Train, and Bus, above) offer half-day itineraries, all of which generally follow the same plan, using comfortable buses staffed with English-speaking guides. Morning tours begin at 9, when buses pick visitors up at the main hotels. The first stop is the cathedral complex, with its bapistry and bell tower, and the Accademia to see Michelangelo's famous statue of David. Next is the Piazzale Michelangelo for a fine view of Florence, then on to the Pitti Palace (or the Museo del Opera del Duomo on Mondays, when the Pitti is closed) for a guided tour of the art. The tours usually end at about 12:30 PM. Afternoon tours stop at the main hotels at 2 PM, begin in Piazza della Signoria, visit the Uffizi Gallery (or the Palazzo Vecchio on Mondays, when the Uffizi is closed), the nearby town of Fiesole, and return to Florence to see the church of Santa Croce, generally ending at about 6 PM.

Excursions Contact the above operators a day in advance, if possible, because excursions are popular. Comfortable buses with English-speaking guides make full-day trips from Florence to Siena and San Gimignano (departure 9 AM, return 6 PM, lunch not included) and afternoon excursions to Pisa (departure 2 PM, return 7 PM), with pickup and return from the main hotels.

Exploring Florence

Orientation

No city in Italy can match Florence's astounding artistic wealth. Important paintings and sculptures are everywhere, and art scholars and connoisseurs have been investigating the subtleties and complexities of these works for hundreds of years. But what makes the art of Florence a revelation to the ordinary sightseer is a simple fact that scholarship often ignores: An astonishing percentage of Florence's art is just plain beautiful. Nowhere in Italy—perhaps in all Europe—is the act of looking at art more rewarding.

But a word of warning is in order here. For some years now, Florentine psychiatrists have recognized a peculiar local malady to which foreign tourists are particularly susceptible. It's called "Stendhal's syndrome," after the 19th-century French novelist, who was the first to describe it in print. The symptoms can be severe: confusion, dizziness, disorientation, depression, and sometimes persecution anxiety and loss of the sense of identity. Some victims immediately suspect food poisoning, but the true diagnosis is far more outlandish. They are suffering from art poisoning, brought on by overexposure to so-called Important Works of High Culture. Consciously or unconsciously, they seem to view Florentine art as an exam (Aesthetics 101, 10 hours per day, self-taught, pass/fail), and they are terrified of flunking.

Obviously, the art of Florence should not be a test. So if you are not an inveterate museum goer or church collector with established habits and methods, take it easy. Don't try to absorb every painting or fresco that comes into view. There is second-rate art even in the Uffizi and the Pitti (*especially* the Pitti), so find some favorites and enjoy them at your leisure. Getting to know a few paintings well will be far more enjoyable than seeing a vast number badly.

And when fatigue begins to set in, stop. Take time off, and pay some attention to the city itself. Too many first-time visitors trudge dutifully from one museum to the next without really seeing what is in between. They fail to notice that Florence the city (as opposed to Florence the museum) is a remarkable phenomenon: a bustling metropolis that has managed to preserve its predominantly medieval street plan and predominantly Renaissance infrastructure while successfully adapting to the insistent demands of 20th-century life. The resulting marriage between the very old and the very new is not always tranquil, but it is always fascinating. Florence the city can be chaotic, frenetic, and full of uniquely Italian noise, but it is alive in a way that Florence the museum, however beautiful, is not. Do not miss the forest for the trees.

The three walking tours outlined in the following pages are best taken a day at a time. Attempts to complete them in fewer than three days will prove frustrating, for many (if not most) Florentine museums and churches close sometime between noon and 2, and only the churches reopen in the late afternoon. If you have only one day, devote it to Tour 1, incorporating a brief detour to see Michelangelo's *David* in the Accademia (located three blocks north of the Piazza del Duomo on the Via Ricasoli and described in Tour 3) after you have visited the Duomo Museum. If there is extra time at the end of the tour (and if you have not been laid low by Stendhal's syndrome), the best place to continue is the church and museum of Santa Croce, described near the end of Tour 3 and located on the Piazza Santa Croce, five blocks west of the Piazza della Signoria.

Highlights for First-Time Visitors

Duomo (Cathedral of Santa Maria del Fiore) (Tour 1: From the Duomo to the Boboli Gardens).

Battistero (Baptistery) (Tour 1: From the Duomo to the Boboli Gardens).

Museo dell'Opera del Duomo (Tour 1: From the Duomo to the Boboli Gardens).

Bargello (Museo Nazionale) (Tour 1: From the Duomo to the Boboli Gardens).

Piazza della Signoria (Tour 1: From the Duomo to the Boboli gardens).

Galleria degli Uffizi (Tour 1: From the Duomo to the Boboli Gardens).

Galleria dell'Accademia (Tour 3: From the Duomo to Santa Croce and Beyond).

Ponte Vecchio (Tour 1: From the Duomo to the Boboli Gardens).

Santa Croce (Tour 3: From the Duomo to Santa Croce and Beyond).

Tour 1: From the Duomo to the Boboli Gardens

Numbers in the margin correspond with points of interest on the Florence map.

The first tour begins with the Cathedral of Santa Maria del Fiore, more familiarly known as the Duomo, located in the Piazza del Duomo, with its accompanying Battistero (Baptistery), the octagonal building that faces the Duomo facade. The Baptistery is one of the oldest buildings in Florence, and local legend has that it was once a Roman temple of Mars; modern excavations, however, suggest its foundation was laid in the sixth or seventh century AD, well after the collapse of the Roman Empire. The round-arched Romanesque decoration on the exterior probably dates from the 11th or 12th century. The interior ceiling mosaics (finished in 1297) are justly famous, but—glitteringly beautiful as they are—they cannot outshine the building's most renowned feature: its bronze Renaissance doors decorated with panels crafted by Lorenzo Ghiberti (1378–1455). The panels are located on the north and east doors of the building (the south door panels are Gothic, designed by Andrea Pisano in 1330), and Ghiberti spent most of his adult life (from 1403 to 1452) working on them. The north doors depict scenes from the life of Christ; the later east doors (the ones facing the Duomo facade) depict scenes from the Old Testament.

Florence

N

Stazione Centrale

V. Vallonda

V. Nazionale

V. Rucellai

V. della Scala

Piazza dell' Unità Italiana

15

V. Palazzuolo

Borgo Ognissanti

Piazza S. Maria Novella

V. d. Belle Donne

V. dei Banchi

V. del Trebbio

V. Rondinelli

16

Piazza Ognissanti

V. d. Porcellana

V. del Sole

Lung. Amerigo Vespucci

V. de Fossi

V. Spada

i

Ponte Vespucci

V. del Moro

18 Vigna Nuova

V. Tornabuoni

17

Arno

Piazza Goldoni

V. d. V. del Purgatorio

V. del Parione

Piazza Santa Trinita

Piazza di Cestello

Lung. Soderini

Ponte alla Carraia

Lung. Corsini

19

Lung.

Borgo S. Frediano

Piazza N. Sauro

Lung. Guicciardini

Ponte S. Trinita

Piazza del Carmine

V. S. Monaca

V. dell'Ardiglione

V. dei Serragli

V. Sant' Agostino

V. Maffia

22

Piazza S. Spirito

21

Borgo Tegolaio

V. Maggio

V. Guicciardini

V. della Chiesa

V. del Campuccio

Torrigiani Gardens

Piazza S. Felice

20

14

V. Romana

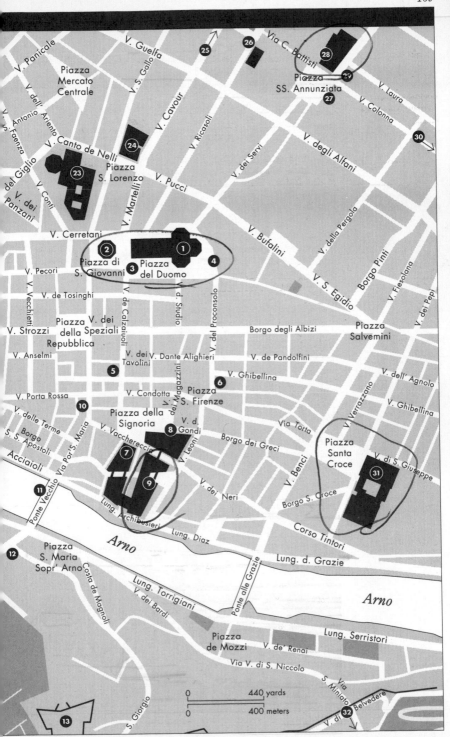

V. Panicale

V. Guelfa

Via C. Battisti

25

26

28

29

Piazza
Mercato
Centrale

Piazza
SS. Annunziata

27

V. Laura

V. S. Gallo

V. Cavour

V. Ricasoli

V. degli Alfani

V. Colonna

30

V. dei Servi

24

Piazza
S. Lorenzo

V. Pucci

23

V. Canto de Nelli

V. del Giglio

V. Conti

V. dei
Panzani

V. Martelli

V.p. Faenza

V.o Antonio Ariento

V. Cerretani

V. Bufalini

V. della Pergola

Borgo Pinti

V. Fiesolana

2

1

4

V. S. Egidio

Piazza di
S. Giovanni

3

Piazza
del Duomo

V. Pecori

V. de Tosinghi

M. d. Studio

V. del Proconsolo

V. dei Pepi

V. Vecchietti

V. Strozzi

Piazza
della
Repubblica

V. dei
Speziali

Borgo degli Albizi

Piazza
Salvemini

V. Anselmi

V. de Calzaiuoli

V. dei
Tavolini

V. Dante Alighieri

V. de Pandolfini

V. dell' Agnolo

5

6

V. Ghibellina

V. Ghibellina

V. Porta Rossa

V. Condotta

Piazza
S. Firenze

10

V. delle Terme

Piazza della
Signoria

V. d.
Gondi

Via Torta

V. Verrazzano

Borgo
S. S. Apostoli

8

V. dei Magazzini

V. Vaccherecci

V. Benci

Piazza
Santa
Croce

31

V. di S. Giuseppe

Acciaioli

7

V. Leoni

Borgo dei Greci

9

V. dei Neri

Borgo S. Croce

11

Ponte Vecchio

Lung. Archibusieri

Lung. Diaz

Corso Tintori

Via Por S. Maria

Arno

12

Piazza
S. Maria
Sopr' Arno

Lung. d. Grazie

Arno

Costa de Magnoli

Lung. Torrigiani

V. dei Bardi

Ponte alle Grazie

Lung. Serristori

Piazza
de Mozzi

V. de' Renai

Via V. di S. Niccolo

S. Giorgio

S. Miniato

Via S. Miniato al Belvedere

0   440 yards

0   400 meters

13

32

The two sets of doors are worth close examination, for they are very different in style and illustrate with great clarity the artistic changes that marked the beginning of the Renaissance. Look, for instance, at the far right panel of the middle row on the earlier north doors (*Jesus Calming the Waters*). Ghiberti here captured the chaos of a storm at sea with great skill and economy, but the artistic conventions he used are basically pre-Renaissance: Jesus is the most important figure, so he is the largest; the disciples are next in size, being next in importance; the ship on which they founder, being least important, is a mere toy. But you can sense Ghiberti's impatience with these artificial spatial conventions. The Cathedral Works Committee made him retain the decorative quatrefoil borders of the south doors for his panels here, and in this scene Ghiberti's storm seems to want to burst the bounds of its frame. It pushes against its artificial borders and seems to be trying to break free of its symbolically stylized world.

On the east doors, the decorative borders are gone. The panels are larger, more expansive, more sweeping, and more convincing. They have, as it were, taken a deep breath, and have sprung to a new kind of pictorial life. Look, for example, at the middle panel on the left-hand door. It tells the story of Jacob and Esau, and the various episodes of the story (the selling of the birthright, Isaac ordering Esau to go hunting, the blessing of Jacob, and so forth) have been merged into a single beautifully realized street scene. A perspective grid is employed to suggest depth, the background architecture looks far more convincing than on the north door panels, the figures in the foreground are grouped realistically, and the naturalism and grace of the poses (look at Esau's left leg) have nothing to do with the sacred message being conveyed. There is a new secular emphasis here that goes far beyond religious symbolism and story telling. Although the religious content remains, man and his place in the natural world are given new prominence and are portrayed with a realism not seen in art since the fall of the Roman Empire, more than a thousand years before.

When Ghiberti was working on these panels, three of his artist friends were bringing the same new humanistic focus to their own very different work. In sculpture, Donato di Niccolo Betto Bardi, known as Donatello, was creating statuary for churches all over town; in painting, Tommaso di Ser Giovanni, known as Masaccio, was executing frescoes at the churches of Santa Maria del Carmine and Santa Maria Novella; in architecture, Filippo Brunelleschi was building the Duomo dome, the Ospedale degli Innocenti, and the church interiors of San Lorenzo and Santo Spirito. They are the fathers of the Renaissance in art and architecture—the four great geniuses who created a new artistic vision—and between them, they began a revolution that was to make Florence the artistic capital of Italy for more than a hundred years.

As a footnote to Ghiberti's panels, one small detail of the east doors is worth a special look. Just to the lower left of the Jacob and Esau panel, Ghiberti placed a tiny self-portrait bust. From either side, the portrait is extremely appealing—Ghiberti looks like everyone's favorite uncle—but the bust is carefully placed so that there is a single spot in front of the doors from which you can make direct eye contact with the tiny head. When that contact is made, the impression of intelligent life—

of *modern* intelligent life—is astonishing. It is no wonder that when these doors were completed, they received one of the most famous compliments in the history of art, from a competitor known to be notoriously stingy with praise: Michelangelo himself declared them so beautiful that they could serve as the Gates to Paradise.

The doors that you see on the Baptistery are exact copies of Brunelleschi's, and they still have the gleam of new bronze. The originals were removed, to protect them from the effects of pollution and acid rain. They have been beautifully restored and are now on display in the Cathedral Museum (to be discussed shortly). *Admission to Baptistery interior free. Open daily 12:30–6:30.*

The immense Duomo—the fourth-largest church in the world—was designed by Arnolfo di Cambio in 1296 but was not consecrated until 1436. The imposing facade dates only from the 19th century; it was built in the neo-Gothic style to complement Giotto's genuine Gothic (14th-century) **Campanile** (Bell Tower), which stands to the right of the church's facade. The real glory of the Duomo, however, is Filippo Brunelleschi's dome, herald of the new Renaissance in architecture, which hovers over the cathedral (and the entire city when seen from afar) with a dignity and grace that few domes, even to this day, can match. It was the first of its kind in the world, and for many people it is still the best.

Brunelleschi's dome was epoch-making as an engineering feat, as well. The space to be enclosed by the dome was so large and so high above the ground that traditional methods of dome construction—wooden centering and scaffolding—were of no use whatever. So Brunelleschi developed entirely new building methods, which he implemented with equipment of his own devising (including the modern crane). Beginning work in 1420, he built not one dome but two, one inside the other, and connected them with common ribbing that stretched across the intervening empty space, thereby considerably lessening the crushing weight of the structure. He also employed a new method of bricklaying, based on an ancient Roman herringbone pattern, interlocking each new course of bricks with the course below in a way that made the growing structure self-supporting. The result was one of the great engineering breakthroughs of all time: Most of Europe's great domes, including St. Peter's in Rome, were built employing Brunelleschi's methods, and today the Duomo has come to symbolize Florence in the same way that the Eiffel Tower symbolizes Paris. The Florentines are justly proud, and to this day the Florentine phrase for "homesick" is *nostalgia del cupolone* (sick for the dome).

The interior is a fine example of Italian Gothic, although anyone who has seen the Gothic cathedrals of France will be disappointed by its lack of dramatic verticality. Italian architecture, even at the height of the Gothic era, never broke entirely free of the influence of Classical Rome, and its architects never learned (perhaps never wanted to learn) how to make their interiors soar like the cathedrals in the cities around Paris.

Most of the cathedral's best-known artworks have now been moved to the nearby cathedral museum. Notable among the works that remain, however, are two equestrian frescoes honoring famous soldiers: Andrea del Castagno's *Niccolo da*

Tolentino, painted in 1456, and Paolo Uccello's *Sir John Hawkwood,* painted 20 years earlier; both are on the left-hand wall of the nave. *Niccolo da Tolentino* is particularly impressive: He rides his fine horse with military pride and wears his even finer hat—surely the best in town—with panache.

If time permits, you may want to explore the upper and lower reaches of the cathedral, as well. Ancient remains have been excavated beneath the nave; the stairway down is near the first pier on the right. The climb to the top of the dome (463 steps) is not for the faint-hearted, but the view is superb; the entrance is on the left wall just before the crossing. *Piazza del Duomo, tel. 055/294514. Excavation admission: 2,000 lire. Ascent admission: 4,000 lire. Duomo open daily 7:30 AM–6:30 PM; open for nonreligious purposes 10–5.*

Leave the Duomo by the right-aisle exit and turn left; at the east end of the piazza, opposite the rear of the cathedral, is the
❹ **Museo dell'Opera del Duomo,** (Cathedral Museum). Its major attractions—other than the Ghiberti door panels mentioned earlier—are two: Donatello's *Mary Magdalen* and Michelangelo's *Pietà* (not to be confused with the more famous *Pietà* in St. Peter's, in Rome). The High Renaissance in sculpture is in part defined by its revolutionary realism, but Donatello's *Magdalen* goes beyond realism: It is suffering incarnate. Michelangelo's heart-wrenching *Pietà* was unfinished at his death; the female figure supporting the body of Christ on the left was added by one Tiberio Calcagni, and never has the difference between competence and genius been manifested so clearly. *Piazza del Duomo 9, tel. 055/2302885. Admission: 4,000 lire; free Sun. Open Mar.–Oct., Mon.–Sat. 9–8, Sun. 10–1; Nov.–Feb., Mon.–Sat. 9–6, Sun. 10–1.*

Return to the Duomo facade, and turn left onto **Via de Calzaiuoli.** This unusually wide street dates from the 14th century and probably represents Florence's first modern city planning. The street received special attention because it ran directly from the city's main religious square to its main civic square, the Piazza della Signoria, where the medieval city hall was located. Both the axis and the city hall remain intact to this day.

A short detour to the west (down Via dei Speziali) leads to the **Piazza della Repubblica.** The piazza's location, if not its architecture, is historically important: Here was located the ancient forum around which lay the original Roman settlement. The street plan in the area around the piazza still reflects the carefully plotted orthogonal grid of the Roman military encampment. The Mercato Vecchio (Old Market), located here since the Middle Ages, was demolished at the end of the last century, and the current piazza was constructed between 1890 and 1917 as a neoclassical showpiece. Nominally the center of town, it has yet to earn the love of most Florentines.

Return to Via de Calzaiuoli and turn right. Just down the street
❺ is the rectangular church of **Orsanmichele,** containing a beautifully detailed 14th-century Gothic tabernacle by Andrea Orcagna. Of particular note here, however, is the building's exterior. Originally a granary, it was transformed in 1336 into a church with 14 exterior niches. Each of the major Florentine trade guilds was assigned its own niche and paid for the statuary the niche contains. All the statuaries are worth examining,

though many are copies, but one deserves special notice: Andrea del Verrocchio's *Doubting Thomas*, dating from around 1470, in the middle niche on the Via de Calzaiuoli. The composition is beautifully controlled: Christ (like the building's other figures) is entirely framed within the niche, but St. Thomas stands on its bottom ledge, with his right foot completely outside the niche frame. This one detail—the positioning of a single foot—brings the whole composition to life, as if St. Thomas, just a moment ago, had stepped into the niche off the busy street to confront his master. It is particularly appropriate that this is the building's only niche to be topped with a classical triangular Renaissance pediment, for it is the revolutionary vitality of sculpture like this that gave the Renaissance its name.

From Via de Calzaiuoli, follow Via dei Tavolini (which turns into Via Dante Alighieri after one block and passes the fraudulently named Casa di Dante on the left) to the intersection of Via del Proconsolo. The church on the southwest corner is the ancient **Badia Fiorentina,** built in 1285; its graceful bell tower (best seen from the interior courtyard) is one of the most beautiful in Florence. The interior of the church proper was half-heartedly remodeled in the Baroque style during the 17th century; its best-known work of art is Filippino Lippi's delicate *Apparition of the Virgin to St. Bernard* (1486), on the left as you enter. The painting—one of Lippi's finest—is in superb condition and is worth exploring in detail. The Virgin's hands are perhaps the most beautiful in the city. (To illuminate, drop a coin in the box near the floor to the painting's right).

On the opposite side of Via del Proconsolo from the Badia is the ❻ **Bargello.** During the Renaissance the building was used as a prison, and the exterior served as a "most-wanted" billboard: Effigies of notorious criminals and Medici enemies were painted on its walls. Today, the building is the **Museo Nazionale,** and houses what is probably the finest collection of Renaissance sculpture in Italy. Michelangelo, Donatello, and Benvenuto Cellini are the preeminent masters here, and the concentration of masterworks, which are beautifully displayed, is remarkable. For Renaissance art lovers, the Bargello is to sculpture what the Uffizi is to painting.

One particular display—easily overlooked—should not be missed. In 1402 Filippo Brunelleschi and Lorenzo Ghiberti competed to earn the most prestigious commission of the day: the decoration of the north doors of the Baptistery in the Piazza del Duomo. For the competition, each designed a bronze bas-relief panel on the theme of the Sacrifice of Isaac; both panels are on display, side by side, in the room devoted to the sculpture of Donatello on the upper floor. The judges chose Ghiberti for the commission; you can decide for yourself whether or not they were right. *Via del Proconsolo 4, tel. 055/210801. Admission: 6,000 lire. Open Tues.–Sat. 9–2, Sun. 9–1.*

Leaving the Bargello, continue south along Via del Proconsolo, to the small Piazza San Firenze. The church of San Firenze, on the left, is one of Florence's few Baroque structures; its steps offer a fine view of the Badia bell tower. From the north end of the piazza, go west on Via Condotta, then left onto Via dei Magazzini, which leads into the **Piazza della Signoria,** recently excavated and then repaved, the most striking square in Florence. It was here, in 1497, that the famous "bonfire of the vanities" took place, when the fanatical monk Savonarola induced his followers to hurl their worldly goods into the flames; it was also here, a year later, that he was hanged as a heretic and, ironically, burned. A bronze plaque in the piazza pavement marks the exact spot of his execution.

Time Out At the west end of the piazza, facing the statuary on the steps of the Palazzo Vecchio, is **Rivoire,** a café famous for its chocolate (both packaged and hot). Its outdoor tables and somewhat less expensive indoor counter are stylish, if pricey, places from which to observe the busy piazza. *Piazza della Signoria.*

7 The statuaries in the square and in the 14th-century **Loggia dei Lanzi** on the south side are variable in quality, with the booby prize indubitably going to Bartolommeo Ammannati's gigantic **Neptune Fountain,** dating from 1565, at the corner of the Palazzo Vecchio. Even Ammannati himself considered it a failure, and the Florentines call it *Il Biancone,* which may be translated as "the big white man" or "the big white lump," depending on your point of view. Benvenuto Cellini's famous bronze *Perseus Holding the Head of Medusa* in the Loggia, however, is far from a failure; even the statue's pedestal is superbly executed (although the statuettes in its niches are recent copies of the originals). Other works in the loggia include *The Rape of the Sabine Women* and *Hercules and the Centaur,* both late–16th-century by Giambologna, and, in the back, a row of sober matrons dating from Roman times. The Loggia recently underwent lengthy structural restorations; many of the statues have been replaced by copies.

Back in the piazza, Giambologna's equestrian statue, to the left of the Neptune Fountain, pays tribute to the Medici Grand Duke Cosimo I; occupying the steps of the Palazzo Vecchio are a copy of Donatello's proud heraldic lion of Florence, known as the *Marzocco* (the original is now in the Bargello); a copy of Donatello's *Judith and Holofernes* (the original is inside the Palazzo Vecchio); a copy of Michelangelo's *David* (original now in the Accademia); and Baccio Bandinelli's *Hercules* (1534).

8 The **Palazzo Vecchio** itself is far from beautiful, but it possesses a more than acceptable substitute: character. The palazzo was begun in 1299 and designed (probably) by Arnolfo di Cambio, and its massive bulk and towering campanile dominate the piazza masterfully. It was built as a meeting place for the heads of the seven major guilds that governed the city at the time; over the centuries it has served lesser purposes, but today it is once again the City Hall of Florence. The interior courtyard is a good deal less severe, having been remodeled by Michelozzo in 1453.

Although most of the interior public rooms are well worth exploring, the main attraction is on the second floor: two adjoining rooms that supply one of the most startling contrasts in Florence. The first is the vast **Sala dei Cinquecento** (Room of the Five Hundred) named for 500 deputies who debated here from 1865 to 1871, when Florence served as the capital of the Kingdom of Italy. The Sala was decorated by Giorgio Vasari, around 1570, with huge frescoes celebrating Florentine history; depictions of battles with neighboring cities predominate. Continuing the martial theme, the Sala also contains Michelangelo's *Victory* group, intended for the never-completed tomb of Pope Julius II, plus miscellaneous sculptures of decidedly lesser quality.

The second room is the little **Studiolo,** entered to the right of the Sala's entrance. This was the study of Cosimo de Medici's son, the melancholy Francesco I, designed by Vasari and decorated by Vasari and Agnolo Bronzino. It is intimate; civilized; and filled with complex, questioning, allegorical art. It makes the vainglorious proclamations next door ring more than a little hollow. *Piazza della Signoria, tel. 055/276–8465. Admission: 8,000 lire. Open Mon.–Fri. 9–7, Sun. 8–1.*

9 Just south of the Palazzo Vecchio is the **Palazzo degli Uffizi,** a U-shaped building fronting on the Arno, designed by Vasari in 1559. Built as an office building—"uffizi" means "offices" in Italian—the palazzo today houses the finest collection of paintings in Italy. Hard-core museum goers will want to purchase the English guide sold outside the entrance.

The collection's highlights include Paolo Uccello's *Battle of San Romano* (its brutal chaos of lances is one of the finest visual metaphors for warfare ever committed to paint); Fra Filippo Lippi's *Madonna and Child with Two Angels* (the foreground angel's bold, impudent eye contact would have been unthinkable prior to the Renaissance); Sandro Botticelli's *Primavera* (its nonrealistic fairy-tale charm exhibits the painter's idiosyncratic genius at its zenith); Leonardo da Vinci's *Adoration of the Magi* (unfinished and perhaps the best opportunity in Europe to investigate the methods of a great artist at work); Raphael's *Madonna of the Goldfinch* (darkened by time, but the tenderness with which the figures in the painting touch each other is undimmed); Michelangelo's *Holy Family* (one of the very few easel works in oil he ever painted, clearly reflecting his stated belief that draftsmanship is a necessary ingredient of great painting); Rembrandt's *Self-Portrait as an Old Man* (which proves that even Michelangelo could, on occasion, be wrong); Titian's *Venus of Urbino* and Caravaggio's *Bacchus* (two very great paintings whose attitudes toward myth and sexuality are—to put it mildly—diametrically opposed); and many, many more. If panic sets in at the prospect of absorbing all this art at one go, bear in mind that the three tours outlined here are structured so as to offer late-afternoon free time, and the Uffizi is (except on Sundays) open late. *Piazzale degli Uffizi 6, tel. 055/218341. Admission: 10,000 lire. Open Tues.–Sat. 9–7, Sun. 9–1.*

Time Out There is a coffee bar inside the Uffizi, near the exit; its terrace offers a fine close-up view of the Palazzo Vecchio. For something more substantial, try lunch at **Cavallino,** a moderately priced restaurant serving Tuscan specialties, overlooking the Piazza della Signoria at Via delle Farine 6/r (closed Wed.).

10 Leave Piazza Signoria at the southeast corner and follow Via Vacchereccia one block west to Via Por Santa Maria. Just north of the intersection is an open-air loggia known as the **Mercato Nuovo** (New Market). It was new in 1551. Today it harbors mostly souvenir stands; its main attraction is Pietro Tacca's bronze *Porcellino* (Piglet) fountain on the south side, dating from around 1612 and copied from an earlier Roman work now in the Uffizi. Rubbing its drooling snout is a Florentine tradition—it is said to bring good luck.

Follow Via Por Santa Maria toward the river, and you will arrive at the **Ponte Vecchio** (the Old Bridge), which is to Florence what Tower Bridge is to London. It was built in 1345 to replace an earlier bridge that was swept away by flood, and its shops housed first butchers, then grocers, blacksmiths, and other merchants. But in 1593 the Medici Grand Duke Ferdinando I, whose private corridor linking the Medici palace (the Palazzo Pitti) with the Medici offices (the Uffizi) crossed the bridge atop the shops, decided that all this plebeian commerce under his feet was unseemly. So he threw out all the butchers and blacksmiths and installed 41 goldsmiths and eight jewelers. The bridge has been devoted solely to these two trades ever since.

In the middle of the bridge, take a moment (better yet, several moments) to study the **Ponte Santa Trinita,** the next bridge downriver. It was designed by Bartolommeo Ammannati in 1567 (possibly from sketches by Michelangelo), blown up by the retreating Germans during World War II and painstakingly reconstructed after the war ended. Florentines like to claim it is the most beautiful bridge in the world. Given the bridge's simplicity, this may sound like idle Tuscan boasting. But if you commit its graceful arc and delicate curves to memory and then begin to compare these characteristics with those of other bridges encountered in your travels, you may well conclude that the boast is justified. The Ponte Santa Trinita is more than just a bridge: It is a beautiful piece of architecture.

A few yards beyond the south end of the Ponte Vecchio (on the left side of Via del Guicciardini) is the church of **Santa Felicita,** in the tiny piazza of the same name. Rarely visited by sightseers, the church contains one of Florence's finest Mannerist masterpieces: Jacopo da Pontormo's *Deposition,* painted around 1526, above the altar in the Capponi Chapel, just to the right of the entrance. The subject matter has recently inspired a particularly droll scholarly debate: Is the body of Christ being lowered from an inexplicably invisible cross, or is it being raised toward God the Father, who was painted on a ceiling dome above that no longer exists? Scholarly debate aside, the painting's swirling design and contorted figures are quintessentially Mannerist. The palette, however, transcends Mannerism: Despite being ill-lit (the lights must be turned on by the sacristan), the altarpiece's luminous colors are among the most striking in Florence.

Like most Italian churches, Santa Felicita closes its doors during the early afternoon. So if you have lingered at the Uffizi or over lunch, you may want to return here at the end of the tour, after exploring the Belvedere Fortress and the Boboli Gardens.

After leaving Santa Felicita, walk along Costa di San Giorgio, which starts as a tiny alley to the left of the church, passes a house once occupied by Galileo (No. 11), and continues on to the Porta San Giorgio entrance in the old city walls. The walk up this narrow street is one of Florence's least-known pleasures. The climb is steep, but just as you begin to wonder when it is going to end, a remarkable transformation takes place: The city falls away, the parked cars disappear, vine-covered walls screening olive trees appear on both sides, birds begin to chirp, and Florence becomes—of all things—tranquil. A narrow

Florentine street has suddenly turned into a picturesque Tuscan country lane.

Just before the costa ends at Porta San Giorgio, turn onto the short lane on the right (Via del Forte di San Giorgio), which **⑬** leads to the main entrance of the **Belvedere Fortress** (down the steps and through the arch). The fortress, which sometimes holds temporary art exhibitions, was built in 1429 to help defend the city against siege. But time has effected an ironic transformation, and what was once a first-rate fortification is now a first-rate picnic ground. Buses carry view-seeking tourists farther up the hill to the Piazzale Michelangelo, but, as the natives know, the best views of Florence are right here. To the north, all the city's monuments are spread out in a breathtaking cinemascope panorama, framed by the rolling Tuscan hills beyond: the squat dome of Santa Maria Novella, Giotto's proud campanile, the soaring dome of the Duomo, the forbidding medieval tower of the Palazzo Vecchio, the delicate Gothic spire of the Badia, and the crenellated tower of the Bargello. It is one of the best city-views in Italy. To the south the nearby hills furnish a complementary rural view, in its way equally memorable. If time and weather permit, a picnic lunch here on the last day of your stay is the perfect way to review the city's splendors and fix them forever in your memory. *Admission free. Open daily 9–sunset.*

Leave the Belvedere Fortress by the north exit, turn left, and **⑭** you will come to the rear entrance of the **Boboli Gardens,** adjacent to the Pitti Palace. Once inside the entrance, follow the path at the far left. The gardens began to take shape in 1549, when the Pitti family sold the palazzo to Eleanor of Toledo, wife of the Medici Grand Duke Cosimo I. The initial landscaping plans were laid out by Niccolo Pericoli Tribolo; after his death in 1550 development was continued by Bernardo Buontalenti; Giulio and Alfonso Parigi; and, over the years, many others. They produced the most spectacular backyard in Florence. The Italian gift for landscaping—less formal than the French but still full of sweeping drama—is displayed here at its best. A description of the gardens' beauties would fill a page but would be self-defeating, for the best way to enjoy a pleasure garden is to wander about, discovering its pleasures for yourself. One small fountain deserves special note, however: the famous *Bacchino*, next to the garden exit at the extreme north end of the palace, nearest the river. It depicts Pietro Barbino, Cosimo's favorite dwarf, astride a particularly unhappy tortoise. It seems to be illustrating—very graphically, indeed—the perils of too much pasta. *Admission free. Open daily 9–one hour before sunset.*

Tour 2: From the Duomo to the Cascine

Tour 2 also begins at the Duomo. From the north side of the Baptistery, walk west along the mostly modern Via de Cerretani; after several blocks it forks. Take the left fork (Via dei Banchi), which leads into the Piazza di Santa Maria Novella, **⑮** dominated by the church of **Santa Maria Novella** on the north side.

The facade of the church looks distinctly clumsy by later Renaissance standards, and with good reason: It is an architectural hybrid. The lower half of the facade was completed mostly in the 14th century; its pointed-arch niches and decorative marble patterns reflect the Gothic style of the day. About a hundred years later (around 1456), architect Leon Battista Alberti was called in to complete the job. The marble decoration of his upper story clearly defers to the already existing work below, but the architectural features he added evince an entirely different style. The central doorway, the four ground-floor half-columns with Corinthian capitals, the triangular pediment atop the second story, the inscribed frieze immediately below the pediment—these are classical features borrowed from antiquity, and they reflect the new Renaissance era in architecture, born some 35 years earlier at the Ospedale degli Innocenti (*see* Tour 3: From the Duomo to Santa Croce and Beyond, below). Alberti's most important addition, however, the S-curve scrolls that surmount the decorative circles on either side of the upper story, had no precedent whatever in antiquity. The problem was to soften the abrupt transition between wide ground floor and narrow upper story. Alberti's solution turned out to be definitive. Once you start to look for them, you will find scrolls such as these (or sculptural variations of them) on churches all over Italy, and every one of them derives from Alberti's example here.

The architecture of the interior is (like the Duomo) a dignified but somber example of Italian Gothic. Exploration is essential, however, because the church's store of art treasures is remarkable. Highlights include the 14th-century stained-glass rose window depicting *The Coronation of the Virgin* (above the central entrance door); the Filippo Strozzi Chapel (to the right of the altar), containing late–15th-century frescoes and stained glass by Filippino Lippi; the chancel (the area around the altar), containing frescoes by Domenico Ghirlandaio (1485); and the Gondi Chapel (to the left of the altar), containing Filippo Brunelleschi's famous wooden crucifix, carved around 1410 and said to have so stunned the great Donatello when he first saw it that he dropped a basket of eggs.

One other work in the church is worth special attention, for it possesses great historical importance as well as beauty. It is Masaccio's *Holy Trinity with Two Donors*, on the left-hand wall, almost halfway down the nave. Painted around 1425 (at the same time as Masaccio was working on his frescoes in Santa Maria del Carmine, described later in this tour), it unequivocally announced the arrival of the Renaissance era. The realism of the figure of Christ was revolutionary in itself, but what was probably even more startling to the contemporary Florentines was the coffered ceiling in the background. The mathematical rules for employing perspective in painting had just been discovered (probably by Brunelleschi), and this was one of the first paintings to employ them with utterly convincing success. As art historian E. H. Gombrich expressed it, "We can imagine how amazed the Florentines must have been when this wall-painting was unveiled and seemed to have made a hole in the wall through which they could look into a new burial chapel in Brunelleschi's modern style." The Renaissance concept of painting as a picture-window through which the viewer looks began here, and it reigned supreme in Western art for a full 500 years.

Leave Piazza di Santa Maria Novella by Via delle Belle Donne, which angles off to the south where you entered the square from Via dei Banchi and leads to a tiny piazza. In the center is a curious column topped by a roofed crucifix, known as the **Croce al Trebbio.** The cross was erected in 1308 by the Dominican Order (Santa Maria Novella was a Dominican church) to commemorate a famous victory: It was here that the Dominican friars defeated their avowed enemies the Patarene heretics in a bloody street brawl.

Beyond the piazza, bear left onto the short Via del Trebbio, then turn right onto Via Tornabuoni. On the left side of the **16** street is the church of **San Gaetano,** with a rather staid Baroque facade (and Albertian scrolls), finished in 1645. Florence never fully embraced the Baroque movement—by the 17th century the city's artistic heyday was long over—but the decorative statuary here does manage to muster some genuine Baroque exuberance. The cherubs on the upper story, setting the coat of arms in place, are a typical (if not very original) Baroque motif.

For those who can afford it, **Via Tornabuoni** is probably Florence's finest shopping street, and it supplies an interesting contrast to the nearby Piazza della Repubblica. There, at the turn of the century, the old was leveled to make way for the new; here, past and present cohabit easily and efficiently, with the oldest buildings housing the newest shops. Ironically, the "modern" Piazza della Repubblica now looks dated and more than a little dowdy, and it is the unrenewed Via Tornabuoni, bustling with activity, that seems up to the minute.

Time Out For a mid-morning pickup, try **Giacosa,** at No. 83 Via Tornabuoni, for excellent coffee, cappuccino, and pastries, or **Procacci,** at No. 64, for finger sandwiches and cold drinks. *Both closed Mon.*

Via Tornabuoni is lined with Renaissance buildings. But its **17** most imposing palazzo is the **Palazzo Strozzi,** a block south, at the intersection of Via Strozzi. Designed (probably) by Giuliano da Sangallo around 1489 and modeled after Michelozzo's earlier Palazzo Medici-Riccardi (*see* Tour 3: From the Duomo to Santa Croce and Beyond, below), the exterior of the palazzo is simple and severe; it is not the use of classical detail but the regularity of its features, the stately march of its windows, that marks it as a product of the early Renaissance. The interior courtyard (entered from the rear of the palazzo) is another matter altogether. It is here that the classical vocabulary—columns, capitals, pilasters, arches, and cornices—is given uninhibited and powerful expression. Unfortunately, the courtyard's effectiveness is all but destroyed by its outlandish modern centerpiece: a brutal metal fire escape. Its introduction here is one of the most disgraceful acts of 20th-century vandalism in the entire city.

One block west, down Via della Vigna Nuova, in the Piazza **18** Rucellai, is Alberti's **Palazzo Rucellai,** which goes a step further than the Palazzo Strozzi, and possesses a more representative Renaissance facade. A comparison between the two is illuminating. Evident on the facade of the Palazzo Rucellai is the ordered arrangement of windows and rusticated stonework seen on the Palazzo Strozzi, but Alberti's facade is far less forbidding. Alberti devoted a far larger proportion of his wall space to windows (which soften the facade's appearance) and filled in the remainder with rigorously ordered classical elements borrowed from antiquity. The end result, though still severe, is far less fortresslike, and Alberti strove for this effect purposely (he is on record as stating that only tyrants need fortresses). Ironically, the Palazzo Rucellai was built some 30 years *before* the Palazzo Strozzi. Alberti's civilizing ideas here, it turned out, had little influence on the Florentine palazzi that followed. To the Renaissance Florentines, power—in architecture, as in life—was just as impressive as beauty.

If proof of this dictum is needed, it can be found several short blocks away. Follow the narrow street opposite the Palazzo Rucellai (Via del Purgatorio) almost to its end, then zigzag right and left to reach the Piazza di Santa Trinita. In the center of the piazza is a column from the Baths of Caracalla, in Rome, given to the Medici Grand Duke Cosimo I by Pope Pius IV in 1560. The column was raised here by Cosimo in 1565, to mark the spot where he heard the news, in 1537, that his exiled Ghibelline enemies had been defeated at Montemurlo, near Prato; the victory made his power in Florence unchallengeable and all but absolute. The column is called, with typical Medici self-assurance, the **Colonna della Giustizia,** the Column of Justice.

(19) Halfway down the block to the right (toward the Arno) is the church of **Santa Trinita.** Originally built in the Romanesque style, the church underwent a Gothic remodeling during the 14th century (remains of the Romanesque construction are visible on the interior front wall). Its major artistic attraction is the cycle of frescoes and the altarpiece in the Sassetti Chapel, the second to the altar's right, painted by Domenico Ghirlandaio, around 1485. Ghirlandaio was a conservative painter for his day, and generally his paintings exhibit little interest in the investigations into the laws of perspective that had been going on in Florentine painting for more than 50 years. But his work here possesses such graceful decorative appeal that his lack of interest in rigorous perspective hardly seems to matter. The wall frescoes illustrate the life of St. Francis, and the altarpiece, *The Adoration of the Shepherds,* seems to stop just short of glowing.

From Santa Trinita, cross the Arno over the Ponte Santa Trinita and continue down Via Maggio until you reach the crossroads of Sdrucciolo de Pitti (on the left) and the short Via dei Michelozzi (on the right). Here you have a choice. If the noon hour approaches, you may want to postpone the next stop temporarily in order to see the churches of Santo Spirito and Santa Maria del Carmine before they close for the afternoon. If this is the case, follow the directions given two paragraphs below and return here after seeing the churches. Otherwise, turn left onto the Sdrucciolo de Pitti.

(20) As you emerge from the Sdrucciolo into the Piazza dei Pitti, you will see unfold before you one of Florence's largest (if not one of its best) architectural set pieces: the famous **Pitti Palace.** The original palazzo, built for the Pitti family around 1460, comprised only the middle cube (on the upper floors the middle seven windows) of the present building. In 1549 the property was sold to the Medici, and Bartolommeo Ammannati was called in to make substantial additions. Although he apparently operated on the principle that more is better, he succeeded only in producing proof that enough is enough.

Today the immense building houses four separate museums: the former **Royal Apartments,** containing furnishings from a remodeling done in the 19th century; the **Museo degli Argenti,** containing a vast collection of Medici household treasures; the **Galleria d'Arte Moderna,** containing a collection of 19th- and 20th-century paintings, mostly Tuscan; and, most famous, the **Galleria Palatina,** containing a broad collection of 16th- and 17th-century paintings. The rooms of the latter remain much as the Medici family left them, but, as Mary McCarthy pointed out, the Florentines invented modern bad taste, and many art lovers view the floor-to-ceiling painting displays here as Italy's most egregious exercise in conspicuous consumption, aesthetic overkill, and trumpery. Still, the collection possesses high points that are very high indeed, including a number of portraits by Titian and an unparalleled collection of paintings by Raphael, among them the famous *Madonna of the Chair. Piazza Pitti, tel. 055/210323. Admission: Galleria Palatina, 8,000 lire; Museo degli Argenti, 6,000 lire; Royal Apartments closed for restoration; Galleria d'Arte Moderna: 4,000 lire. Open Tues.–Sat. 9–2, Sun. 9–1.*

Return to Via Maggio from the Pitti, take Via dei Michelozzi, a short street that leads into Piazza Santo Spirito; at the north **㉑** end rises the church of **Santo Spirito.** Its unfinished facade gives nothing away, but, in fact, the interior, although appearing chilly (or even cold) compared with later churches, is one of most important pieces of architecture in all Italy. One of a pair of Florentine church interiors designed by Filippo Brunelleschi in the early 15th century (the other, San Lorenzo, is described in Tour 3: From the Duomo to Santa Croce and Beyond, below) it was here that Brunelleschi supplied definitive solutions to the two main problems of interior Renaissance church design: how to build a cross-shaped interior using classical architectural elements borrowed from antiquity and how to reflect in that interior the order and regularity that Renaissance scientists (of which Brunelleschi was one) were at the time discovering in the natural world around them.

Brunelleschi's solution to the first problem was brilliantly simple: Turn a Greek temple inside out. To see this clearly, look at one of the stately arch-topped arcades that separate the side aisles from the central nave. If you imagine the arches above the columns filled in down to the level of the top of the column capitals, then the architrave, frieze, and cornice immediately above the capitals would stretch uninterruptedly from one end of the nave to the other, and you would be looking at the side exterior of a Greek temple. Brunelleschi thus transformed an exterior Greek colonnade into an interior Renaissance arcade. Whereas the ancient Greek temples were walled buildings surrounded by classical colonnades, Brunelleschi's churches were classical arcades surrounded by walled buildings. This was perhaps the single most brilliant architectural idea of the early Renaissance, and its brilliance overthrew the previous era's religious taboo against pagan architecture once and for all, triumphantly reclaiming that architecture for Christian use.

Brunelleschi's solution to the second problem—making the entire interior orderly and regular—was mathematically precise: He designed the ground plan of the church so that all its parts are proportionally related. The transepts and nave have exactly the same width; the side aisles are exactly half as wide as the nave; the little chapels off the side aisles are exactly half as deep as the side aisles; the chancel and transepts are exactly one-eighth the depth of the nave; and so on, with dizzying exactitude. For Brunelleschi, such a design technique would have been far more than a convenience; it would have been a matter of passionate conviction. Like most theoreticians of his day, he believed that mathematical regularity and aesthetic beauty were opposite sides of the same coin, that one was not possible without the other. The conviction was both revolutionary and powerful, and the measured dignity of the architecture it produced in buildings such as this one was overwhelmingly convincing. The conviction stood unchallenged for a hundred years, until Michelangelo turned his hand to architecture and designed the Medici Chapel and the Biblioteca Laurenziana in San Lorenzo across town (*see* Tour 3: From the Duomo to Santa Croce and Beyond, below), and thereby unleashed a revolution of his own that spelled the end of the Renaissance in architecture and the beginning of the Baroque.

Leave Piazza Santo Spirito by Via Sant'Agostino, diagonally across the square from the church entrance, and follow it to Via de Serragli. You are now in the heart of a working-class neighborhood known as the Oltrarno, which is to Florence what Trastevere is to Rome: unpretentious, independent, and proud. Cross Via de Serragli and follow Via San Monaca to Piazza del Carmine. The church of **Santa Maria del Carmine** at the south end contains, in the Brancacci Chapel, at the end of the right transept, a masterpiece of Renaissance painting, a fresco cycle that changed art forever. Fire almost destroyed the church in the 18th century; miraculously, the Brancacci Chapel survived almost intact.

The cycle is the work of three artists: Masaccio and Masolino, who began it in 1423, and Filippino Lippi, who finished it, after a long interruption during which the sponsoring Brancacci family was exiled, some 50 years later. It was Masaccio's work that opened a new frontier for painting; tragically, he did not live to experience the revolution his innovations caused, for he was killed in 1428 at the age of 27.

Masaccio collaborated with Masolino on several of the paintings, but by himself he painted *The Tribute Money* on the upper-left wall; *Peter Baptizing the Neophytes* on the upper altar wall; *The Distribution of the Goods of the Church* on the lower altar wall; and, most famous, *The Expulsion of Adam and Eve* on the chapel's upper-left entrance pier. If you look closely at the latter painting and compare it with some of the chapel's other works, you will see a pronounced difference. The figures of Adam and Eve possess a startling presence, a presence primarily due to the dramatic way in which their bodies seem to reflect light. Masaccio here shaded his figures consistently, so as to suggest emphatically a single, strong source of light within the world of the painting but outside its frame. In so doing, he succeeded in imitating with paint the real-world effect of light on mass, and he thereby imparted to his figures a sculptural reality unprecedented in its day. He brought a new sense of order to the art of shading, and to contemporary Florentines his Adam and Eve must have seemed surrounded by light and air in a way that was almost magical. All the painters of Florence came to look.

These matters have to do with technique, and Masaccio's achievement in the Brancacci frescoes announced a technical breakthrough of epoch-making proportions. But with *The Expulsion of Adam and Eve*, his skill went beyond technical innovation, and if you look hard at the faces of Adam and Eve, you will see more than just finely modeled figures. You will see terrible shame and terrible suffering, and you will see them depicted with a humanity rarely achieved in art. *Admission to Brancacci Chapel: 5,000 lire. Open Mon. and Wed.–Sat. 10–5, Sun. 1–5.*

Time Out   A popular spot for lunch on Piazza del Carmine is **Carmine,** a moderately priced restaurant with outdoor tables during the warmer months. It is located at the end of the piazza's northern extension. *Closed Sun.*

From Piazza del Carmine, return to Via de Serragli and walk back across the river over the Ponte alla Carraia (with a fine view of the Ponte Santa Trinita, to the right) to Piazza Carlo Goldoni, named for the 18th-century Italian dramatist. Here you again have a choice: You can turn left to explore the Cascine, a vast (2-mile-long) park laid out in the 18th century on the site of the Medici dairy farms (it begins some 10 blocks downriver, at the Piazza Vittorio Veneto), or, if you have not overdosed on art, you can turn right and return to the Uffizi, which is open all day on most days (and which is usually far less crowded in the late afternoon than in the morning).

Tour 3: From the Duomo to Santa Croce and Beyond

Like the other two tours, Tour 3 begins at the Duomo. From the west side of the Baptistery, follow Borgo San Lorenzo north one block to Piazza San Lorenzo, in which stands a bustling outdoor clothing market overlooked by the unfinished facade of the church of **San Lorenzo.** Like Santo Spirito on the other side of the Arno, the interior of San Lorenzo was designed by Filippo Brunelleschi in the early 15th century. The two church interiors are similar in design and effect and proclaim with ringing clarity the beginning of the Renaissance in architecture. (If you have not yet taken Tour 2, you might want to read its entry on Santo Spirito now; it describes the nature of Brunelleschi's architectural breakthrough, and its main points apply equally well here. *See* Tour 2: From the Duomo to the Cascine, above) San Lorenzo possesses one feature that Santo Spirito lacks, however, which considerably heightens the dramatic effect of the interior: the grid of dark, inlaid marble lines on the floor. The grid makes the rigorous regularity with which the interior was designed immediately visible and offers an illuminating lesson on the laws of perspective. If you stand in the middle of the nave at the church entrance, on the line that stretches to the high altar, every element in the church—the grid, the nave columns, the side aisles, the coffered nave ceiling—seems to march inexorably toward a hypothetical vanishing point beyond the high altar, exactly as in a single-point-perspective painting.

The church complex contains two other important interiors, designed by Michelangelo, which contrast markedly with the interior of the church proper and which in their day marked the end of Brunelleschi's powerful influence and the end of the

High Renaissance in architecture. The first is the **Biblioteca Laurenziana,** the Laurentian Library and its famous anteroom, entered from the church cloister (exit the church through the door at the left side of the nave just before the crossing, take an immediate right, climb the stairs to the cloister balcony, and enter the first door to the right). Michelangelo the architect was every bit as original as Michelangelo the sculptor. Unlike Brunelleschi, however, he was not interested in expressing the ordered harmony of the spheres in his architecture. He was interested in experimentation and invention and in expressing a personal vision that was at times highly idiosyncratic.

It was never more idiosyncratic than here. This strangely shaped anteroom has had scholars scratching their heads for centuries. In a space more than two stories high, why did Michelangelo limit his use of columns and pilasters to the upper two-thirds of the wall? Why didn't he rest them on strong pedestals instead of on huge, decorative curlicued scrolls, which rob them of all visual support? Why did he recess them into the wall, which makes them look weaker still? The architectural elements here do not stand firm and strong and tall, as inside the church next door; instead, they seem to be pressed into the wall as if into putty, giving the room a soft, rubbery look that is one of the strangest effects ever achieved by classical architecture. It is almost as if Michelangelo purposely set out to defy his predecessors—intentionally to flout the conventions of the High Renaissance in order to see what kind of bizarre, mannered effect might result. His innovations were tremendously influential and produced a period of architectural experimentation—the Mannerist era in architecture—that eventually evolved into the Baroque. As his contemporary Giorgio Vasari (the first art historian) put it, "Artisans have been infinitely and perpetually indebted to him because he broke the bonds and chains of a way of working that had become habitual by common usage."

Many critics have thought that the anteroom is a failure and have complained that Michelangelo's experiment here was willful and perverse. But nobody has ever complained about the room's staircase (best viewed head-on), which emerges from the library with the visual force of an unstoppable flow of lava. In its highly sculptural conception and execution, it is quite simply one of the most original and beautiful staircases in the world. *Admission free. Open Mon.–Sat. 9–1.*

The other Michelangelo interior is San Lorenzo's **New Sacristy,** so called to distinguish it from Brunelleschi's **Old Sacristy** (which can be entered from inside the church at the end of the left transept). The New Sacristy is reached from outside the rear of the church, through the imposing **Cappella dei Principi,** the Medici mausoleum that was begun in 1605 and kept marble workers busy for several hundred years.

Michelangelo received the commission for the New Sacristy in 1520 from Cardinal Giulio de Medici, who later became Pope Clement VII and who wanted a new burial chapel for his father, Giuliano, his uncle Lorenzo the Magnificent, and two recently deceased cousins. The result was a tour de force of architecture and sculpture. Architecturally, Michelangelo was as original and inventive here as ever, but it is—quite properly—the powerful sculptural compositions of the side wall tombs that dominate the room. The scheme is allegorical: On the wall tomb to the right are figures representing day and night, and on the wall tomb to the left are figures representing dawn and dusk; above them are idealized portraits of the two cousins, usually interpreted to represent the active life and the contemplative life. But the allegorical meanings are secondary; what is most important is the intense presence of the sculptural figures, the force with which they hit the viewer. Michelangelo's contemporaries were so awed by the impact of this force (in his sculpture here and elsewhere) that they invented an entirely new word to describe the phenomenon: *terribilità* (dreadfulness). To this day it is used only when describing his work, and it is in evidence here at the peak of its power. *Piazza di Madonna degli Aldobrandini, tel. 055/213206. Admission: 8,500 lire. Open Tues.–Sat. 9–2, Sun. 9–1.*

Just north of the Medici Chapel (a block down Via dell'Ariento) is Florence's busy main food market, the **Mercato Centrale.** If a reminder that Florence is more than just a museum is needed, this is the perfect place for it. There is food everywhere, some of it remarkably exotic, and many of the displays verge on the magnificent. At the Mercato Nuovo, near Ponte Vecchio, you will see tourists petting the snout of the bronze boar for good luck; here you will see Florentines petting the snout of a real one, very recently deceased and available for tonight's dinner.

Time Out The **Mercato Centrale** has a number of small coffee bars scattered about; there is even one upstairs among the mountains of vegetables. Have a coffee, watch the activity, and enjoy the fact that for once there is not a painting in sight.

Return to the clothing market in front of San Lorenzo, and from the north end of the piazza follow Via de Gori east one block, and turn left onto Via Cavour. As you turn the corner, **㉔** you will pass **Palazzo Medici-Riccardi** (entrance on Via Cavour). Begun in 1444 by Michelozzo for Cosimo de Medici, the main attraction here is the interior chapel on the upper floor. Painted onto its walls is Benozzo Gozzoli's famous *Procession of the Magi*, finished in 1460 and celebrating both the birth of Christ and the greatness of the Medici family, whose portraits it contains. Like his contemporary Ghirlandaio, Gozzoli was not a revolutionary painter and is today considered less than first rate because of his old-fashioned (even for his day) technique. Gozzoli's gift, however, was for entrancing the eye, not challenging the mind, and on those terms his success here is beyond question. The paintings are full of activity yet somehow frozen in time in a way that fails utterly as realism, but succeeds triumphantly as soon as the demand for realism is set aside. Entering the chapel is like walking into the middle of a magnificently illustrated child's storybook, and the beauty of the illustrations makes this one of the most unpretentiously enjoyable rooms in the entire city. *Via Cavour 11, tel. 055/27601. Admission free. Open Mon.–Tues., Thurs.–Sat. 9–12:45, 3–4:45, Sun. 9–noon.*

From Palazzo Medici-Riccardi, follow Via Cavour two blocks north to Piazza San Marco. At the north end of the square is the church of San Marco; attached to the church (entrance just to the right of the church facade) is a former Dominican monastery that now houses the **Museo San Marco.** The museum—in **㉕** fact, the entire monastery—is a memorial to Fra Angelico, the Dominican monk who, when he was alive, was as famous for his piety as for his painting. When the monastery was built in 1437, he decorated it with his frescoes, which were meant to spur religious contemplation; when the building was turned into a museum, other works of his from all over the city were brought here for display. His paintings are simple and direct and furnish a compelling contrast to the Palazzo Medici-Riccardi Chapel (Fra Angelico probably would have considered the glitter of Gozzoli's work there worldly and blasphemous). The entire monastery is worth exploring, for Fra Angelico's paintings are everywhere, including the Chapter House, at the top of the stairs leading to the upper floor (the famous *Annunciation)*, in the upper-floor monks' cells (each monk was given a different religious subject for contemplation), and in the gallery just off the cloister as you enter. The latter room contains, among many other works, his beautiful *Last Judgment;* as usual with Last Judgments, the tortures of the damned are far more inventive than the pleasures of the redeemed. *Piazza San Marco 1, tel. 055/210741. Admission: 6,000 lire. Open Tues.–Sat. 9–2, Sun. 9–1.*

From Piazza San Marco, take a short detour a half-block down Via Ricasoli (which runs back toward the Duomo from the square's east side) to the **Galleria dell'Accademia.** The museum contains a notable collection of Florentine paintings dating from the 13th to the 18th centuries, but it is most famous for its collection of statues by Michelangelo—including the unfinished *Slaves*—which were meant for the tomb of Michelangelo's patron and nemesis Pope Julius II (and which seem to be fighting their way out of the marble), and the original *David*, which was moved here from the Piazza della Signoria in 1873. The *David* was commissioned in 1501 by the Opera del Duomo (Cathedral Works Committee), which gave the 26-year-old sculptor a leftover block of marble that had been ruined by another artist. Michelangelo's success with the defective block was so dramatic that the city showered him with honors, and the Opera del Duomo voted to build him a house and a studio in which to live and work.

Today the *David* is beset not by Goliath but by tourists, and seeing the statue at all—much less really studying it—can be a trial. But a close look is worth the effort it takes to combat the crowd. The statue is not quite what it seems. It is so poised and graceful and alert—so miraculously *alive*—that it is often considered the definitive embodiment of the ideals of the High Renaissance in sculpture. But its true place in the history of art is a bit more complicated.

As Michelangelo well knew, the Renaissance painting and sculpture that preceded his work were deeply concerned with ideal form. Perfection of proportion was the ever-sought Holy Grail; during the Renaissance, ideal proportion was equated with ideal beauty, and ideal beauty was equated with spiritual perfection. In painting, Raphael's tender Madonnas are perhaps the preeminent expression of this philosophy: They are meant to embody a perfect beauty that is at once physical and spiritual.

But Michelangelo's *David*, despite its supremely calm and dignified pose, departs from these ideals. As a moment's study will show, Michelangelo did not give the statue ideal proportions. The head is slightly too large for the body, the arms are slightly too large for the torso, and the hands are dramatically too large for the arms. By High Renaissance standards these are defects, but the impact and beauty of the *David* are such that it is the *standards* that must be called into question, not the statue. Michelangelo was a revolutionary artist (and the first Mannerist) because he brought a new expressiveness to art: He created the "defects" of the *David* intentionally. He knew exactly what he was doing, and he did it in order to express and embody, as powerfully as possible in a single figure, an entire biblical story. David's hands *are* too big, but so was Goliath, and these are the hands that slew him. *Via Ricasoli 60, tel. 055/214375. Admission: 10,000 lire. Open Tues.–Sat. 9–2, Sun. 9–1.*

From the Accademia, return to Piazza San Marco and turn right on Via Battisti, which leads into the Piazza della Santissima Annunziata. The building directly across the square as you enter is the **Ospedale degli Innocenti,** or Foundling Hospital, built by Brunelleschi in 1419. He designed the building's portico with his usual rigor, building it out of the two shapes he considered mathematically (and therefore philosophically and aesthetically) perfect: the square and the circle. Below the level of the arches, the portico encloses a row of perfect cubes; above the level of the arches, the portico encloses a row of intersecting hemispheres. The whole geometric scheme is articulated with Corinthian columns, capitals, and arches borrowed directly from antiquity. At the time he designed the portico, Brunelleschi was also designing the interior of San Lorenzo, using the same basic ideas. But since the portico was finished before San Lorenzo, the Ospedale degli Innocenti takes the historical prize: It is the very first Renaissance building.

The church at the north end of the square is **Santissima Annunziata;** it was designed in 1447 by Michelozzo, who gave it an uncommon (and lovely) entrance cloister. The interior is an extreme rarity for Florence: a sumptuous example of the Baroque. But it is not really a fair example, since it is merely 17th-century Baroque decoration applied willy-nilly to an earlier structure—exactly the sort of violent remodeling exercise that has given the Baroque a bad name ever since. The **Tabernacle of the Annunziata,** immediately inside the entrance to the left, illustrates the point. The lower half, with its stately Corinthian columns and carved frieze bearing the Medici arms, was built at the same time as the church; the upper half, with its erupting curves and impish sculpted cherubs (badly in need of a bath), was added 200 years later. Each is effective in its own way, but together they serve only to prove that dignity is rarely comfortable wearing a party hat.

One block east of the entrance to Santissima Annunziata (on the left side of Via Colonna) is the **Museo Archeologico.** If time and interest permit, a visit here is unquestionably worthwhile. The collection contains Etruscan, Egyptian, and Greco-Roman antiquities; guidebooks in English are available. The Etruscan collection is particularly notable—the largest in northern Italy—and includes the famous bronze *Chimera,* which was discovered (without the tail, which is a reconstruction) in the 16th century. *Via della Colonna 36, tel. 055/247–8641. Admission: 6,000 lire. Open Tues.–Sat. 9–2, Sun. 9–1.*

Follow Via Colonna east to Borgo Pinti and turn right, following Borgo Pinti through the arch of San Piero to the small Piazza San Pier Maggiore. The tower at the south end is the

30 **Torre dei Corbizi,** dating from the Middle Ages. During the Guelph-Ghibelline conflict of the 13th and 14th centuries, Florence was a forest of such towers—more than 200 of them, if the smaller three- and four-story towers are included. Today only a handful survive.

Time Out Have lunch at **I Ghibellini** (closed Wed.), a moderately priced restaurant overlooking the Piazza San Pier Maggiore. For dessert, follow Via Palmieri to No. 7/r Via Isola delle Stinche, and have an ice cream at **Vivoli,** Florence's most famous *gelateria.*

From Piazza San Pier Maggiore, Via Palmieri (which becomes Via Isola delle Stinche) leads to Via Torta, which curves around to the left—it takes its shape from the outline of a Roman amphitheater once located here—and opens out onto Piazza Santa Croce.

31 Like the Duomo, the church of **Santa Croce** is Gothic, but (also like the Duomo) its facade dates only from the 19th century. The interior is most famous for its art and its tombs. As a burial place, the church is a Florentine pantheon and probably contains a larger number of important skeletons than any church in Italy. Among others, the tomb of Michelangelo is immediately to the right as you enter (he is said to have chosen this spot so that the first thing he would see on Judgment Day, when the graves of the dead fly open, would be Brunelleschi's Duomo dome through Santa Croce's open doors); the tomb of Galileo Galilei, who produced evidence that the earth is not the center of the universe (and who was not granted a Christian burial until 100 years after his death because of it), is on the left wall, opposite Michelangelo; the tomb of Niccolo Machiavelli, the Renaissance political theoretician whose brutally pragmatic philosophy so influenced the Medici, is halfway down the nave on the right; the grave of Lorenzo Ghiberti, creator of the Gates of Paradise doors to the Baptistery, is halfway down the nave on the left; the tomb of composer Gioacchino Rossini, of "William Tell Overture" fame, is at the end of the nave on the right. The monument to Dante Alighieri, the greatest Italian poet, is a memorial rather than a tomb (he is actually buried in Ravenna); it is located on the right wall near the tomb of Michelangelo.

The collection of art within the church and church complex is by far the most important of that in any church in Florence. Historically, the most significant works are probably the Giotto frescoes in the two adjacent chapels immediately to the right of the altar, which illustrate scenes from the lives of St. John the Evangelist and St. John the Baptist (in the right-hand chapel) and scenes from the life of St. Francis (in the left-hand chapel). Time has not been kind to them; over the centuries wall tombs were introduced into the middle of them, whitewash and plaster covered them, and in the 19th century they underwent a clumsy restoration. But the reality that Giotto introduced into painting can still be seen. He did not paint beautifully stylized symbols of religion, as the Byzantine style that preceded him prescribed; he instead painted drama—St. Francis surrounded by grieving monks at the very moment of his death. This was a radical shift in emphasis, and it changed the course of art. Before him, the role of painting was to symbolize the attributes of God; after him, it was to imitate life. The style of his work is indeed primitive, compared with later painting, but in its day (the Proto-Renaissance of the early 14th century), it caused a sensation that was not equalled for another 100 years. He was for his time the equal of both Masaccio and Michelangelo.

Among the church's other highlights are Donatello's **Annunciation,** one of the most tender and eloquent expressions of surprise ever sculpted (located on the right wall two-thirds of the way down the nave); Taddeo Gaddi's 14th-century frescoes illustrating the life of the Virgin, clearly showing the influence of Giotto (in the chapel at the end of the right transept); Donatello's *Crucifix,* criticized by Brunelleschi for making Christ look like a peasant (in the chapel at the end of the left transept); Giovanni Cimabue's 13th-century *Triumphal Cross,* badly damaged by the flood of 1966 (in the church museum off the cloister); and the *Pazzi Chapel,* yet another of Brunelleschi's crisp exercises in architectural geometry (also off the cloister, at the east end). *Piazza Santa Croce 16, tel. 055/ 244619. Church Cloister and Museum admission: 2,000 lire. Open Mar.–Sept., Thurs.–Tues. 10–12:30, 2:30–6:30; Oct.– Feb., Thurs.–Tues. 10–12:30, 3–5.*

After leaving Santa Croce, you have a choice. If you have a fair amount of stamina left, you can cross the river at the Ponte alle Grazie (west of the church complex) and climb the Monte alle Croci above it to investigate the view from the **Piazzale Michelangelo** and the church of **San Miniato al Monte;** the latter is a famous example of Romanesque architecture dating from the 11th century and contains a fine 13th-century apse mosaic. If the climb seems too arduous, you can (as always) return to the Uffizi.

Shopping

Since the days of the medieval guilds, Florence has been synonymous with fine craftsmanship and good business. Such time-honored Florentine specialties as antiques (and reproductions), bookbinding, jewelry, lace, leather goods, silk, and straw attest to that. More recently, the Pitti fashion shows and the burgeoning textile industry in nearby Prato have added fine clothing to the long line of merchandise available in the shops of Florence.

Another medieval feature is the distinct feel of the different shopping areas, a throwback to the days when each district supplied a different product. Florence's most elegant shops are concentrated in the center of town, with Via Tornabuoni leading the list for designer clothing. Borgo Ognissanti and Via Maggio across the river have the city's largest concentration of antiques shops, and the Ponte Vecchio houses the city's jewelers, as it has since the 16th century. Boutiques abound on Via della Vigna Nuova and in the trendy area around the church of Santa Croce. In the less-specialized, more residential areas near the Duomo and in the area south of the Arno, known as the Oltrarno, just about anything goes on sale.

Those with a tight budget or a sense of adventure may want to take a look at the souvenir stands under the loggia of the Mercato Nuovo, the stalls that line the streets between the church of San Lorenzo and the Mercato Centrale, or the open-air market that takes place in the Cascine park every Tuesday morning.

Shops in Florence are generally open from 9 to 1 and 3:30 to 7:30 and closed Sundays and Monday mornings most of the year. During the summer the hours are usually 9 to 1 and 4 to 8, with closings on Saturday afternoons but not Monday mornings. When locating the stores, remember that the addresses with "r" in them will be indicated in red, a separate numbering system from the black residential addresses. Most shops take major credit cards and will ship purchases, though it's wiser to take your purchases with you. If not, try the little man in Vicolo de' Cavallari near the Battistero, who wraps packages with a true Florentine flourish.

Via Tornabuoni   **Gucci** (Via Tornabuoni 73/r, 57/r). The Gucci family is practically single-handedly responsible for making designers' initials (in this case the two interlocking "Gs") a status symbol. These Florence stores are the ones that started it all, and prices here are slightly better than elsewhere on their clothing and leather goods.

Casadei (Via Tornabuoni 33/r). The ultimate fine leathers are crafted into classic shapes here, winding up as women's shoes and bags.

Ugolini (Via Tornabuoni 20/r). This shop once made gloves for the Italian royal family, but now anyone who can afford it can have the luxury of its exotic leathers, as well as silk and cashmere ties and scarves.

Settepassi-Faraone (Via Tornabuoni 25/r). One of Florence's oldest jewelers, Settepassi-Faraone has supplied Italian (and other) royalty with finely crafted gems for centuries. Its selection of antique-looking classics has been updated with a choice of contemporary silver.

Ferragamo (Via Tornabuoni 16/r). Born near Naples, the late Salvatore Ferragamo made his fortune custom-making exotic shoes for famous feet, especially Hollywood stars, and so this establishment knows about less-than-delicate shoe sizes. His palace at the end of the street has since passed on to his wife, Wanda, and displays designer clothing, but the elegant footwear still underlies the Ferragamo success.

Via della Vigna Nuova   **Il Bisonte** (Via del Parione). The street address is just off Via della Vigna Nuova; Il Bisonte is known for its natural-look leather goods, all stamped with the store's bison symbol.

Filpucci (Via della Vigna Nuova 14/r). This is Italy's largest manufacturer of yarns. Its nearby factories producing skeins of the stuff for Italy's top designers, and the extensive stock of its retail outlet in Florence encourages the talented to create their own designs.

Escada (Via della Vigna Nuova 71/r). An elegant boutique, Escada has a reputation for the quality and understatement that is the hallmark of Florentine women's fashions.

Alinari (Via della Vigna Nuova 46/r). This outlet is one of Florence's oldest and most prestigious photographers, and in this store, next to its museum, prints of its historic photographs are sold along with books and posters.

Et Cetera (Via della Vigna Nuova 82/r). In a city of papermakers, this store has some of the most unusual such items, most of which are handmade and some of which have made it into the design collection of New York's Museum of Modern Art.

Antico Setificio Fiorentino (Via della Vigna Nuova 97/r). This fabric outlet really *is* antique, having been producing antique fabrics for over half a millenium. Reams of handmade material of every style and description are on sale, and the decorative tassels make lovely, typically Florentine, presents as well.

Borgo Ognissanti **Pratesi** (Lungarno Amerigo Vespucci 8/r). The name Pratesi is a byword for luxury, in this case linens that have lined the beds of the rich and famous, with an emphasis on the former.

Giotti (Piazza Ognissanti 3/r). The largest selection of Bottega Veneta's woven-leather bags are stocked at this shop, which carries a full line of the firm's other leather goods, as well as its own leather clothing.

Loretta Caponi (Borgo Ognissanti 12/r). Signora Caponi is synonymous with Florentine embroidery, and her luxury lace, linens, and lingerie have earned her a worldwide reputation.

Fallani Best (Borgo Ognissanti 15/r). The eclectic collection of antiques, while concentrating on 18th- and 19th-century Italian paintings, has enough variety to appeal to an international clientele.

Paolo Ventura (Borgo Ognissanti 16/r). Specialties here are antique ceramics from all periods and places of origin. As with the other shops, the rule of thumb is that the Italian goods are best, and, in this case, such items as a Giacomo Balla coffee service is outstanding.

Alberto Pierini (Borgo Ognissanti 22/r). The rustic Tuscan furniture here is all antique, and much of it dates back to the days of the Medici.

Duomo **Bartolini** (Via dei Servi 30/r). For housewares, nothing beats this shop, which has a wide selection of well-designed, practical items.

Emilio Pucci (Via dei Pucci 6/r). Originally from the Marches, Pucci is another household name in Florence, presiding over the opening ceremonies of the Renaissance *Calcio in Costume* festivities each year. He became an international name during the dolce vita era of the early '60s, when his prints and "palazzo pajamas" were all the rage. His shop in the family palazzo still sells the celebrated silks, and recently he added a line of designer wines (red, white, and rosé) from his estate in Chianti to his stock.

Calamai (Via Cavour 78/r). One of Florence's largest gift shops, Calamai carries everything from inexpensive stationery to housewares in bright, bold colors and designs in its largest of three stores.

Pineider (Piazza della Signoria 14/r and Via Tornabuoni 76/r). Pineider now has shops throughout the world, but it began in Florence and still does all its printing here. Personalized stationery and business cards are its main business, but the stores also sell fine desk accessories.

Casa dello Sport (Via dei Tosinghi 8/r). Here you'll find lines of casual wear for the entire family—sporty clothes by some of Italy's most famous manufacturers.

Santa Croce **Salimbeni** (Via Matteo Palmieri 14/r). Long one of Florence's best art bookshops, Salimbeni specializes in publications on Tuscany; it publishes many itself.

I Maschereri (Borgo Pinti 18/r). Spurred on by the revival of Carnival in recent years, I Maschereri has begun to produce fanciful masks in *commedia dell'arte* and contemporary styles.

Sbigoli Terrecotte (Via Sant'Egidio 4/r). This crafts shop carries a wide selection of terra-cotta and ceramic vases, pots, cups, and saucers.

Leather Guild (Piazza Santa Croce 20/r). This is one of many such shops throughout the area that produce inexpensive, antique-looking leather goods of mass appeal, but here you can see the craftspersons at work, a reassuring experience.

Ponte Vecchio   **Gherardi** (Ponte Vecchio 5). The king of coral in Florence has the city's largest selection of finely crafted and encased specimens, as well as other precious materials such as cultured pearls, jade, and turquoise.

Piccini (Ponte Vecchio 23/r). This venerable shop has literally been crowning the heads of Europe for almost a century, and combines its taste for the antique with contemporary jewelry.

Melli (Ponte Vecchio 44/r). Antique jewelry is the specialty here; it is displayed alongside period porcelains, clocks, and other museum-quality objects.

Della Loggia (Ponte Vecchio 52/r). For a contemporary look, try this store, which combines precious and semiprecious stones in settings made of precious and nonprecious metals, such as the gold and steel pieces usually on display in its windows.

Oltrarno   **Centro Di** (Piazza dei Mozzi 1). Its name stands for Centro di Documentazione Internazionale, and it publishes art books and exhibition catalogues for some of the most important organizations in Europe. Centro Di stocks its own publications along with many others.

Giannini (Piazza Pitti 37/r). One of Florence's oldest paper-goods stores, Giannini is *the* place to buy the marbleized version, which comes in a variety of forms, from flat sheets to boxes and even pencils.

Galleria Luigi Bellini (Lungarno Soderini 5). The Galleria claims to be Italy's oldest antiques dealer. Whether or not it's true, what matters is that the merchandise is genuine, and since father Mario Bellini was responsible for instituting Florence's international antiques biennial, there's a good chance he's right.

Via Maggio   **Giovanni Pratesi** (Via Maggio 13/r). This shop specializes in Italian antiques, in this case furniture with some fine paintings, sculpture, and decorative objects turning up from time to time.

Guido Bartolozzi (Via Maggio 18/r). Vying with Luigi Bellini as one of Florence's oldest antiques dealers, Bartolozzi's collection of predominately Florentine objects from all periods is as highly selected as it is priced.

Paolo Paoletti (Via Maggio 30/r). Look for Florentine antiques, with an emphasis on Medici-era objects from the 15th and 16th centuries.

Soluzioni (Via Maggio 82/r). This offbeat store displays some of the most unusual items on this staid street, ranging from clocks to compacts, all selected with an eye for the eccentric.

Sports

Bicycling   Bikes are a good way of getting out into the hills, but the scope for biking is limited in the center of town. *See* Getting Around in Essential Information, above, for information on where to rent bicycles.

Canoeing Those who get the urge to paddle on the Arno can try **Società Canottieri Comunali** (Lungarno dei Medici 8, tel. 055/282130) near the Uffizi.

Golf **Golf Club Ugolino** (Via Chiantigiana 3, Impruneta, 055/205–1009) is a hilly 18-hole course in the heart of Chianti country just outside town. It is open to the public.

Jogging Don't even think of jogging on city streets, where tour buses and triple-parked Alfa Romeos leave precious little space for pedestrians. Instead, head for the **Cascine**, the park along the Arno at the western end of the city. You can jog to the Cascine along the Lungarno (stay on the sidewalk), or take bus No. 17 from the Duomo. A cinder track lies on the hillside just below **Piazzale Michelangelo**, across the Arno from the city center. The views of the Florence skyline are inspirational, but the locker rooms are reserved for members, so come ready to run.

Swimming There are a number of pools open to foreigners who want to beat the Florentine heat, among them **Bellariva** (Lungarno Colombo 6, tel. 055/677521), **Circolo Tennis alle Cascine** (Viale Visarno 1, tel. 055/356651), **Costoli** (Viale Paoli, tel. 055/675–744), and **Le Pavoniere** (Viale degli Olmi, tel. 055/367506).

Tennis The best spot for an open court is **Circolo Tennis alle Cascine** (Viale Visarno 1, tel. 055/356651). Other centers include **Tennis Club Rifredi** (Via Facibeni, tel. 055/432552) and **Il Poggetto** (Via Mercati 24/B, tel. 055/460127).

Spectator Sports

Horse Racing You can make your bets at the **Ippodromo Visarno** (Piazzale delle Cascine, tel. 055/360056). Check with the local papers to see when they're running.

Soccer *Calcio* (soccer) is a passion with the Italians, and the Florentines are no exception. A medieval version of the game is played in costume each year, but if you want to see the modern-day equivalent, go and watch the Fiorentina team at the Stadio Comunale (Viale M. Fanti). The big games are played on Sunday afternoons, and the season runs from about late August to May.

Dining

Florentines are justifiably proud of their robust food, claiming that it became the basis for French cuisine when Catherine de Médici took a battery of Florentine chefs with her when she reluctantly relocated to become Queen of France in the 16th century.

A typical Tuscan repast starts with an antipasto of *crostini* (toasted bread spread with a chicken liver pâté) or cured meats such as *prosciutto crudo* (a salty prosciutto), *finocchiona* (salami seasoned with fennel), and *salsiccia di cinghiale* (sausage made from wild boar). This is the time to start right in on the local wine—Chianti, *naturalmente*. Don't be surprised if the waiter brings an entire straw-covered flask to the table. Customers are charged only for what they consume (*al consumo*, the arrangement is called), but it's wise to ask for a flask or bottle to be opened then and there, since leftover wines are often mixed together.

Primi piatti (first courses) can consist of excellent local versions of risotto or variations of pasta dishes available throughout Italy. Peculiar to Florence, however, are the vegetable-and-bread soups such as *pappa al pomodoro* (tomatoes, bread, olive oil, onions, and basil), *ribollita* (white beans, bread, cabbage, and onions), or, in the summer, *panzanella* (tomatoes, onions, vinegar, oil, and bread). Before they are eaten, these soups are often christened with *un "C" d'olio*, a generous C-shaped pouring of the excellent local olive oil from the ever-present tabletop cruet.

Second to none among the *secondi piatti* (main courses) is *bistecca alla fiorentina*—a thick slab of local Chianina beef, grilled over charcoal, seasoned with olive oil, salt, and pepper, and served rare. *Trippa alla fiorentina* (tripe stewed with tomatoes in a meat sauce) and *arista* (roast loin of pork seasoned with rosemary) are also regional specialties, as are many other roasted meats that go especially well with the Chianti. These are usually served with a *contorno* (side dish) of white beans, sauteed greens, or artichokes in season, all of which can be drizzled with more of that wonderful olive oil.

Tuscan desserts are typically Spartan. The cheese is the hard *pecorino*, and locals like to go for the even tougher *biscottini di Prato*, which provide an excuse to dunk them in the potent sweet dessert wine called *vin santo*, made of dried grapes, which they say will bring the dead back to life!

Remember that dining hours are earlier here than in Rome, starting at 12:30 for the midday meal and from 7:30 on in the evening. Many of Florence's restaurants are small, so reservations are a must. When going to the restaurants, note that the "r" in some of the following addresses indicates the red numbering system used for Florentine businesses, which differs from the black numbers used for residences.

Highly recommended restaurants in each price category are indicated by a star ★ .

Category	Cost*
Very Expensive	over 110,000 lire
Expensive	70,000–110,000 lire
Moderate	30,000–70,000 lire
Inexpensive	under 30,000 lire

*per person, for a three-course meal, including house wine and taxes

Very Expensive
★

Enoteca Pinchiorri. A sumptuous Renaissance palace bursting with bouquets is the setting for this restaurant, considered one of the best in Italy. The "enoteca" part of the name comes from its former incarnation as a wineshop under owner Giorgio Pinchiorri, who still keeps a stock of 70,000 bottles in the cellar. Wife Annie Feolde has recently added her refined interpretations of Tuscan cuisine—*triglie alla viareggina* (mullet with tomato sauce) and *arrosto di coniglio* (roast rabbit)—to a nouvelle menu that includes *ravioli di melanzane* (ravioli stuffed with eggplant), *petto di piccione* (pigeon breast), and *formaggio alle erbette* (cheese with herbs). *Via Ghibellina 87, tel. 055/242757. Reservations required. Jacket and tie re-*

quired. AE, V. Closed Sun. and Mon. lunch, all Aug., Dec. 24-28.

Expensive **La Capannina di Sante.** Florence's best fish restaurant is situ-
★ ated, not surprisingly, along a quiet stretch of the Arno, with
indoor tables in an ample, unpretentious trattoria-type setting
and a few tables outdoors under the pergola during the warmer
months. Risotto and various types of pasta are combined with
seafood, and the *grigliata mista di pesce*, or mixed grill of fish,
is among the standouts. *Piazza Ravenna, tel. 055/683345. Reservations advised for dinner. Dress: casual. AE, DC, MC, V.
Closed Sun., Mon. lunch and one week in Aug., Dec. 23-30.*

Il Cestello. Located across the Arno from the church of San
Frediano in Cestello, the restaurant is part of the Excelsior hotel and moves to the roof during the warmer months to enjoy a
stupendous view of the city E. M. Forster would envy. Its Tus-
can-based menu features delicious risotto and pasta dishes (including an exemplary *pasta e fagioli*, pasta with beans), a rare
selection of seafood, and an ever-changing sampling of whatever is fresh from the market. *Hotel Excelsior, Piazza
Ognissanti 3, tel. 055/264201. Reservations recommended for
nonguests of the hotel. Jacket and tie required. AE, DC, MC,
V.*

★ **Da Dante-Al Lume di Candela.** Everything from pasta to dessert is homemade here. The menu is Florentine and includes
such specialties as a simple soup called *acquacotta*, literally
"cooked water" but actually a vegetable soup in a meat broth,
and an excellent selection of meat dishes such as ossobuco and
bistecca alla fiorentina. The restaurant has an elegant setting
in a medieval tower. *Via delle Terme 23/r, tel. 055/294566. Reservations required. Jacket and tie required. AE, DC, MC, V.
Closed Sun., Mon. lunch, and Aug. 10-25.*

Relais le Jardin dell'Hotel Regency. Another hotel restaurant,
this one with a turn-of-the-century, stained-glass-and-wood-
paneling setting, stands on its own. Its *crespelle*, or crepes,
come highly recommended in their infinite variety, as do the
medaglioni di vitello al rabarbo (medallions of veal with rhu-
barb) and other aromatic meat dishes. *Piazza Massimo
D'Azeglio 5, tel. 055/245247. Reservations required for nonguests of the hotel. Jacket and tie required. AE, DC, MC, V.
Closed Sun.*

Sabatini. A Florentine tradition not without its detractors, the
restaurant maintains a high standard of excellence that, while
predictable (a recent innovation was its own version of a Bellini, called a Sabatini, made with spumante and strawberry
juice), is reassuring in its consistency. *Risotto ai funghi*, or risotto with mushrooms, is one specialty, as are all the Florentine dishes prepared and served with classic Old World style.
*Via dei Panzani 9/a, tel. 055/211559. Reservations advised.
Jacket and tie required. AE, DC, MC, V. Closed Mon. and
July 1-15.*

Moderate **Buca dell'Orafo.** One of the best of the Florentine *buca*, meaning hole, restaurants, Buca dell'Orafo is set in the cellar of a former goldsmith's shop near the Ponte Vecchio. It offers all the
Florentine specialties and prides itself on its bistecca. *Via dei
Girolami 28, tel. 055/213619. Reservations advised. Dress: casual. Closed Sun., Mon., and all Aug.*

Camillo. Bright and bustling, this popular restaurant does a
swift business in classic Tuscan dishes (the house has its own

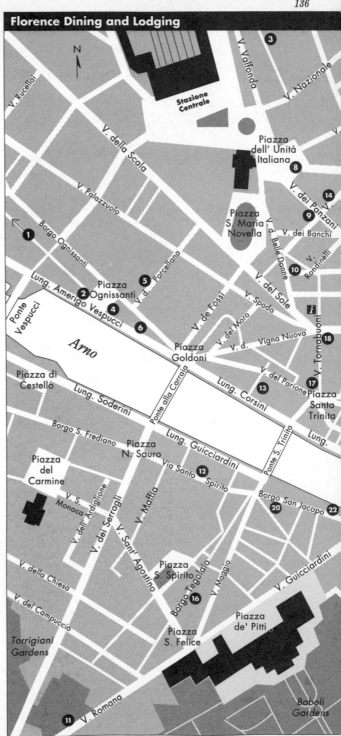

Florence Dining and Lodging

Dining
Acqua al Due, **33**
Angiolino, **12**
Buca dell'Orafo, **24**
Camillo, **20**
Cantinetta
Antinori, **10**
Coco Lezzone, **13**
Da Dante–Al Lume
di Candela, **21**
Da Noi, **37**
Enoteca Pinchiorri, **38**
Harry's Bar, **6**
Il Cestello, **4**
Il Cibreo, **39**
La Capannina
di Sante, **42**
Le Fonticine, **7**
La Loggia, **43**
La Vecchia Cucina, **36**
Mario da Ganino, **27**
Perbacco, **16**
Relais Le Jardin
dell'Hotel Regency, **30**
Sabatini, **9**
Sostanza detto
Il Troia, **5**
Za Za, **15**

Lodging
Annalena, **11**
Astoria Pullman, **14**
Baglioni, **8**
Beacci Tornabuoni, **17**
Bellettini, **19**
Bencistà, **29**
Excelsior, **4**
Grand Hotel, **2**
Grand Hotel Villa
Cora, **41**
Kraft, **1**
La Residenza, **18**
Liana, **32**
Loggiato dei Servi, **25**
Lungarno, **22**
Monna Lisa, **35**
Palazzo Vecchio, **3**
Pitti Palace, **23**
Plaza Hotel
Lucchesi, **40**
Quisisana e Ponte
Vecchio, **26**
Regency Umbria, **31**
Rigatti, **34**
Villa San Michele, **28**

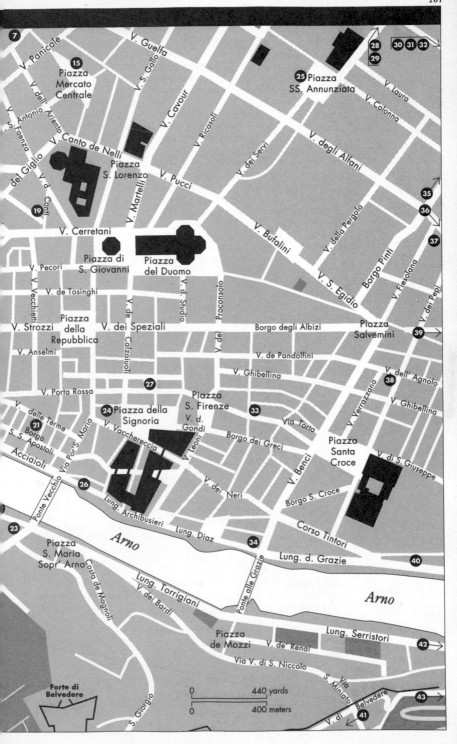

7

V. Panicale

15 Piazza Mercato Centrale

V. Guelfa

V. S. Gallo

V. dell' Ariento

V. S. Antonio

V. Faenza

del Giglio

V. d. Conti

V. Canto de Nelli

Piazza S. Lorenzo

V. Cavour

V. Ricasoli

V. dei Servi

25 Piazza SS. Annunziata

V. Laura

V. Colonna

V. degli Alfani

V. Martelli

V. Pucci

19

V. Cerretani

Piazza di S. Giovanni

Piazza del Duomo

V. Bufalini

V. della Pergola

35

36

37

V. Pecori

V. Vecchietti

V. de Tosinghi

V. d. Studio

V. Proconsolo

V. S. Egidio

Borgo Pinti

V. Fiesolana

V. Strozzi

Piazza della Repubblica

V. dei Speziali

V. de Calzaiuoli

V. de

Borgo degli Albizi

Piazza Salvemini

V. dei Pepi

39

V. Anselmi

V. de Pandolfini

V. Ghibellina

V. dell' Agnolo

38

V. Ghibellina

V. Porta Rossa

27

Piazza S. Firenze

33

V. Verrazzano

V. delle Terme

21 Borgo S. S. Apostoli

24 Piazza della Signoria

Via Por S. Maria

V. Vacchereccia

V. d. Gondi

V. Leoni

Via Torta

Borgo dei Greci

V. Benci

Piazza Santa Croce

V. di S. Giuseppe

Acciaioli

Ponte Vecchio

26

Lung. Archibusieri

V. dei Neri

Borgo S. Croce

23

Piazza S. Maria Sopr' Arno

Costa de Magnoli

Arno

Lung. Diaz

34

Corso Tintori

Lung. d. Grazie

40

Lung. Torrigiani

V. dei Bardi

Ponte alle Grazie

Arno

Lung. Serristori

Piazza de Mozzi

V. de' Renai

42

Via V. di S. Niccolò

Forte di Belvedere

S. Giorgio

0   440 yards

0   400 meters

S. Miniato

V. di Belvedere

41

43

28

29

30 **31** **32**

olive oil and Chianti), including *fegatini di pollo* (sautéed chicken livers) and porcini mushrooms with parmigiano cheese. *Borgo San Jacopo 57/r, tel. 055/212427. Reservations advised. AE, DC, MC, V. Closed Wed., Thurs., Aug., and Dec.*

Cantinetta Antinori. Set on the ground floor of a Renaissance palace, this is an elegant place for ladies (and gentlemen) who lunch after shopping in nearby Via Tornabuoni. The Antinori family is best known as wine producers, and their wares may be sampled with light salads, bread, sausage, and cheese snacks or more complete meals. *Piazza Antinori 3, tel. 055/292234. Reservations advised. Dress: casual. AE, DC, MC, V. Closed Sat., Sun., and Aug.*

★ **Il Cibreo.** Located near the Sant'Ambrogio market, Il Cibreo uses the freshest ingredients to prepare updated versions of Florentine classics, presented in an upscale trattoria-style dining room or in a piazza overlooking the market during the warmer months. The *pappa al pomodoro*, presented as a thick red dollop on a sparkling white Ginori plate, and inventive dishes such as *anatra farcita di pinoli e uvetta* (duck stuffed with pine nuts and raisins) are two of many specialties. A café annex serves drinks and snacks all day. *Via dei Macci 118/r, tel. 055/234-1100. Reservations advised for dinner. Dress: casual. Closed Sun., Mon., and Aug. 1–Sept. 10. AE, DC, MC, V.*

Coco Lezzone. The name roughly translates as "big smelly cook," a self-effacing image that this whitewashed, red-checked-tablecloth hole-in-the-wall, a few Gucci-shod steps off Via Tornabuoni, deems appropriate. It serves classic Florentine dishes such as pappa al pomodoro and arista. *Via del Parioncino 26/r, tel. 055/287178. Dress: casual. Closed Tues. dinner, Sun. (in summer, Sat. and Sun.), and Aug. No credit cards.*

★ **Le Fonticine.** Owner Silvano Bruci is from Tuscany, wife Gianna from Emilia-Romagna, and the restaurant combines the best of both worlds in a trattoria-type setting liberally hung with Silvano's extensive collection of paintings. Emilia-Romagna specialties such as tortellini ready the taste buds for Tuscan grilled porcini mushrooms so meaty they provide serious competition for the bistecca alla fiorentina. *Via Nazionale 79/r, tel. 055/282106. Reservations advised. Dress: casual. AE, V. Closed Sun., Mon, and July 20–Aug. 20.*

Harry's Bar. Americans love it, and it *is* the only place in town to get a perfect martini or a hamburger or a club sandwich—if that's what you want. The small menu also has well-prepared international offerings, and the bar is open until midnight. *Lungarno Vespucci 22/r, tel. 055/239-6700. Reservations required. Dress: casual. AE, MC. Closed Sun. and Dec. 10–Jan. 15.*

La Loggia. Though it may be crowded and somewhat rushed, La Loggia is worth the wait for the view of Florence from atop the Piazzale Michelangelo, especially during the summer when there are tables outdoors. The food is almost incidental, but sticking to such Florentine classics as porcini mushrooms and bistecca alla fiorentina makes for a thoroughly memorable evening. *Piazzale Michelangelo 1, tel. 055/234-2832. Dress: casual. AE, DC, MC, V. Closed Wed. and Aug. 10–25.*

Mario da Ganino. On a side street between the Duomo and Palazzo Vecchio, this trattoria is informal, rustic and cheerful. You are offered a taste of mortadella (at no charge) to start off your meal, which might include some of the homemade pasta on the menu. *Gnudoni* (ravioli without the pasta casing) are a specialty, as is cheesecake for dessert. Main courses uphold Florentine tradition, with grilled steak and chops and bean dishes. Get there early; it seats only about 35, and double that number in good weather at outside tables. *Piazza dei Cimatori 4/r, tel. 055/214125. Reservations advised. Dress: casual. AE, DC. Closed Sun. and Aug. 15–25.*

Da Noi. Efficiently run by a renegade Swede from Enoteca Pinchiorri and her Italian husband, this tiny restaurant presents such self-consciously creative items as *tagliatelle di segale al pâté di fegato* (rye-flour tagliatelle pasta with liver pâté) and *quaglie al ginepro* (quail with juniper) in a hushed environment popular with Americans who read food magazines diligently. *Via Fiesolana 46/r, tel. 055/242917. Reservations required. Dress: casual. No credit cards. Closed Sun., Mon., and Aug.*

Sostanza detto Il Troia. Equally famous for its brusque service as it is for its bistecca alla fiorentina, Il Troia is Florence's oldest restaurant, founded in 1869. Its menu is still strictly Florentine, and all the local classics are served at communal tables, with no frills, to a clientele of out-of-towners and tourists. *Via del Porcellana 25/r, tel. 055/212691. Reservations advised. Dress: casual. No credit cards. Closed Sat. evening, Sun., and Aug.*

★ **La Vecchia Cucina.** Located in an out-of-the-way part of town near the Campo di Marte, this restaurant draws a loyal crowd of devotees of its highly inventive variations on Italian themes. The menu changes every other week, since it features seasonal foods such as asparagus and porcini mushrooms, but always includes pasta made by the owner's mother, who is from Emilia-Romagna. The olive oil is of the highest quality, the wine list has an excellent selection of Italian wines, and the homemade dessert pastries are miniature masterpieces. *Viale de Amicis 1/r, tel. 055/660143. Reservations necessary. Dress: casual. V. Closed Sun. and Aug.*

Inexpensive **Acqua al Due.** You'll find this tiny restaurant near the Bargello. It serves an array of Florentine specialties in a lively, very casual setting. Acqua al Due is popular with young Florentines, partly because it's air-conditioned in the summer and always open late. *Via dell'Acqua 2/r, tel. 055/284170. No reservations. Dress: casual. No credit cards. Closed Mon., and Aug.*

Angiolino. This bustling little trattoria in the Oltrarno district is popular with locals and visitors. It has a real charcoal grill and an old woodburning stove to keep customers warm on nippy days. The menu offers Tuscan specialties such as *ribollita* (minestrone) and a classic bistecca alla fiorentina. The bistecca can push the check up into the Moderate range. *Via Santo Spirito 36/r, 055/298976. Reservations advised in the evening. Dress: casual. No credit cards. Closed Sun. dinner, Mon., and last 3 weeks in July.*

Perbacco. Between Piazza Pitti and Santo Spirito, an unimposing entrance and steep stairs lead down into an authentic wine cellar with vaulted ceilings. Choose the house wine or one of some 30 Tuscan vintages to go with such hearty Tuscan country dishes as *gran farro* (thick wheat soup with beans) and *buglione* (stew of mixed meat and vegetables). A special wine is included with the daily fixed-price menu. *Via Borgo Tegolaio 21/r. tel. 055/218511. No reservations. Dress: Casual. No credit cards. Evenings only. Closed Sun.*

Za-Za. Slighty more upscale than neighboring trattorias, Za-

Za attracts white-collar workers and theater people. Posters of movie stars hang on wood-paneled walls, and classic Florentine cuisine is served at communal tables. *Piazza Mercato Centrale 16/r, tel. 055/215411. Reservations advised. Dress: casual. AE, DC, MC, V. Closed Sun. and Aug.*

Wine Shops In addition, there are many wine shops where you can have a snack or sandwich. Of these, **Le Cantine** (Via dei Pucci) is stylish and popular, as is **Cantinone del Gallo Nero** (Via Santo Spirito 6), which also serves meals in a brick-vaulted wine cellar. More modest are **Borgioli** (Piazza dell'Olio), **Fiaschetteria** (Via dei Neri), **Fratellini** (Via dei Cimatori), **Nicolino** (Volta dei Mercanti), and **Piccolo Vinaio** (Via Castellani).

Lodging

Florence's importance not only as a tourist city but as a convention center and the site of the Pitti fashion collections throughout the year has guaranteed a variety of accommodations, many in former villas and palazzos. However, these very factors mean that reservations are a must at all times of the year.

If you do find yourself in Florence with no reservations, go to the **Consorzio ITA** office in the train station. It's open every day from 9 AM to 8:30 PM. If the office is shut, your best bet is to try some of the inexpensive (but clean) accommodations at a *pensione* or a *locanda* (inn); many are located on **Via Nazionale** (which leads east from Piazza Stazione) and on **Via Faenza,** the second left off Via Nazionale.

Highly recommended lodgings in each price category are indicated by a star ★.

Category	Cost*
Very Expensive	over 380,000 lire
Expensive	270,000–380,000 lire
Moderate	130,000–270,000 lire
Inexpensive	under 130,000 lire

*All prices are for a double room for two, including tax and service.

Very Expensive **Excelsior.** Traditional Old World charm finds a regal setting at
★ the Excelsior, a neo-Renaissance palace complete with painted wooden ceilings, stained glass, and acres of Oriental carpets strewn over marble floors in the public rooms. The rooms are furnished with the chaises-longues, classical decorations, and long mirrors of the Empire style. This is characteristic of the CIGA hotel chain that owns it and is especially appropriate here, since Napoleon's sister Caroline was once the proprietress of the property. Plush touches include wall-to-wall carpeting in the rooms and thick terrycloth towels on heated racks in the bathrooms. Its Il Cestello restaurant serves excellent food and in summer moves up to the roof for a wonderful view. *Piazza Ognissanti 3, tel. 055/264201, fax 055/210278. 205 rooms with bath. Facilities: restaurant with piano bar. AE, DC, MC, V.*
Grand Hotel. Across the piazza from the Excelsior, this Florentine classic, also owned by the CIGA chain, provides all the lux-

urious amenities of its sister. Most rooms and public areas are decorated in sumptuous Renaissance style, many with frescoes. Baths are in marble. Some rooms have balconies overlooking the Arno. *Piazza Ognissanti 1, tel. 055/288781, fax 055/217400. 107 rooms with bath. Facilities: restaurant, winter garden, bar, parking. AE, DC, MC, V.*

Grand Hotel Villa Cora. Built near the Boboli Gardens and Piazzale Michelangelo in the mid-19th century when Florence was briefly the capital of Italy, the Villa Cora retains the opulence of that era. The decor of its remarkable public and private rooms runs the gamut from neoclassical to rococo and even Moorish, and reflects the splendor of such former guests as the Empress Eugénie, wife of Napoleon III, and Madame Von Meck, Tchaikovsky's mysterious benefactress. *Viale Machiavelli 18, tel. 055/2298451, fax 055/229086. 48 rooms with bath. Facilities: restaurant, garden, swimming pool, piano bar, car service. AE, DC, MC, V.*

Regency. Undisturbed sleep is almost guaranteed at this hotel, which is tucked away in a respectable residential district near the synagogue. The rooms are decorated in flamboyant but tasteful fabrics and antique-style furniture faithful to the hotel's incarnation in the 19th-century as a private mansion. It has one of Florence's best hotel restaurants. *Piazza Massimo D'Azeglio 3, tel. 055/245247, fax 055/234-2938. 38 rooms with bath. Facilities: garden, restaurant. AE, DC, MC, V.*

Villa San Michele. The setting for this hideaway is so romantic—nestled in the hills of nearby Fiesole—that it once attracted Brigitte Bardot for her honeymoon (even today guests sleep on linen sheets). The villa was originally a monastery whose facade and loggia have been attributed to Michelangelo: The rooms now contain sumptuous statuary, paintings, Jacuzzis, and Savonarola chairs that would put their namesake to shame. Many of the rooms have a panoramic view of Florence, others face an inner courtyard, and a luxuriant garden surrounds the whole affair. The restaurant is excellent, and MAP is mandatory. *Via Doccia 4, Fiesole, tel. 055/59451, fax 055/598734. 28 rooms with bath. Facilities: restaurant, piano bar, swimming pool, garden, courtesy bus service. AE, DC, MC, V. Open mid-Mar.–mid-Nov.*

Expensive   **Astoria Pullman.** Decorated with the classic Tuscan *pietra serena* (a gray sandstone), white stucco walls, and terracotta floors, the hotel resembles an ancient Florentine palace (complete with a copy of Botticelli's *Primavera)*, and no wonder, since that's precisely what it was. Parts of the original building go back to 1176, with the Palazzo Gaddi wing a relative newcomer dating from the 17th century. And though John Milton wrote much of *Paradise Lost* here, that would hardly describe the recently remodeled hotel's present condition, with modern, comfortable facilities and rooms with a view on the top floors. *Via del Giglio 9, tel. 055/2398022, fax 055/214632. 91 rooms with bath. Facilities: hairdresser, sauna, garden. AE, DC, MC, V.*

★ **Baglioni.** This large turn-of-the-century building was conceived in the European tradition of grand hotels; it's located between the train station and the cathedral. The charming roof terrace has the best view in Florence and is home to the Terrazza Brunelleschi restaurant. The hotel is spacious and elegant, with well-proportioned rooms decorated tastefully in antique Florentine style, and many have leaded glass windows.

Fourth-floor rooms have been completely done over in pastel tones harmonizing with the floral carpeting or mellow parquet. The hotel has a full range of conference facilities, which makes it a favorite of businesspeople. *Piazza dell'Unità Italiana 6, tel. 055/218441, fax 055/215695. 197 rooms with bath. Facilities: roof garden restaurant. AE, DC, MC, V.*

Hotel Lungarno. In the Oltrarno section, hanging right over the Arno, fifty yards from the Ponte Vecchio, this comfortable hotel has a devoted return clientele. The lobby-cum-breakfast room is filled with comfortable sofas and easy chairs, the newspapers hang nearby, and the friendly management even permits pets. Some of the rooms are in a beautifully restored trecento tower, and from some of them you could fish in the river. Breakfast is included. *Borgo San Jacopo 14, tel. 055/264211, fax 055/268437. 66 rooms. Facilities: air conditioning, cable TV, meeting room, garage next door. AE, DC, MC, V.*

Kraft. The efficient and comfortable Kraft has many period-style rooms with balconies overlooking the Arno. Its location near the Teatro Comunale (it is also next to the U.S. consulate) gives it a clientele from the music world. *Via Solferino 2, tel. 055/284273, fax 055/298267. 68 rooms with bath. Facilities: rooftop restaurant, swimming pool. AE, DC, MC, V.*

★ **Monna Lisa.** Housed in a Renaissance palazzo, the hotel retains its original *pietra serena* staircase, terra-cotta floors, and painted ceilings and was once the home of Sant' Antonino, who became bishop of Florence. Its rooms still have a rather homey quality, and though on the small side, many have contemplative views of a lovely garden. The ground-floor lounges give you the feel of living in an aristocratic town house. *Borgo Pinti 27, tel. 055/2479751, fax 055/247–9755. 20 rooms with bath. Facilities: garden, bar. AE, DC, MC, V.*

Plaza Hotel Lucchesi. This comfortable hotel, just a short walk beyond the Uffizi along the Arno, was completely renovated recently. Now its modern rooms with wonderful views of the river are soundproof as well, as are the ones overlooking the red-tiled roofs extending toward Santa Croce. *Lungarno della Zecca Vecchia 38, tel. 055/264141, fax 055/248–0921. 97 rooms with bath. Facilities: restaurant. AE, DC, MC, V.*

Moderate **Annalena.** The entrance to the hotel, just beyond the Pitti Palace, faces the Boboli Gardens, while the hotel's rear rooms look out on the largest private garden in Florence. Once part of the Medici holdings, it has been everything from a convent to a hiding place for refugees. Its distinguished past is reflected in an authentic antique decor steeped in character, and it attracts a worldly, bohemian clientele. *Via Romana 34, tel. 055/222402, fax 055/222403. 20 rooms with bath. Facilities: breakfast room on terrace. AE, DC, MC, V.*

Beacci Tornabuoni. This is perhaps *the* classic Florentine *pensione* (although by law all lodgings have been reclassified as hotels of various categories). Set in a 14th-century palazzo, it contains a series of quaint, old-fashioned rooms, renovated a few years ago, all presided over by a *signora* full of personality. Half board is required, but the food is good and can also be brought to the rooms, most of which have views of the red-tiled roofs in the neighboring downtown area. *Via Tornabuoni 3, tel. 055/212645. 30 rooms, with bath. Facilities: restaurant, bar. AE, DC, MC, V.*

Bencistà. Below the luxurious Villa San Michele in Fiesole, this hotel has the same tranquil setting and is even two centuries older. The rooms are furnished with antiques, and half board is required. *Via Benedetto da Maiano 4, Fiesole, tel. 055/59163, fax 055/59163. 40 rooms, 24 with bath. No credit cards.*

★ **Loggiato dei Serviti.** A relatively new and charming hotel, the Loggiato dei Servi is tucked away under a historic loggia in one of the city's quietest and loveliest squares. Vaulted ceilings and tasteful furnishings, some of them antiques, make this a hotel for those who want to get the feel of Florence and will appreciate a 19th-century town house look while enjoying modern creature comforts. The hotel has no restaurant. *Piazza Santissima Annunziata 3, tel. 055/289592, fax 055/289595. 29 rooms with bath. AE, DC, MC, V.*

Pitti Palace. Run by an American and her Italian husband, the hotel combines modern efficiency with Old World warmth, providing friendly service along with a lovely roof terrace overlooking the Arno from the Pitti Palace side. *Via Barbadori 2, tel. 055/282257. 40 rooms, 29 with bath. AE, V.*

Quisisana e Ponte Vecchio. The hotel gets the first part of its name from the Italian for "here one heals," the second part from its location near the city's most famous bridge. Comfortable rooms furnished in mahogany, a central location, and a loggia with views of the Arno make it a pleasant place to stay. *Lungarno Archibusieri 4, tel. 055/216692, fax 055/268303. 36 rooms, 33 with bath. Facilities: terrace. AE, DC, MC, V.*

La Residenza. Located just down the street from the Beacci, on Florence's most elegant shopping street, is La Residenza: The top floor has a charming roof garden and rooms with even better views for fewer lire. The *signora* here is equally accommodating, the decor equally antique, and the plumbing up to date. *Via Tornabuoni 8, tel. 055/284197. 24 rooms with bath. Facilities: roof garden, garage. AE, DC, V.*

Inexpensive **Bellettini.** You couldn't ask for anything more central; this small hotel occupies two floors of a well-kept but centuries-old building near the church of San Lorenzo, in a neighborhood with plenty of inexpensive eating places. The good-sized rooms have Venetian or Tuscan provincial decor; bathrooms are bright and modern. Air-conditioning is available at an extra charge. *Via dei Conti 7, tel. 055/213561, fax 055/283551. 28 rooms with bath. Facilities: bar and lounge area. DC, MC, V.*

Liana. This small hotel, located near the English Cemetery, is in a quiet 19th-century villa that formerly housed the British Embassy. Its clean and pleasant rooms all face a stately garden. *Via Vittorio Alfieri 18, tel. 055/245303. 20 rooms, 18 with bath. AE, V.*

Palazzo Vecchio. The decor is minimal in this rather starkly furnished small hotel near the station. It's handy for everything; the proprietor owns a restaurant a block or two away; and there's a tiny parking area next to the building, a rare commodity in Florence. *Via Cennini 4, tel. 055/212182. 16 rooms with bath or shower, 2 without. AE, DC, MC, V.*

Rigatti. Occupying the top two floors of the 19th-century Palazzo Alberti, between Palazzo Vecchio and Santa Croce, this elegantly furnished hotel has wonderful views of the Arno from its tiny front terrace, as well as five quiet rooms overlooking a garden in back. The rooms are spacious and tastefully furnished, with modern bathrooms. *Lungarno Diaz 2, tel. 055/213022. 28 rooms, 14 with bath. No credit cards.*

The Arts and Nightlife

The Arts

Theater **Estate Fiesolana.** From June through August, this festival of theater, music, dance, and film takes place in the churches and the archaeological area of Fiesole (Teatro Romano, Fiesole, tel. 055/599931).

Concerts **Maggio Musicale Fiorentina.** This series of internationally acclaimed concerts and recitals is held in the **Teatro Comunale** (Corso Italia 16, tel. 055/277–9236) from late April through June. During the same period, there is a concert season of the Orchestra Regionale Toscana, in the church of **Santo Stefano al Ponte** (tel. 055/2420). Amici della Musica organizes concerts at the **Teatro della Pergola** (box office Via della Pergola 10/r, tel. 055/241881).

Opera Operas are performed in the Teatro Comunale from December through February.

Film **Florence Film Festival.** An international panel of judges gathers in late spring at the Forte di Belvedere to preside over a wide selection of new releases.

Festival del Popolo. This festival, held each December, is devoted to documentaries and is held in the Fortezza da Basso.

Nightlife

Unlike the Romans and Milanese, the frugal and reserved Florentines do not have a reputation for an active nightlife; however, the following places attract a mixed crowd of Florentines and visitors.

Piano Bars Many of the more expensive hotels have their own piano bars, where nonguests are welcome to come for an *aperitivo* or an after-dinner drink. The best view is from the bar at the **Excelsior** (Piazza Ognissanti 3, tel. 055/264201), on a roof garden overlooking the Arno. **Caffé Pitti** (Piazza Pitti 9, tel. 055/296241), an informal bar, is a popular afternoon and evening gathering place for Florence's international colony. **Il Barretto** (Via del Parione 50/r, tel. 055/294122) is an intimate, wood-paneled spot.

Jazz Clubs **Playgin** (Piazza Santa Maria Novella 26/r, tel. 055/211590) has live jazz on weekends. The generically named **Jazz Club** (Via Nuova de Caccini 33, tel. 055/247–9700) also has live music and closes only on Monday.

Discos The two largest discos, with the youngest crowds, are **Yab Yum** (Via Sassetti 5r, tel. 055/282018) and **Space Electronic** (Via Palazzuolo 37, tel. 055/295082). Less frenetic alternatives are **Jackie O'** (Via Erta Canina 24, tel. 055/2342442) and **Full Up** (Via della Vigna Vecchia 21/r, tel. 055/293006).

5 Venice

Introduction

Venice today is in one important way the same as it was more than 1,000 years ago, when inhabitants from the mainland defied the sea to build a city on forests of tree trunks driven into the mud flats of a treacherous lagoon. The intervening centuries saw the development of some of the world's most inspired architecture, but water remains the city's defining feature.

You must walk everywhere in Venice, and where you cannot walk, you go by water. Occasionally, from fall to spring, you have to walk *in* water, when extraordinarily high tides known as *acque alte* invade the lower parts of the city, flooding Piazza San Marco for a few hours. Unless you're lucky to find one of the makeshift plank bridges that appear from nowhere to keep certain busy routes open, you'll have to take off your socks and shoes, roll up your pantlegs, and wade in with everyone else. The problem of protecting Venice and its lagoon from dangerously high tides has generated extravagant plans and so many committee reports that the city may sink as much under the weight of paper as under that of the water.

Then there are the hordes of tourists from all over the world that flow through Piazza San Marco and eddy wide-eyed around stern guides imparting succinct history lessons in a babble of languages. Like the Venetians, you will have to adapt to the crowds, visiting the major sights at odd hours, when the tour groups are still at breakfast or have boarded buses on their return to the mainland (most of them are day-trippers). Get away from Piazza San Marco when it's crowded; you'll be surprised to find many areas of Venice practically deserted. Explore the districts of Cannaregio or Castello, quiet areas where you can find the time and space to sit and contemplate the watercolor pages of Venetian history.

The resourceful Venetians who built this island city during Europe's Dark Ages used their navigational and trading talents to turn an out-of-the-way refuge against the marauding Goths into a staunch—and very rich—bulwark of Christendom that held against the tides of Turkish expansion. Early in its history the city called in Byzantine artists to decorate its churches with brilliant mosaics, still glowing today. Then the influence of Lombard-Romanesque architecture from the 11th to 13th centuries gave rise to the characteristic type of palace for which Venice is famous the world over. Many of the sumptuous palaces along the Grand Canal were built at that time, strong reminders of Venice's control of all major trading routes to the East. Subsequently, Gothic styles from elsewhere in Europe were adapted to create a new kind of Venetian Gothic art and architecture. Venice attained a peak of power and wealth in the 15th and 16th centuries. It extended its domain inland to include all of what is now known as the Veneto region and even beyond. In the last half of the 15th century, the Renaissance arrived in Venice, and its artists began to write a new and important chapter in the history of painting.

The decline of Venice came slowly. For 400 years the powerful maritime city-republic had held sway. After the 16th century the tide changed. The Ottoman Empire blocked Venice's Mediterranean trade routes, and the rest of Europe had to look to new Atlantic routes for its goods. Like its steadily dwindling fortunes, Venice's art and culture began a prolonged decline, leaving only the splendid monuments to recall a glorious past.

You can see the panoply of history by visiting only the major museums and churches, but if you want a fuller picture of the districts that keep this a living city, get off the beaten track as often as you can. You'll need a detailed map showing most, if not all, street names and *vaporetto* (water bus) routes, but you'll probably get lost anyway (everyone does). Ask directions from shopkeepers or at a café where locals outnumber the tourists; chances are, they will admire your initiative and put you back on the right track.

Essential Information

Arriving and Departing by Plane

Airports and Airlines Domestic and some Alitalia international flights arrive at **Marco Polo** airport at Tessera, about 10 kilometers (6 miles) north of the city on the mainland. For information, call tel. 041/661111.

Between the Airport and Downtown ACTV (the municipal transit authority) provides regular bus service between the airport and Piazzale Roma, which is the end of the road, just at the mainland entrance to Venice itself.

By Bus The fare is about 800 lire. The direct nonstop ATVO bus connects the airport with Piazzale Roma in 20 minutes; fare is about 4,500 lire.

By Taxi A yellow taxi from the airport to Piazzale Roma costs about 40,000 lire.

By Boat This is the best way to get to Venice from the airport. The most direct way is by the fast **Cooperativa San Marco** launch, with regular scheduled service throughout the day, until midnight; the landing in Venice is just off Piazzetta San Marco, and the fare is 13,000 lire per person, including bags. A **water taxi** (a sleek modern motorboat known as a *motoscafo*) from the airport costs more than 100,000 lire, and overcharging is common. Always agree on a water-taxi fare before boarding.

Arriving and Departing by Car, Train, and Bus

By Car You are strongly advised not to bring a car to Venice. You'll have to pay for a garage or parking space during your stay. If there's space, you can park in one of the multistory garages at Piazzale Roma or in the adjacent, less expensive parking lot of Tronchetto. On holiday weekends, traffic backs up on the causeway between Venice and Mestre; electronic signs advise whether and where parking space is available. From the Tronchetto parking lot you can get a Line 34 vaporetto (water bus) direct to San Marco; otherwise take bus No. 17 or walk about 500 yards to Piazzale Roma, where other vaporetti stop. You can take your car to the Lido, the long, narrow island guarding the Venetian lagoon; the car ferry (Line 17) leaves about every 50 minutes from a landing at Tronchetto.

By Train **Santa Lucia** station is on the Grand Canal in the northwest corner of the city. Make sure your train is bound for this station. Some through trains to points north leave you at the Venezia-Mestre station on the mainland, where you have to change to a local train to get to the Venezia–Santa Lucia station. For train information, call tel. 041/715555.

By Bus The bus terminal is at Piazzale Roma, near the vaporetto stop of that name. Express buses operated by SITA connect Venice with every major Italian city.

Porters Because cars are not allowed in Venice, many people need porters to help negotiate the footbridges and staircases. Porters wear badges and blue shirts or smocks. You will find them at the airport and train stations and also at some of the principal vaporetto landings. They charge about 8,000 lire for one or two bags, extra at night and on holidays. Since you can't always count on finding a porter when you need one, a folding luggage cart will prove invaluable (suitcases with wheels are not the answer on uneven paving stones and over bridges).

However you arrive in Venice, get information before you arrive on the location of your hotel and exactly how to get there. Depending on its location, regardless of whether you take a vaporetto or water taxi to the nearest landing, you may have to walk some distance from the landing to reach it, with or without the help and guidance of a porter. Be prepared to find your way on your own or to call the hotel for instructions when you arrive.

Getting Around

First-time visitors find that getting around Venice presents some unusual problems: The layout is complex; the waterborne transportation can be bewildering; the house-numbering system is totally illogical; street names in the six districts are duplicated; and often you must walk, whether you want to or not. It's essential that you have a good map showing all street names and vaporetto routes; buy one at a newsstand.

By Vaporetto ACTV vaporetti run the length of the Grand Canal and circle the city. You can buy a map and timetable of the network at newsstands. There are more than 20 lines, some of which connect Venice with the major and minor islands in the lagoon. Line 1 is the Grand Canal local. Line 5 goes to the island of Murano. Timetables are posted on all landing stages, where ticket booths are located (open early morning–9 PM). Buy single tickets or books of 10, and count your change carefully; short-changing is a nasty habit in these parts. The fare is 1,800 lire on most lines; 2,500 lire for the Line 2 express connecting the train station, Rialto, San Marco, and the Lido. Stamp your ticket in the machine on the landing stage. A daily tourist ticket costs 10,000 lire. A 3-day tourist ticket costs 17,000 lire. Vaporetti run every 10 minutes or so during the day; Lines 1, 2, and 5 run every hour between midnight and dawn. Landing stages are clearly marked with name and line number and serve boats going in both directions.

By Motoscafo These stylish powerboats are expensive, and the fare system is as complex as Venice's layout. A minimum fare of about 50,000 lire gets you nowhere, and you'll pay three times as much to get from one end of the Grand Canal to the other. Always agree on the fare before starting out. To avoid arguments, overcharging, and rip-offs, avoid motoscafi altogether.

By Traghetto Few tourists know about the two-man gondolas that ferry people across the Grand Canal at various fixed points. They are the cheapest and shortest gondola ride in Venice and can save a lot of walking. The fare is 400 lire, which you hand to the gondolier when you get on. Look for traghetto signs.

By Gondola No visit to Venice is complete without a gondola ride. But not many visitors know that the best time for one is in the late afternoon or early evening hours, when the Grand Canal isn't so heavily trafficked, or that it's best to start from a station on the Grand Canal because the lagoon is usually choppy. Make it clear that you want to see the smaller canals and come to terms on the cost and duration of the ride before you start. Gondoliers are supposed to charge a fixed minimum of about 70,000 lire for up to five passengers for 50 minutes. In practice they ask double that for a 30- to 40-minute ride. After 9 PM the rate goes up. Bargaining may get you a better price.

On Foot This is the only way to reach many parts of Venice, so wear comfortable shoes. Invest in a good map that names all streets, and count on getting lost more than once.

Important Addresses and Numbers

Tourist Information The main tourist office is at Calle Ascensione 71C (tel. 041/522–6356), just off Piazza San Marco, under the arcade in the far left corner opposite the basilica. *Open Apr.–Oct., Mon.–Sat. 8:30–7:30; Nov.–Mar., Mon.–Sat. 8:30–1:30.*

There are other information booths at the Santa Lucia train station (tel. 041/715016), in the bus terminal at Piazzale Roma (tel. 041/522–7402), at Marco Polo airport (no phone), and at Tronchetto parking lot (no phone).

Consulates U.K. (Campo Santa Maria della Carita 1051, Dorsoduro, tel. 041/522–7207). There is no U.S. or Canadian consular service.

Emergencies Police, tel. 113.
Ambulance, tel. 041/523–0000.

Doctors and Dentists Dial the number for ambulances (*see* above) and ask the **Croce Azzurra** (Blue Cross) to recommend a doctor or dentist convenient for your location. The British consulate can also recommend doctors and dentists.

Late-Night Pharmacies Venetian pharmacies take turns opening late or on Sundays; dial 192 for information on which are open. Alternatively, the daily list of late-night pharmacies is posted on the front of every pharmacy. Two with English-speaking staff are **Farmacia Italo-Inglese** (Calle della Mandola, tel. 041/522–4837) and **International Pharmacy** (Calle Lunga San Marco, tel. 041/522–2311).

English-Language Bookstores Venice's centuries of experience in dealing with foreign visitors mean that bookstores and newsstands throughout the city are well stocked with publications in English. **Fantoni,** on Salizzada San Luca, specializes in art books and has an excellent selection of collections by famous writers and photographers. **O. Bohm,** just behind Piazza San Marco on Salizzada San Moise, has English-language books and a large selection of antique prints of Venice. **Libreria San Barnaba,** on Fondamenta Gherardini, near Campo San Barnaba, has shelves full of paperbacks and books on Venice in English.

Good general-interest bookstores include **Serenissima** (San Zulian), near San Marco; **Studium** (Calle Canonica), off Piazzetta dei Leoncini; and **Zanco** (Campo San Bartolomeo), near the Rialto Bridge.

Travel Agencies **American Express** (San Moisè 1471, tel. 041/520–0844); **CIT** (Piazza San Marco 4850, tel. 041/528–5480); **Wagons Lits/Cook** (Piazzetta dei Leoncini 289, tel. 041/522–3405).

Guided Tours

Orientation **American Express** and **CIT** offer two-hour walking tours of the San Marco area, taking in the basilica and the Doge's Palace (about 45,000 lire). Tours usually begin at 10 AM from the main offices of these companies, but it is safer to contact them beforehand. American Express has an afternoon walking tour that ends with a gondola ride and a glassblowing demonstration (Apr.–Oct., about 50,000 lire).

Special-Interest American Express, CIT, and other operators offer group gondola rides with serenades. Assemble at sunset by the Rialto Bridge (about 32,000 lire).

During July and August, free guided tours (some in English) of **St. Mark's Basilica** are offered several times a day by the Patriarchate of Venice; information is available in the atrium of the church. *Tel. 041/520–0333. No tours Sun.*

Bassani (Calle Larga XXII Marzo 2414, near San Marco, tel. 041/520–3644) offers two offbeat tours to help visitors to Venice get the feel of the city. *A Day in Venice* tour takes you to some hidden corners and includes lunch (about 80,000 lire). *A Night in Venice* includes dinner, a gondola serenade, and music at a night spot (about 95,000 lire). Both are available May–October.

Excursions Don't take organized tours to the islands of Murano, Burano, or Torcello. They are annoyingly commercial and emphasize glass-factory showrooms, pressuring you to buy. You can easily visit these islands on your own (*see* Tour 5: Islands of the Lagoon in Exploring Venice, below).

American Express offers an excursion by bus to the Venetian villas and Padua (about 65,000 lire. *Tours Apr.–Oct., Tues., Thurs., Sat., Sun.*

CIT runs an excursion on the Brenta Canal on the Burchiello motorlaunch to Padua. The return trip is by bus (about 125,000 lire; tours Apr.–Oct., Tues., Thurs., Sat.).

Personal Guides **American Express** and **CIT** can provide guides for walking or gondola tours of Venice or cars with driver and guide for tours of the mainland. You can get a list of licensed guides and their rates from the main tourist office in Piazza San Marco (tel. 041/522–6356).

Exploring Venice

Orientation

The church of St. Mark's is unquestionably the heart of Venice, but venturing even 50 yards from it can sometimes lead to confusion because of the bewildering combination of alleys, canals, and dead ends throughout the city. The narrow canalside streets seem to behave quite differently from their counterparts on maps, and the street-numbering system, alleged to refer to each block, is more trouble than it is worth to try to understand. Use the tall spire of the St. Mark's bell tower as your landmark while you try to find out how you managed to get so far from where you meant to be. Keep a map of vaporetto lines with you at all times because the best way back to St. Mark's or your hotel may well be along one of these routes.

Our first two tours should help you find your bearings. Tour 1 takes in the sights around the San Marco district, the geographic and spiritual center of the city. Tour 2 takes to the water along the Grand Canal, the main artery of Venice, linking many of its major sights. Tours 3 and 4 take you east and west, respectively, giving you the chance to explore some of the more offbeat sights and areas, as well as the less central churches and art collections. The last tour takes you to the other major islands of the Venetian lagoon, places where the pace of life is slower and the crafts that helped establish Venice's trading reputation are still practiced.

Highlights for First-Time Visitors

Accademia Gallery (Tour 4: The Western and Northern Districts).
Campanile of St. Mark's (Tour 1: The San Marco District).
Campo Santi Giovanni e Paolo (Tour 3: To the Arsenal and Beyond).
Frari Church (Tour 4: The Western and Northern Districts).
Murano, Burano, and Torcello (Tour 5: Islands of the Lagoon).
Palazzo Ducale (Tour 1: The San Marco District).
Piazza San Marco (Tour 1: The San Marco District).
Ponte di Rialto (Tour 2: The Grand Canal).
St. Mark's Basilica (Tour 1: The San Marco District).
Scuola di San Rocco (Tour 4: The Western and Northern Districts).

Tour 1: The San Marco District

Numbers in the margin correspond with points of interest on the Venice map.

① **Piazza San Marco** (St. Mark's Square) is the heart of Venice, perpetually animated during the day, when it's crowded with people and pigeons. It can be magical at night, especially in the winter, when melancholy mists swirl around the lampposts and bell tower. Historically and geographically, it's the logical place to start exploring the city. Go to the tourist information office in the far left corner of the piazza at the end opposite the church (*see* Important Addresses and Numbers in Essential Information, above). It can provide a list of current museum opening hours, which can change overnight if renovations are under way. While there, pick up a copy of *A Guest in Venice*, a free information booklet (also available at your hotel).

② At the other end of the square is **St. Mark's Basilica,** one of Europe's most beautiful churches, an opulent synthesis of Byzantine and Romanesque styles. It was begun in 1063 to house the remains of St. Mark the Evangelist, which were filched from Alexandria two centuries earlier by two agents of the doge (the annually elected ruler of Venice). The story goes that they stole the saint's remains and hid them in a barrel under

Venice

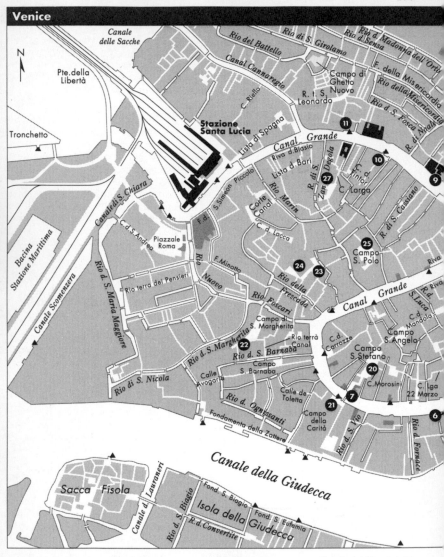

Sacca della Misericordia

Canale delle Navi

San Michele

0 — 440 yards
0 — 400 meters

Racchetta
Fondamente
Rio S. Caterina
28
29
R. d. Gesuiti Nuove
Rio della Panada
C. d. Squero
Canale delle Navi

Strada Nuova
Rio d. Santi Apostoli
Campo d. Pescheria
Erberia
26
del Vin
8
del Carbon
Merceria
R. d. Fava
Sol. di S. Lio
C. d. Bande
Campo Manin
Fabbri
Frezzaria
R. d. S. Moisè

13
C. d. Testa
R. Barbaria delle Tole
Campo Santi Giovanni e Paolo
14
Rio d. S. Marina
Rughe Giuffa
R. d. S. Severo
R. d. S. Lorenzo
12
Guistina
R. d. S.
15
R. d. S. Francesco
Canale d. Galeazze
C. Lion
19
C. d. Furlani
R. d. Scudi
R. d. Greci
R. d. Pietà
R. d. Gorna
Fond. Osmarin
4
1
2
3
5
7
R. d. Palazzo
Molo
Riva degli
Schiavoni
16
17
R. d. l'Arsenale
Piazza San Marco
Darsena Grande
Rio d. Vergini
Rio d. S. Daniele
C. di S. Pietro
18
Rio della Tana
V. Garibaldi
Riva dei Sette Martiri
Rio d. S. Anna
R. d. S. Giuseppe
R. d. Giardini

Canale di S. Marco

Isola di S. Giorgio Maggiore

Fond. delle Zitelle

Calle Michelangelo

Viale Trieste

Fond. delle Zitelle

▲ Boat stop

layers of pickled pork to get them past Islamic guards. That account and another legend connected with St. Mark's vision of an angel are illustrated in mosaics in the lunettes (semicircular decorations) over the main doors. Over the years the church has been endowed with all the riches Venetian admirals and merchants could carry off from the Orient. Among its treasures are the four gilded bronze horses in the church's upstairs museum, as well as precious columns and rare marbles; gem-studded icons seized in the sack of Constantinople in 1202; and the Pala d'Oro, a dazzling 10th-century altarpiece in gold and silver, encrusted with precious gems and enamels. In the dim light it's not easy to make out the figures in the mosaics that sheathe the upper walls and the domes, but their gold background gleams subtly even on the grayest day. Try to see the interior on a sunny day or during solemn services, when it is fully lit and presents a memorable spectacle. Be warned: Guards at the door turn away any visitors, male or female, wearing shorts or inappropriate clothing. *Open Mon.–Sat. 9:30–5:30, Sun. 2:30–5:30. Free guided visits in English (subject to the formation of English-speaking groups) are offered Mon.–Sat. at 11; groups form on the left in the atrium.*

The earliest mosaics in St. Mark's are those of Mary and the Apostles in the atrium of the church above the main door; they date back to the 11th century. Inside, the mosaics on the great domes were done in the 12th and 13th centuries. You can see how they contrast in style with the much later mosaics, those based on drawings by such masters as Titian and Tintoretto and easily distinguishable by their movement and color. Be sure to see the **Pala d'Oro** (Golden Altarpiece). The admission ticket is also valid for entrance to the **Treasury,** which contains some exquisite pieces, but lines may be long. *Pala d'Oro and Treasury. Admission: 2,000 lire. Open Apr.–Sept., Mon.–Sat. 9:30–5:30; Sun. 1:30–5:30; Oct.–Mar., Mon.–Sat. 10–5, Sun. 2–5.*

From the atrium, climb the steep stairway to the **Museo Marciano** (St. Mark's Museum) for a look at the interior of the church from the organ gallery and a sweeping view of Piazza San Marco and the Piazzetta dei Leoncini from the outdoor gallery. The highlight of the museum is the close-up of the four magnificent gilded bronze horses that once stood outside on the gallery, where copies now stand. The originals were probably cast in Constantinople in the 4th century AD, but some hold that they are Greek works of the 3rd century BC. *Admission: 2,000 lire. Open Apr.–Sept., daily 9:30–5:30; Nov.–Mar., daily 10–5.*

❸ Just outside St. Mark's is the tall brick **Campanile (Bell Tower),** a reconstruction of the original, which stood for 1,000 years before it collapsed one morning in 1912, practically without warning. In the 15th century, clerics found guilty of immoral behavior were suspended in wooden cages from the tower, sometimes to subsist on bread and water for as long as a year, sometimes to starve to death. The pretty marble loggia (covered gallery) at its base was built in the early 16th century by Florentine architect Jacopo Sansovino (1486–1570): It, too, has been carefully restored. The view from the tower on a clear day is worth the price of admission. You get a pigeon's-eye view of the city, the Lido, the lagoon, and the mainland as far as the distant Alps. Oddly, you can't see the myriad canals that snake through the 117 islets on which Venice is built. *Piazza San Marco, tel. 041/522-4064. Admission: 3,000 lire. Open Apr.–Oct., daily 9:30–7:30; Nov.–Mar., daily 10–4.*

Next look at Piazza San Marco, which abuts the Campanile and St. Mark's. The vast square is flanked by arcaded 16th-century buildings designed to house the administrative and judicial offices from which magistrates and clerks ran Venice's extensive empire. On the left of the square as you look toward St. Mark's is the **Torre dell' Orologio** (Clock Tower), erected in 1496 and endowed with an enameled timepiece and animated figures of Moors that strike the hour. During Ascension Week and on Epiphany (Jan. 6), an angel and three wise men go in and out of the doors and bow to the virgin. When Napoleon entered Venice with his troops in 1797, he dubbed Piazza San Marco "the world's most beautiful drawing room" and promptly gave orders to redecorate it. His architects demolished an old church at the far end of the square, opposite St. Mark's, and put up the Ala Napoleonica (Napoleonic Wing or Fabbrica Nuova) uniting the two elongated 16th-century buildings on either side.

A massive marble staircase in the Fabbrica Nuova leads to the **④ Museo Correr,** an interesting and varied collection of historical items and paintings by old masters, once the private collection of the aristocrat Teodoro Correr, who donated them to the city in 1830. Exhibits range from the absurdly high-soled shoes worn by 16th-century Venetian ladies (who had to be supported by a servant on each side in order to walk on these precarious perches) to fine artworks by the talented Bellini family of Renaissance painters. *Piazza San Marco, Ala Napoleonica, tel. 041/522-5625. Admission: 5,000 lire. Open Mon., Wed.–Sat. 10–4; Sun. 9–12:30.*

Time Out The obvious choice for a pleasant pause is one of the cafés on the square. **Florian** (closed Wed.) is the oldest and most famous; it's a historic coffeehouse where Casanova was a customer. All the cafés are fairly expensive, and all charge an additional tax for entertainment when the orchestra is playing. Like a gondola ride, this may be a splurge, but it's a treat you shouldn't miss. And, remember, you can linger as long as you like.

The square that leads from Piazza San Marco down to the waters of St. Mark's Basin is called the **Piazzetta San Marco.** **⑤** Above it rises the **Palazzo Ducale** (Doge's Palace), a Gothic-Renaissance fantasia of pink-and-white marble, a majestic expression of the prosperity and power attained by Venice during its most glorious period. Its top-heavy design (the dense upper floors rest on the graceful ground-floor colonnade) has always confounded architectural purists, who insist that proper architecture be set out the other way around. The palace was the residence of the doges, Venice's elected rulers, and the seat of the city's highest-ranking magistrates. You enter the palace at the ornate Gothic Porta della Carta (Gate of the Paper), which opens onto an immense courtyard. Ahead is the **Scala dei Giganti** (Stairway of the Giants), guarded by huge statues of Mars and Neptune. These were the work of Jacopo Sansovino. The palace is a magnificent maze of vast halls, monumental staircases, secret corridors, state apartments, and sinister prison cells. It's lit mainly by natural light, so try to see it on a bright day. Among the highlights are richly carved ceilings throughout, many of them framing paintings by Paolo Veronese

(1528–88) and other masters. The huge *Paradise* on the end wall of the **Great Council Hall** is by Jacopo Tintoretto (1518–94): It is a dark, dynamic masterpiece. This is the world's largest oil painting (23 by 75 feet), a vast work commissioned for a vast hall. Step onto the balcony of the Great Council Hall for a view of St. Mark's Basin, its waters churning with the wakes of countless boats. Look at the frieze of portraits of the first 76 doges around the upper part of the walls. One portrait is missing: Only a black void near the left-hand corner of the wall opposite Tintoretto's painting marks the spot where the portrait of doge Marin Falier should be. A Latin inscription bluntly explains that Falier was executed for treason in 1355. The Republic never forgave him.

At the ticket office of the Doge's Palace you can book a guided tour of the palace's secret rooms; it takes you to the doge's private apartments, up into the attic and Piombi prison, from which Casanova escaped, and through hidden passageways to the torture chambers, where prisoners were interrogated. Unfortunately, the tour is offered only in Italian. From the east wing of the Doge's Palace, the enclosed marble **Ponte dei Sospiri** (Bridge of Sighs) arches over a narrow canal to the cramped, gloomy cell blocks of the so-called New Prison. (The bridge was named for the sighs of those being led to prison.) On your way to the exit on the ground floor of the palace, you can see the **Pozzi Prison**—18 dark, dank cells that were set aside for the most hardened criminals. *Piazzetta San Marco, tel. 041/ 522–4951. Admission: 8,000 lire. Open daily May–Sept. 9–6, Oct.–Apr. 9–3. Secret Itineraries Tour 4 times daily; reserve at least a day ahead if possible. Cost: 5,000 lire.*

Tour 2: The Grand Canal

Catch Vaporetto Line 1 at the San Marco landing stage for a leisurely cruise along the **Grand Canal**, Venice's main thoroughfare. This 2-mile ribbon of water loops through the city. When the canal is busiest, usually in the morning, large and small craft crisscross its waters, stirring up a maelstrom that sets gondolas rocking and sends green waves slapping at the seaweed-slippery foundations of palaces. The quietest and most romantic time to ride in a gondola along the Grand Canal is about an hour or so before sunset: this is an experience you shouldn't miss. However, for an overall sightseeing tour of the canal, you get a better, more extensive view from the vaporetto—which is both higher in the water and much less expensive. Try to get one of the coveted seats in the prow, where you have a clear view.

The Grand Canal has an average depth of about 9 feet and varies from 40 to 76 yards in width. It winds like an inverted letter *S* through Venice, from the San Marco landing to the landing at the train station (Ferrovia), passing under three bridges and between 200 palaces dating from the 14th century to the 18th century, most of them in Venetian Gothic or Renaissance style. Don't even try to identify them; just take in the unparalleled magnificence of the scene, and enjoy watching the action along this unique watery avenue.

There are a few easily recognizable sights on the Grand Canal that may serve as landmarks when you venture out to explore the city: Starting from San Marco, look left for **Santa Maria del-**

la Salute, the huge, white, domed 17th-century church designed by the only great Venetian Baroque architect, Baldassare Longhena (1598–1682). On the same side is the low white
marble wall marking the never-completed palace that houses
the Peggy Guggenheim collection of modern art. On the left
❼ side of the first bridge you come to—the **Accademia Bridge**—is
the **Accademia Gallery.** The gallery is a treasure house of Venetian painting (*see* Tour 4: The Western and Northern Districts,
below). The canal narrows and boat traffic increases as you ap-
❽ proach the **Rialto Bridge.** The bridge was built in 1592, and the
vegetable and fish markets are on the left. This is a commercial
hub of the city, heart of a good shopping district.

The Ca'd'Oro landing on the right, just beyond the Rialto, iden-
❾ tifies the lovely Venetian Gothic palace of **Ca'd'Oro,** adorned
with marble traceries and ornaments that were once embel-
lished with pure gold. Not far beyond, on the left, another
❿ white church is adorned with Baroque statues; this is **San Stae,**
and the landing here is a gateway to a part of Venice that most
tourists never see, a neighborhood of narrow canals, airy
squares, and good *trattorie.* Another vaporetto stop away is
⑪ **San Marcuola,** on the right. This unfinished brick church is
guarded by cats and pigeons, and it marks the edge of another
district that is off the beaten track and well worth exploring:
Cannaregio and the old Jewish ghetto.

Tour 3: To the Arsenal and Beyond

To explore the city's eastern districts and see some of its most
beautiful churches, head out of Piazza San Marco under the
clock tower into the **Merceria,** one of Venice's busiest streets.
At Campo San Zulian and the church of San Giuliano, turn right
onto Calle Guerra and Calle delle Bande to reach the graceful
⑫ white marble church of **Santa Maria Formosa.** It's on a lively
square with a few sidewalk cafés and a small vegetable market
on weekday mornings. Follow Calle Borgoloco into Campo San
Marina, where you turn right, cross the little canal, and take
⑬ Calle Castelli to the church of **Santa Maria dei Miracoli.** Per-
fectly proportioned and sheathed in marble, it's an early-Ren-
aissance gem, decorated inside with exquisite marble reliefs.

Behind the church, bear right to Calle Gallina, which leads to
Campo Santi Giovanni e Paolo, site of the massive Dominican
church of San Giovanni e Paolo, or San Zanipolo, as it's known
in the slurred Venetian dialect. The powerful equestrian **monument of Bartolomeo Colleoni** by Florentine sculptor Andrea del
Verrocchio (1435–88) stands in the square. Colleoni had served
Venice well as a *condottiere,* or mercenary commander (the Venetians preferred to pay others to fight for them and had the
money to do it). When he died in 1475, he left his fortune to
the city on the condition that a statue be erected in his honor "in
the piazza before St. Mark's." The republic's shrewd administrators coveted Colleoni's ducats but had no intention of honoring anyone, no matter how valorous, with a statue in Piazza San
Marco. So they commissioned the statue and put it up in the piazza before the Scuola di San Marco, headquarters of a charitable confraternity that happened to have the right name,
⑭ enabling them to collect the loot. The Church of **Santi Giovanni
e Paolo** is a kind of pantheon of the doges and contains a wealth
of artworks. Don't miss the Rosary Chapel, off the left cross-

ing; it's a sumptuous study in decoration, built in the 16th century to commemorate the victory of Lepanto in western Greece in 1571, when Venice led a combined European fleet in destroying the Turkish navy.

⑮ Continue beyond Santi Giovanni e Paolo to another large church, **San Francesco della Vigna,** built by Sansovino in 1534. A pretty cloister opens out from the severely simple gray-and-white interior. Not many tourists find their way here, and local youngsters play ball in the square shadowed by the church's austere classical Palladian facade.

⑯ Go left as you leave the church to begin the 500-yard walk to the **Campo dell'Arsenale,** at the main entrance to the **Arsenal,** an immense dockyard founded in 1104 to build and equip the fleet of the Venetian republic. Four stone lions from ancient Greece guard the great Renaissance gateway.

⑰ The **Museo Navale** (Naval Museum) on nearby Campo San Biagio has four floors of full-scale boat models, from gondolas and doges' ceremonial boats to Chinese junks, as well as other smaller boats guaranteed to fascinate children—and boat lovers. *Campo San Biagio, tel. 041/520–0276. Admission: 1,000 lire. Open Mon.–Fri. 9–1, Sat. 9–noon.*

⑱ If you still have time and energy, go east to the island and church of **San Pietro di Castello.** Two footbridges lead to this island. The church served as Venice's cathedral for centuries; now it presides over a picturesque workaday neighborhood, and its tipsy bell tower leans over a grassy square.

Time Out If you're this far afield, you may need sustenance to get you back to the center of town. There are several moderately priced snack bars and trattorie on Via Garibaldi, midway between the Arsenal and the island of San Pietro. **Sottoprova** (closed Tues.) has tables outdoors.

⑲ About midway between the Arsenal and St. Mark's, on your way back from the eastern district, is the **Scuola di San Giorgio degli Schiavoni,** one of six *scuole* built during the time of the Republic. These weren't schools, as the present-day Italian word would imply, but confraternities devoted to charitable works. Each scuola was decorated lavishly, both in the private chapels and in the meeting halls where work was discussed. The Scuola di San Giorgio degli Schiavoni features works by Vittore Carpaccio (ca. 1465–1525), a local artist who often filled his otherwise devotional paintings with acutely observed details of Venetian life. Study the exuberance of his *St. George* as he slays the dragon or the vivid colors and details in *The Funeral of St. Jerome* and *St. Augustine in His Study. Calle dei Furlani, tel. 041/522–8828. Admission: 3,000 lire. Open Tues.–Sat. 9:30–12:30, 3:30–6:30, Sun. 10–12:30.*

Tour 4: The Western and Northern Districts

If churches, art, and sculpture and further ramblings through the back streets and along the old canals of Venice continue to interest you, head out of Piazza San Marco under the arcades of the Fabbrica Nuova at the far end of the square. If you want to make a detour for an expensive drink at **Harry's Bar,** just turn left down Calle Valleresso, behind the Hotel Luna. Then head ⑳ for **Campo Morosini,** which everyone calls by its old name, Campo San Stefano, in honor of the 14th-century church off to one side of the square; stop in to see the ship's-keel roof, a type found in several of Venice's older churches and the work of its master shipbuilders.

Time Out **Café Paolin,** with tables occupying most of one end of the square, is reputed to have Venice's best ice cream. It's a pleasant place to sit and watch the passing parade.

⓴ Join the stream of pedestrians crossing the Grand Canal on the Accademia Bridge (under which you pass on Tour 2) and head for the **Accademia Gallery,** Venice's most important picture gallery. It has an extraordinary collection of Venetian paintings, attractively displayed and well lit. Highlights include works from 14th-century altarpieces and Giovanni Bellini's 15th-century oils, aglow with color, to the Golden Age of the 16th century, with the colorful and expressive works of Tiziano Vecellio (Titian 1487–1576) and Jacopo Tintoretto, and the grand compositions of Paolo Veronese. The 18th century is well represented by Giovanni Battista Tiepolo (1696–1770) and his followers. Be sure to see the *Tempest,* by Giorgione (1477–1510), and Veronese's monumental canvas, recently cleaned, *The Feast in the House of Levi.* This last painting was commissioned as a Last Supper, but the Inquisition took issue with Veronese's inclusion of jesters and German soldiers in the painting. Veronese avoided the charge of sacrilege by changing the title, and the picture was then supposed to depict the bawdy, but still biblical, feast of Levi. *Campo della Carità, tel. 041/522–2247. Admission: 8,000 lire. Open Mon.–Sat. 9–2, Sun. 9–1.*

Time Out Between the Accademia and San Barnaba, on Calle Toelletta, is **Ae Meravegie** (closed Sun.), a coffee bar and sandwich shop with a variety of tasty sandwiches, quiches, and beer.

Off Campo San Barnaba, on Fondamenta Gherardini, you'll see a floating fruit and vegetable market tied up in the canal. It's one of the few left in Venice. Continue toward Campo Santa Margherita; on your way you can look for two of Venice's best mask shops (*see* Shopping, below). **Cà Macana** is on Calle Boteghe; here you can see how masks are made. **Mondonovo,** on Rio Terra Canal, displays inventive masks.

⓶⓶ At **Campo Santa Margherita,** a busy neighborhood shopping square, stop in to see Tiepolo's ceiling paintings in the **Scuola dei Carmini.** The paintings, now displayed on the second floor, were commissioned to honor the Carmelite order by depicting prominent Carmelites in conversation with saints and angels. Tiepolo's vivid techniques transformed some unpromising religious themes into flamboyant displays of color and movement. Mirrors are available on the benches to make it easier to see the ceiling without getting a sore neck. *Campo dei Carmini, tel. 041/528–9420. Admission: 5,000 lire. Open Mon.–Sat. 9–noon, 3–6.*

⓶⓷ Continue on to the **Frari,** an immense Gothic church built in the 14th century for the Franciscans. In keeping with the austere principles of the Franciscan order, the Frari is quite stark inside, with much less ornamentation than other Venetian churches. The relative absence of decoration gives a select feeling to the church paintings, such as Bernini's *Madonna and*

Four Saints in the sacristy. The most striking is Titian's large *Assumption* over the main altar. Titian cleverly used the design of the church interior to frame his painting. The *Pesaro Madonna* over the first altar on the left nave near the main altar is also by Titian; his wife, who died shortly afterward in childbirth, posed for the figure of Mary. On the same side of the church, look at sculptor Canova's spooky pyramid-shape tomb.

㉔ Behind the Frari is the **Scuola di San Rocco,** filled with dark, dramatic canvases by Tintoretto. In 1564, the Venetian-born artist beat other painters competing for the commission to decorate this building by submitting not a sketch but a finished work, which he additionally offered free of charge. The more than 50 paintings took a total of 23 years to complete. These works, depicting Old and New Testament themes, were restored in the 1970s, and Tintoretto's inventive use of light has once more been revealed. *Campo San Rocco, tel. 041/523–4864. Admission: 5,000 lire. Open daily 10–1, 3:30–6:30.*

The area around San Rocco is well off the normal tourist trail, with narrow alleys and streets winding alongside small canals to little squares, where posters advertising political parties and sports events seem to be the only signs of life. Head back
㉕ past the Frari by way of Rio Terrà **Campo San Polo,** one of Venice's largest squares, and a favorite playground for neighborhood children. From here you take Calle della Madonetta, Calle dell'Olio, Ruga Ravano, and Ruga Vecchia San Giovanni
㉖ in the **Rialto** shopping district, where you can cross the Grand Canal for the shortcut back to San Marco. Alternatively, you can go north from Campo San Polo by way of Calle Bernardo, Calle del Scaleter, Rio Terrá Parrucchetta, and Calle del
㉗ Tintor to **Campo San Giacomo dell'Orio,** where the 13th-century church of San Giacomo stands on a charming square that few tourists ever find. Here you're not far from the **San Stae** vaporetto landing, so you can take the boat back along the Grand Canal to the heart of the city.

Tour 5: Islands of the Lagoon

Narrow channels help boats negotiate the shallow waters of the Venetian lagoon, with its islands of San Michele, Murano, Burano, and Torcello. These islands are famous for their handicrafts—notably glass and lace—but guided tours here usually involve high-pressure attempts to make you buy, with little time left for anything else. It's much cheaper and more adventurous to make your own way around the islands, using the good vaporetto connections. Services to and from Venice use the landing stage at Fondamente Nuove, almost due north of St. Mark's. The most distant island, Torcello, is ideal for picnics but has no food stores. Buy provisions in Venice if you plan to picnic there.

㉘ If you're making your way on foot to Fondamente Nuove, stop at the church of the **Gesuiti,** which dominates the Campo dei Gesuiti. This 18th-century church is built in an extravagantly Baroque style; the classical arches and straight lines of the Renaissance have been abandoned in favor of flowing, twisting forms. The marble of the gray-and-white interior is used like brocade, carved into swags and drapes. Titian's *Martyrdom of St. Lawrence,* over the first altar on the left, is a dramatic example of the great artist's feel for light and movement.

㉙ From **Fondamente Nuove** you have a choice of vaporetti. Line 5 goes to San Michele and Murano; Line 12, which you can join at Murano, skips San Michele and goes to Murano, Burano, and Torcello.

Numbers in the margin correspond with points of interest on the Venetian Lagoon map.

㉚ It's only a five-minute ride to **San Michele,** the smallest of the islands, which is taken up almost completely with the pretty Renaissance church of **San Michele in Isola,** designed by Coducci in 1478, and Venice's **cemetery.** It is a moving experience to walk among the gravestones, with the sound of lapping water on all sides. Ezra Pound, the great Russian impresario, art critic Sergey Diaghilev, and Igor Stravinsky are buried here.

㉛ Another five minutes on Line 5 takes you to **Murano,** which, like Venice, is made up of a number of smaller islands, linked by bridges. Murano is known exclusively for its glassworks, which you can visit to see how glass is made. Many of these line the **Fondamenta dei Vetrai,** the canalside walkway leading away from the landing stage. The houses along this walk are much more colorful—and a lot simpler—than their Venetian counterparts; traditionally they were workmen's cottages. Just before the junction with Murano's Grand Canal—250 yards up from the landing stage—is the church of **San Pietro Martire.** This 16th-century reconstruction of an earlier Gothic church has two works by Venetian masters: the *Madonna and Child,* by Giovanni Bellini, and *St. Jerome,* by Veronese.

Cross the Ponte Vivarini and turn right onto **Fondamenta Cavour.** About 100 yards up on the left is the **Museo Vetrario** (Glass Museum), with a collection of Venetian glass that ranges from priceless antique to only slightly less expensive modern. The museum gives you a good idea of the history of Murano's glassworks, which were moved here from Venice in the 13th century because they were a fire risk. It's useful, too, to get a clear idea of authentic Venetian styles and patterns if you're planning to make some purchases later. *Admission: 5,000 lire. Open Mon., Tues., Thurs.–Sat. 10–4, Sun. 9–12:30.*

㉜ Make your way back along the same route to the landing stage and take Line 12 to **Burano,** which is about 30 minutes from Murano. It's a small island fishing village with houses painted in cheerful colors and a raffishly raked bell tower on the main square, about 100 yards from the landing stage and clearly visible. Lace is to Burano what glass is to Murano, but be prepared to pay a lot for the real thing. Stalls line the way from the landing stage to **Piazza Galuppi,** the main square; the vendors, many of them fishermen's wives, are generally good-natured and unfamiliar with the techniques of the hard sell.

The **Consorzio Merletti di Burano** (Lace Museum) on Piazza Galuppi is the best place to learn the intricacies of the lace-making traditions of Burano. It is also useful for learning the nature of the skills involved in making the more expensive lace, in case you intend to buy some lace on your way back to the vaporetto. *Piazza Galuppi. Admission: 4,000 lire. Open daily 9–6.*

Venetian Lagoon

MESTRE
Marco Polo Airport
Torcello 33
Burano 32
Murano 31
San Michele 30
Malcontenta
Cavallino
VENICE ○ Lido
○ Malamocco
○ Alberoni
Golfo di Venezia
N
○ Pellestrina
○ Chióggia
Laguna Veneta
0   4 miles
0   6 km

Time Out Among the pleasant *trattorie* on Piazza Galuppi are **Ai Pescatori** (closed Mon.) and **Romano** (closed Tues.). Both serve seafood specialties à la carte, but keep your eye on the costs.

Vaporetto Line 12 continues from the Burano landing stage to the sleepy green island of **Torcello,** about 10 minutes farther. This is where the first Venetians landed in their flight from the barbarians 1,500 years ago. Even after many settlers left to found the city of Venice on the island of Rivo Alto (Rialto), Torcello continued to grow and prosper, until its main source of income, wool manufacturing, was priced out of the marketplace. It's hard to believe now, looking at this almost deserted island, that in the 16th century it had 20,000 inhabitants and 10 churches.

A brick-paved lane leads up from the landing stage and follows the curve of the canal toward the center of the island. You pass **Locanda Cipriani,** an inn famous for its good food and the patronage of Ernest Hemingway, who often came to Torcello for the solitude. These days Locanda Cipriani is about the busiest spot on the island, as well-heeled customers arrive on high-speed powerboats for lunch.

Just beyond is the grassy square that holds the only surviving monuments of the island's past splendor. The low church of **Santa Fosca,** on the right, dates back to the 11th century. Next to it is the **cathedral,** also built in the 11th century: The ornate Byzantine mosaics are testimony to the importance and wealth of an island that could attract the best artists and craftsmen of its day. The vast mosaic on the inside of the facade depicts the

Last Judgment as artists of the 11th and 12th centuries imagined it: Figures writhe in vividly depicted contortions of pain. Facing it, as if in mitigation, is the calm mosaic figure of the Madonna, alone in a field of gold above the staunch array of Apostles.

The trip back from Torcello retraces the route from Venice. Boats leave every hour, and the trip takes about 50 minutes.

Venice for Free

The bad news is that the lack of cars and trucks in Venice pushes prices up considerably, at least in the realm of food and drink. What cannot be ferried to a restaurant or shop doorstep must be pushed or carried through the narrow streets of the city; the consumer is the one who pays for this increased labor cost. The good news is that once you've arrived in Venice, you're standing in the greatest attraction—the city itself—and individual sights are almost like icing on the cake.

Churches, of course, are free. While some are outstandingly decorated or filled with historical significance, the only money you'll pay will be the 100- or 200-lire coins needed to throw some light on a side chapel.

Collezione Peggy Guggenheim. Entrance is free on Saturday evenings from 6 to 9.

What to See and Do with Children

The whole experience of a visit to Venice should provide excitement for a child. For the parent it means trading one constant warning ("Look both ways before crossing") for another ("Stay away from the edge of that canal"). Wandering over the many footbridges and along narrow alleyways leading nowhere, children get a chance to burn off a lot of excess energy, and sometimes their aimless rambles lead to an unexpected square or little church. But there are not many activities aimed at children.

Glassblowing. Go to one of the showrooms with demonstrations along Fondamenta dei Vetrai in Murano. (*See* Tour 5: Islands of the Lagoon, above).

Gondola ride. Your child will probably have suggested this more than once, long before you even arrive in Venice. Gondoliers usually perform well for children, demonstrating how they steer and calling out to other traffic as they near a junction.

Lion Statues. These guardians of the Arsenal are a reminder of Venice's glorious naval past (*See* Tour 3: To the Arsenal and Beyond, above). The lions in Piazzetta dei Leoncini are fine mounts for tots (*see* Tour 1: The San Marco District, above).

Museo Navale (*See* Tour 3: To the Arsenal and Beyond, above).

Torre dell'Orologio. The hourly display when the bronze bell is struck always draws a crowd of young and old (*See* Tour 1: The San Marco District, above).

Winter Carnival. A Ferris wheel hung with colored lights and a merry-go-round come to Riva degli Schiavoni every February. Children also enjoy dressing up in masks or full costume during the carnival festivities during the two weeks before Ash Wednesday.

Off the Beaten Track

Fort of San Andrea. Built on the island of Certosa just northeast of Venice, this great fort dates from the 16th century, when Venetian naval power reached its peak. Huge chains were stretched from the fort to the Lido to prevent enemy ships from entering the Lagoon. These days it serves a more peaceful purpose, as a quiet spot for picnics or just getting away from crowds. *Take Vaporetto 14 from San Nicolò on the Lido (see Lido, below).*

The Ghetto. In 1516, Venice's Great Council ordered all Jews to be confined to a small island in Cannaregio. They were not allowed to leave this area after sunset, when the huge gates were barred until dawn. Jewish physicians, whose services were favored by the aristocrats, were the only exception. The ghetto expanded to Ghetto Vecchio and Ghetto Novissimo. In 1797 Napoleon's troops freed the people, but by that time their synagogues and homes were rooted in these neighborhoods. The **Museo Ebraico** is in one corner of Campo Ghetto Nuovo, a pretty square with a fountain and a few trees. From the museum, you can join a guided tour of the synagogues; tours are in English and are given several times a day. *From the Cannaregio Canal, cross Ponte dei Tre Archi and follow the canal as far as Sottoportego del Ghetto. Campo del Ghetto Nuovo, tel. 041/521-5359. Open mid-Mar.–mid-Nov., weekdays 10:30–1, 2:30–5, Sun. 10:30–1; closed Sat. and Jewish holidays. Mid-Nov.–mid-Mar., weekdays and Sun. 10–12:30; closed Sat. and Jewish holidays.*

Giudecca. Eight islands make up this eel-shape strip of land, which lies across the San Marco Basin from the heart of Venice. Slightly removed from the city, it has always been seen as a place apart, first as a colony for Jews in the 13th century (possibly leading to its name) and later as a pleasure garden for wealthy Venetians, during the long and luxurious decline of the Republic. The Giudecca is dominated by the church of **Il Redentore.**

Isola di San Giorgio Maggiore. When you look out into the Canal of San Marco, you can see this island, separated by a small channel from the Giudecca. It is dominated by the Palladian church of San Giorgio Maggiore and the former Benedictine monastery. Inside the airy and simply decorated church, look for Tintoretto's *Last Supper* and *Shower of Manna.* The church's bell tower affords a great view of Venice and its harbor, and on a clear day you can see the Dolomites in the distance. An elevator takes you to the top. The monastery now houses an artistic foundation and usually is closed to the public. *Take a vaporetto from Riva degli Schiavoni or Fondamenta delle Zitelle. Admission to Bell Tower: 2,000 lire. Open daily 9–12:30, 2–6.*

Lido. This island, forming the north–south barrier for the Lagoon, has the best beaches for sunbathing, but the Adriatic Sea is too polluted for swimming anywhere near Venice. There are municipal tennis courts and a horse-riding club. Hotels Des Bains and Cipriani have exclusive clubs with lovely swimming pools. The famous Lido Casino operates during the summer months only. The church and monastery of San Nicolo are on the northern end of the island; during the week, this is a pleasant place for a walk and lunch. Avoid the Sunday crowds; most restaurants are closed on Monday. *Take vaporetto 2 or 4 to Piazzale Maria Elisabetta. Bus A goes north to San Nicolo.*

Madonna dell'Orto. This was Tintoretto's parish church; he was buried just to the right of the main altar. On each side of the altar are his paintings *The Last Judgment* and *Adoration of the Golden Calf.* In the latter, he supposedly painted his own face (with a black beard) on one of the pagans holding the calf. There are several more of his paintings and work by other artists here. *Cannaregio district, off Fondamenta Madonna dell'Orto, across the canal from the Palazzo Mastelli.*

Shopping

Shopping in Venice is part of the fun of exploring the city, and you're sure to find plenty of interesting shops and boutiques as you explore. It's always a good idea to mark on your map the location of a shop that interests you; otherwise, you may not be able to find it again in mazelike Venice. Shops are usually open 9–1 and 3:30 or 4–7:30 and are closed Sunday and on Monday morning. However, many tourist-oriented shops are open all day, every day. Food shops are closed Wednesday afternoon, except in July and August, when they close Saturday afternoon. Some shops close for both a summer and a winter vacation.

Shopping Districts The main shopping areas are the **Mercerie,** the succession of narrow and crowded streets winding from Piazza San Marco to the Rialto, and the area around Campo San Salvador, Calle del Teatro, Campo Manin, and Campo San Fantin. If you can't face the crowds on the Mercerie, go a little out of the way to the **Strada Nuova,** between Santi Apostoli and the train station, where many Venetians shop. The **San Marco** area is full of shops and top-name boutiques, such as Missoni, Valentino, Fendi, and Versace.

Department Stores The only thing approximating a department store here is **Coin,** at the Rialto bridge, featuring men's and women's fashions. The **Standa** stores on Campo San Luca and Strada Nuova have a wide range of goods at moderate prices.

Food Markets The open-air fruit and vegetable market at **Rialto** is colorful and animated throughout the morning, when Venetian housewives come to pick over the day's offerings and haggle with vendors. The adjacent fish market offers a vivid lesson in ichthyology, presenting some species you've probably never seen (open mornings Mon.–Sat.). At the other end of Venice, in the Castello district, is **Via Garibaldi,** the scene of another lively food market on weekday mornings.

Specialty Stores Glass, most of it made in Murano, is Venice's number-one prod-
Glassware uct, and you'll be confronted by mind-boggling displays of traditional and contemporary glassware, often kitsch. Take your time and be selective. Should you buy glass in Venice's shops or in the showrooms of Murano's factories? You will probably find that prices are pretty much the same; showrooms in Venice that are outlets of Murano glassworks sell at the same prices as the factories. However, because of competition, shops in Venice

stocking wares from various glassworks may charge slightly lower prices.

In Venice, **Venini** (Piazzetta dei Leoncini 314), **Pauli** (Calle dell'Ascensione 72), and **Salviati** (Piazza San Marco 78 and 110) are reliable and respected firms. For chic, contemporary glassware, **Carlo Moretti** is a good choice; his signature designs are on display at **Isola** (Campo San Moisè). For stunning glass beads and jewelry, go to **Archimede Seguso** (Piazza San Marco); **Vetri d'Arte** (Piazza San Marco) offers moderately priced glass jewelry. In a category all his own is **Gianfranco Penzo** (Campo del Ghetto Nuovo 2895), who decorates Jewish ritual vessels in glass, makes commemorative plates, and takes special orders.

In Murano, most of the glass factories have showrooms where glassware is sold. The **Domus** shop (Fondamenta dei Vetrai) has a selection of smaller objects and jewelry from the best glassworks.

Lace Venice's top name is **Jesurum,** with a shop at Piazza San Marco 60 and a much larger establishment at Ponte Canonica, behind St. Mark's. **Martinuzzi, Fabris,** and **Tokatzian,** all on Piazza San Marco, also have a good selection. Remember that much of the lace and embroidered linen sold in Venice and on Burano is made in China or Taiwan. For the same sumptuous brocades, damasks, and cut velvets used by the world's most prestigious decorators, go to **Lorenzo Rubelli** (Campo San Gallo 1089), just off Piazza San Marco. At **Norelene** (Campo San Maurizio 2606), you'll find stunning hand-printed fabrics.

Masks These are a tradition in Venice; they were worn everywhere during the 18th century, especially by theatergoers, gamblers, and carnival revelers. Shops throughout the city sell masks of all types. Among the most interesting are **Mondonovo** (Rio Terra Canal), **Cà Macana** (Calle delle Botteghe, near San Barnaba), and **Laboratorio Artigiano Maschere** (Barbaria delle Tole), near Santi Giovanni e Paolo).

Prints An old print of Venice makes a distinctive gift or souvenir. There's an excellent selection at **O. Bohm** (Salizzada San Moisè, just off Piazza San Marco). Hand-printed paper and desk accessories, memo pads, and address books abound at the well-known **Piazzesi** shop (Campiello della Feltrina, near Santa Maria del Giglio).

Sports

Golf The **Golf Club Lido di Venezia,** an 18-hole course, is located on the Lido island. *Via del Forte, Alberoni, Lido, tel. 041/731015.*

Horseback Riding **Circolo Ippico Veneziano** (tel. 041/765162) is located at Ca' Bianca on the Lido. It is open all year.

Jogging The best spot to jog is along the waterfront walkway of the Giudecca (*see* Off the Beaten Track, above); it's probably the longest uninterrupted stretch of sidewalk in Venice, and it rarely gets crowded.

Swimming Considering the polluted state of the Adriatic, the only place to swim is at a pool. Venice's public pool is the **Piscina Gandini** (tel. 041/523-1932), located on Isola di San Giorgio. The deluxe hotels **Excelsior** (tel. 041/526-0201) and **Des Bains** (tel. 041/

765921) are both located on Lungomare Marconi on the Lido; their pools are open to nonguests.

Tennis The municipal courts on **Lungomare d'Annunzio** (tel. 041/ 709955), on the Lido, are open only in the summer. The **Hotel des Bains** (*see* Swimming, above) and the exclusive **Sea Gull Club** of the Hotel Cipriani (tel. 041/520–7744) will let nonguests play for a fee.

Dining

The general standard of Venetian restaurants has suffered from the onslaught of mass tourism. It is very difficult to eat well in Venice at moderate prices. Although seafood is a specialty here, it's no bargain, and you will find some fish dishes very expensive, especially those that are priced by weight (mainly baked or steamed fish). Under the auspices of the restaurant association, most of the city's restaurants offer special tourist menus, moderately priced according to the level of the restaurant and generally representing good value. It's always a good idea to reserve your table or have your hotel *portiere* do it for you. Dining hours are short, starting at 12:30 or 1 for lunch and ending at 2:30, when restaurants close for the afternoon, opening up again to start serving at about 8 and closing again at 11 or midnight. Most close one day a week and are also likely to close without notice for vacation or renovation. Few have signs on the outside, so when the metal blinds are shut tight, you can't tell a closed restaurant from a closed TV-repair shop. This makes them hard to spot when you are exploring the city. You may not find a cover charge (*pane e coperto*), but a service charge of 15%–20% will almost surely be on the check.

Venetian cuisine is based on seafood, with a few culinary excursions inland. Antipasto may take the form of a seafood salad, *prosciutto di San Daniele* (cured ham) from the mainland, or pickled vegetables. As a first course Venetians favor risotto, a creamy rice dish that may be cooked with vegetables or shellfish. Pasta, too, is good with seafood sauces; Venice is *not* the place to order spaghetti with tomato sauce. *Pasticcio di pesce* is pasta baked with fish, usually *baccalà* (dried cod). A classic first course is *pasta e fagioli* (thick bean soup with pasta). *Bigoli* is strictly a local pasta, made of whole wheat, usually served with a salty *tonno* (tuna) sauce. Polenta, made of cornmeal, is another pillar of regional cooking. It's often served as an accompaniment to *fegato alla veneziana* (liver with onion, Venetian style). Local seafood includes *granseola* (crab) and *seppie* or *seppioline* (cuttlefish).

The dessert specialty in Venice is *tiramesù* (a heavenly concoction of creamy cheese, coffee, and chocolate with pound cake); the recipe originated on the mainland, but the Venetians have adopted it enthusiastically. Local wines are the dry white Tocai and Pinot from the Friuli region and bubbly white Prosecco, a naturally fermented sparkling white wine that is a shade less dry. The best Prosecco comes from the Valdobbiadene; Cartizze, which is similar, is considered superior by some. You can sample all of these and more in Venice's many wineshops, where wine is served by the glass and accompanied by *cicchetti* (assorted tidbits), often substantial enough for a light meal.

Highly recommended restaurants in each price category are indicated by a star ★.

Category	Cost*
Very Expensive	over 150,000 lire
Expensive	90,000–150,000 lire
Moderate	50,000–90,000 lire
Inexpensive	under 50,000 lire

per person, including three courses, wine, and service

Very Expensive

★ **Antico Martini.** A Venetian institution known for good food, Antico Martini has an elegant look, neoclassical columns, and a pretty pink-accented dining terrace overlooking La Fenice theater. In the winter you dine in cozy wood-paneled salons. Specialties are seasonal and might include *petti di pollo San Giorgio* (breast of chicken with cream and mushrooms), kidneys flambé, and vegetarian ravioli. A four-course *menu gastronomico* (fixed-price menu) is an excellent value at about 60,000 lire, including cover and service charges. *Campo San Fantin 1983, tel. 041/522–4121. Reservations advised. Jacket and tie required. AE, DC, MC, V. Closed Tues., Wed. lunch, Dec.–mid Mar. but open for Christmas and Carnival seasons.*

Danieli Terrace. The famous Danieli Hotel provides a superlative location for a very special meal, which you can enjoy on the terrace in fair weather or in the pastel-toned dining room. Either way you have a picture-postcard view of San Giorgio and the lagoon. Cuisine and prices are on a par with the ambience. *Branzino al forno* (baked sea bass) and scampi take the honors here, and the desserts are as dreamy as the view. *Hotel Danieli, Riva degli Schiavoni 4196, tel. 041/522–6480. Reservations advised. Jacket and tie required. AE, DC, MC, V.*

La Caravella. One of Venice's top locales, near St. Mark's, is the setting for this small and intimate restaurant with old-time sailing-ship decor. La Caravella has a reputation for fine food and cordial, courteous service. Among the specialties on the vast menu are the very Venetian *taglierini alla granseola* (delicate pasta with crab sauce) and scampi in port sauce. *Calle Larga XXII Marzo 2397, tel. 041/5208901. Reservations required. Dress: casual. AE, DC, MC, V. Closed Wed. from Nov. to Apr.*

Expensive

Arturo. The cordial proprietor of this tiny restaurant near Campo Sant'Angelo has the distinction (in Venice) of not serving seafood. Instead, spaghetti with seasonal vegetables and meat dishes, such as *braciolona di maiale* (pork chop in vinegar), are tasty, as are the *porcini* mushrooms, in season. *Rioterrà degli Assassini, tel. 041/528–6974. Reservations required. Dress: casual. No credit cards. Closed Sun., Dec., Aug.*

Cortile. Set in a lovely garden court shaded by awnings and bright with blossoms, this open-air restaurant is refreshing by day and romantic by night, when you dine by candlelight. In the winter it moves indoors to wood-paneled Venetian-style salons. The specialties are *crespelle* (crepes) and flambé dishes; it shares the kitchen of La Caravella but its prices are a notch lower. *Calle Larga XXII Marzo 2402, tel. 041/5208738. Reser-*

vations not necessary. Dress: casual. AE, DC, MC, V. Closed Wed.

Do Forni. The entrance and one dining room (there are several, ranging in decor from Venetian provincial to classic trattoria) are replicas of the dining car of the *Orient Express.* The menu is enormous, but the courteous waiters will help you choose among Venetian specialties such as *zuppa di mare alla chioggiotta* (fish stew) and *rombo Do Forni* (turbot) and other Italian dishes. There's a wide choice of desserts and a fizzy house Prosecco that is very pleasant. *Calle dei Specchier 468, tel. 041/523-7729. Reservations not necessary. Dress: casual. AE, DC, MC, V. Closed Thurs. (open daily in summer) and Nov. 20–Dec. 6.*

★ **Fiaschetteria Toscana.** You'll soon see why this is one of the most popular restaurants with the Venetians themselves, whether you eat in the upstairs dining room or under the arbor on the square. Cheerful, courteous waiters may suggest the delicate *tagliolini alla buranella* (thin noodles with shrimp) or *rombo* (turbot) with capers. The local clientele insists on good value and a friendly atmosphere. *Campo San Giovanni Crisostomo, tel. 041/528-5281. Reservations advised. Dress: casual. AE, DC, MC, V. Closed Tues., July 1–15.*

★ **Noemi.** Centrally located, near St. Mark's, this attractive restaurant is in the tourist mainstream but maintains high standards of cuisine and service. The menu gastronomico (about 60,000 lire) offers several choices in a four-course framework, and there's a three-course lunch menu of Venetian specialties (about 40,000 lire). Otherwise you order à la carte. Specialties are *cannelloni allo smeraldino* (with chopped chicken, cheese, and spinach) and veal chop *alla zingara* (with olives and capers). *Calle dei Fabbri, tel. 041/522-5238. Reservations advised. Dress: casual. AE, DC, MC, V. Closed Sun. and Mon. lunch, Dec. 15–Jan. 31.*

Moderate **Corte Sconta.** Near the Arsenale, this very Venetian trattoria isn't easy to find, but is worth the effort. It has been a favorite with locals for many years and has gradually been discovered by enterprising tourists. The atmosphere and service are informal, and seafood is the specialty (it would be the only thing on the menu, if there were a menu). Take along your travel dictionary, for the waitress will recite the list of fish dishes depending on what was in the market that morning. Try *spaghetti con nero di seppie* (with a sauce of squid ink), roast fish or *baccalà mantecato*, (salt cod pounded to a paste). *Calle del Pestrin 3886, Castello (near San Giovanni in Bragora), tel. 041/522-7024. Reservations advised. Dress: casual. AE, MC, V.*

Da Fiore. Long a favorite with Venetians, Da Fiore has been discovered by tourists, so it's imperative to reserve for an excellent seafood dinner, which might include such specialties as *pasticcio di pesce* (fish pie) and *seppioline* (cuttlefish). Not easy to find, it's near Campo San Polo. *Calle Scalater 2202, tel. 041/721308. Reservations necessary. Dress: casual. AE, DC, V. Closed Sun., Mon., Aug. 10–early Sept., and Dec. 25–Jan. 15.*

Da Ignazio. Smallish, pleasant, and handy to the Rialto district, Ignazio is reliable for good food at reasonable prices, barring expensive fish dishes. The cuisine is classic Venetian here, from pasta or risotto with seafood sauce to *fegato alla veneziana* (liver with onions), but there are standard Italian items as well. *Calle dei Saoneri 2749, tel. 041/523-4852. Reservations advised. Dress: casual. AE, DC, MC, V. Closed Sat.*

Venice Dining and Lodging

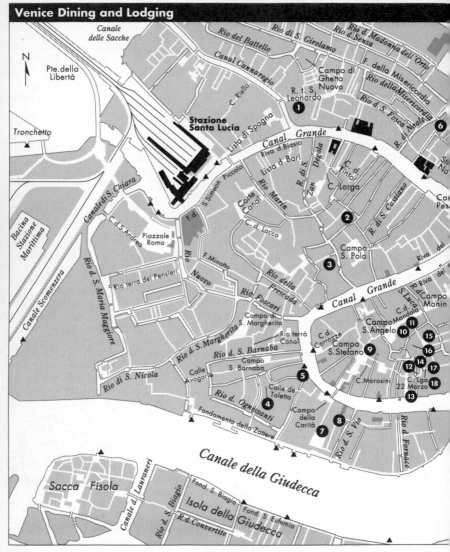

Dining
Ai Cugnai, **8**
Antica Adelaide, **6**
Antico Martini, **15**
Arturo, **11**
Corte Sconta, **28**
Cortile, **14**
Da Fiore, **2**

Da Ignazio, **3**
Danieli Terrace, **23**
Do Forni, **21**
Fiaschetteria
Toscana, **19**
Gazebo, **1**
La Caravella, **17**
Montin, **4**
Noemi, **20**
Vino Vino, **10**

Lodging
Accademia, **5**
Alboretti, **7**
Cipriani, **24**
Danieli, **23**
Fenice, **16**
Flora, **18**
Gritti Palace, **13**

La Residenza, **27**
Londra Palace, **25**
Metropole, **26**
San Stefano, **9**
Saturnia
Internazionale, **14**
Scandinavia, **22**
Torino, **12**

Sacca
della
Misericordia

Canale delle Navi

San
Michele

0 ⊢————————————⊣ 440 yards
0 ⊢————————————⊣ 400 meters

Ci Pacchetta
Fondamente
Rio S. Caterina

R. d. Gesuiti Nuove

Fondamente Nuove

Strada
Nova

Rio d. Santi Apostoli

R. d. della Panada

C. d. Testa

C. d. Squero

R. dei Mendicanti

Campo d.
escheria

Campo Santi
Giovanni e Paolo

19

Rio d. S. Marina

R. d. Barbaria delle Tole

R. d. S. Giustina

Campo
di
S. Maria
Formosa

22

R. d. S. Severo

R. d. S. Lorenzo

R. d. S.
Francesco

Canale
d. Galeazze

al Vin

R. d. Fava

Sol. di S. Lio

d. Carbon

C. d. Bande

C. Lion

C. d.
Furlani

R. d. Pietà

R. d. Scudi

R. d. Corna

**Darsena
Grande**

Rio d. Vergini

Colle dei

C. d.
Specchier

in

C. d.
Pestrin

di S. Pietro

Rio d. S. Daniele

o

21

R. d. Palazzo

Fond.
Osmarin

R. d. Greca

C. d.

28

di S.

20

Frezzaria

23

R. d. Moisè

Molo

25

Riva degli

26

Schiavoni

27

R. d. Arsenale

Rio della Tana

Rio d. S. Anna

R. d. S. Giuseppe

Rio dei Giardini

i

**Piazza
San Marco**

V. Garibaldi

Riva dei Sette Martiri

Viale Trieste

Canale di S. Marco

**Isola di
S. Giorgio
Maggiore**

Fond.
delle Zitelle

Ci

Calle
Michelangelo

24

▲ Boat stop

Montin. Despite being a little out of the way, this old inn is popular with Venetians and tourists alike. Inside, walls are covered with paintings; outside, you dine under an elongated arbor. The specialties are *rigatoni ai quattro formaggi* (with cheese, mushrooms, and tomato) and *antipasto Montin* (seafood antipasto). *Fondamenta Eremite 1147, tel. 041/522–7151. Reservations advised. Dress: casual. AE, DC, MC, V. Closed Tues. evening, Wed., all Jan.*

Inexpensive **Ai Cugnai.** The "management," a bevy of friendly and efficient ladies, lends a homey air to proceedings in this popular neighborhood tavern near the Accademia. You eat in the modest dining room and "garden" courtyard. The limited menu offers such Venetian specialties as spaghetti *alle seppie* (with cuttlefish sauce) and *granseole* (crabs). *Calle San Vio, tel. 041/528–9238. Reservations advised in evening. Dress: casual. No credit cards. Closed Mon. and all Jan.*

Antica Adelaide. This informal tavern serves a limited range of well-prepared dishes such as *pasticcio alla gorgonzola* (pasta baked with cheese) and *fritto di pesce* (fried fish). In fair weather you dine in a garden courtyard. To find this inconspicuous establishment, look for the barrel in front of the entrance. *Calle Priuli, off Strada Nova, tel. 041/520–3451. Reservations advised in evening. Dress: casual. No credit cards. Closed Mon.*

★ **Gazebo.** You'll find Gazebo near the train station and Ponte delle Guglie. It is a friendly trattoria that's several cuts above the others on this main pedestrian route. It offers outdoor dining in a garden courtyard and courteous service. Spaghetti *al cartoccio* (steamed in foil with seafood) is the specialty, and there's pizza, too. *Rio Terrà San Leonardo 1333/A (Strada Nova), tel. 041/716380. Reservations advised. Dress: casual. AE, DC, MC, V. Closed Thurs.*

Vino Vino. The annex of the famous Antico Martini restaurant, this is a highly informal wine bar where you can sample Italian vintages and munch on a limited selection of dishes from the kitchens of its upscale big sister, next door. It's open nonstop 10 AM–1 AM. *Campo San Fantin, Calle del Caffettier 2007/a, tel. 041/523–7027. No reservations. Dress: casual. AE, DC, MC, V. Closed Tues.*

Lodging

Most of Venice's hotels are in renovated palaces. The top hotels are indeed palatial, although some "Cinderella" rooms may be small and dowdy. In lower categories, space is at a premium; some rooms may be cramped, and not all hotels have lounging space. Because of conservation laws, some cannot install elevators. Air-conditioning is essential for survival in summer heat; many hotels charge a hefty supplement for it. Although it has no cars, Venice does have boats plying the canals and pedestrians chattering in the streets, even late at night. Don't be surprised if your room is noisy (earplugs help).

The busiest times for hotels are March 15–November 2; December 20–January 2; and the two-week Carnival period leading up to Ash Wednesday, usually in February. Book well in advance. If you don't have reservations, you can almost always get a room in any category by going upon arrival to the AVA (Hotel Association) booths at the train station, airport, and at the municipal parking garage at Piazzale Roma. The 10,000, 20,000, or 30,000-lire deposit (depending on the category of the hotel) is rebated on your bill. The booths are open daily 9–9.

Most hotels quote rates inclusive of breakfast. Rates are generally higher than in Rome or Florence, but you can save considerably in the off season. Remember that it is essential to know how to get to your hotel when you arrive in Venice.

Highly recommended lodgings in each price category are indicated by a star ★.

Category	Cost*
Very Expensive	over 400,000 lire
Expensive	220,000–400,000 lire
Moderate	100,000–220,000 lire
Inexpensive	under 100,000 lire

All prices are for a standard double room for two, including taxes and service.

Very Expensive
★ **Cipriani.** It's impossible to feel stressed in this sybaritic oasis of stunningly decorated rooms and suites, some with garden patios. The Cipriani is located on the Giudecca, across St. Mark's Basin from the heart of Venice, with views of San Giorgio and the lagoon. The hotel launch whisks you back and forth to St. Mark's at any hour of the day or night, but the Cipriani is not for anyone who wants to feel Venice's heartbeat. Cooking courses and fitness programs help keep guests occupied. *Giudecca 10, tel. 041/520–7744, fax 041/5203930. 98 rooms or suites with bath. Facilities: outdoor swimming pool, gardens, tennis courts. AE, DC, MC, V. Closed Nov.–Mar.*

Danieli. This famous hotel is a collage of newer buildings around a 15th-century palazzo, which is loaded with sumptuous Venetian decor and atmosphere. Some of the suites are positively palatial, but lower-priced rooms may not be. The salons and bar are chic places to relax and watch the celebrities go by, and the dining terrace, like many rooms, has a fabulous view of San Giorgio and St. Mark's Basin. *Riva degli Schiavoni 4196, tel. 041/522–6480, fax 041/5200208. 230 rooms or suites with bath. Facilities: bar, restaurant, terrace. AE, DC, MC, V.*

Gritti Palace. The atmosphere of an aristocratic private home pervades this quietly elegant hotel. Fresh flowers, fine antiques, sumptuous appointments, and Old World service give guests the feeling of being very special people. The dining terrace on the Grand Canal is best in the evening when the boat traffic dies down. *Campo Santa Maria del Giglio 2467, tel. 041/794611, fax 041/5200942. 98 rooms or suites with bath. Facilities: bar, restaurant, canalside terrace. AE, DC, MC, V.*

Expensive **Londra Palace.** This grand hotel commands a fine view of San Giorgio and St. Mark's Basin and has a distinguished ambience. The rooms are decorated in dark paisley prints, with sophisticated touches, and the rooftop suite is a honeymooner's dream. The *Deux Lions* restaurant offers the best French cuisine in Venice, and the piano bar is open late. Guest perks include a complimentary Mercedes for one-day excursions and free entrance to the city Casino. *Riva degli Schiavoni 4171, tel. 041/520–0533, fax 041/5225032. 69 rooms and suites with bath. Fa-*

cilities: piano bar, restaurant, terrace, solarium. AE, DC, MC, V.

★ **Metropole.** Everything about the Metropole has the distinctive atmosphere of a small, exclusive hotel. It is decorated with subtle color-coordinated fabrics and run with careful attention to detail. It overlooks St. Mark's Basin, but the quiet, spacious rooms on the garden are especially inviting. You can step from your watertaxi or gondola directly into the hotel lobby. *Riva degli Schiavoni 4149, tel. 041/520–5044, fax 041/522–3679. 64 rooms with bath. Facilities: bar, grill room. AE, DC, MC, V.*

Saturnia Internazionale. There's lots of Old World charm in this historic palace, which is quietly but centrally located near St. Mark's. Its beamed ceilings, damask-hung walls, and authentic Venetian decor impart real character to the solid comfort of its rooms and salons. Many rooms, among them numbers 80, 82, and 84, have been extensively redecorated and endowed with more glamorous—and much larger—bathrooms. *Calle Larga XXII Marzo 2398, tel. 041/520–8377, fax 041/520–7131. 95 rooms with bath. Facilities: bar, 2 restaurants. AE, DC, MC, V.*

Moderate **Accademia.** One of Venice's most charming hotels, the Accad-
★ emia is also one of its most popular, so early reservations are a must. It is located in a 17th-century villa near the Accademia Gallery and the Grand Canal. Lounges, bar, and wood-paneled breakfast room are cheery, with fresh flowers everywhere. You can even have breakfast outside on the garden terrace in good weather. Bedrooms are ample and comfortably furnished, whether in the traditional wood-paneled style or in the bright contemporary look of the air-conditioned top floor. A gracious private-home atmosphere and reasonable rates in this category make this one a gem. *Fondamenta Bollani 1058, tel. 041/523–7846, fax 041/523–9152. 26 rooms, most with bath or shower. Facilities: bar, 2 gardens, landing on canal. AE, DC, MC, V.*

Fenice. The hotel takes its name from the Fenice Theater, which is nearby. There is a slightly bohemian air to the place, perhaps because of the theatrical clientele, so don't be shocked to find other guests in 18th-century costume if you arrive during the Carnival season. Rooms are individually decorated; those in the older wing have more character. *Campiello Fenice 1936, tel. 041/523–2333, fax 041/520–3721. 60 rooms with bath. MC, V.*

Flora. This hotel has what many in this category lack: plenty of sitting rooms and a pretty garden with wrought-iron coffee tables. It's in a quiet, though central, location near San Moisé and St. Mark's. Rooms have Venetian period decor, which some might find a bit dark; some are rather small, with tiny bathrooms. But the location and relaxing atmosphere should be enough to make up for these shortcomings. *Calle Bergamaschi 2283 (off Calle Larga XXII Marzo), tel. 041/520–5844, fax 041/ 522–8217. 30 rooms with bath or shower. Facilities: garden. AE, DC, MC, V. Closed mid-Nov.–Jan.*

Scandinavia. Glass chandeliers shed their light on dizzying combinations of Venetian damask patterns on walls, floor, divans, and chairs. The somewhat overpowering decor confirms that you're in the heart of Venice, just off charming Campo Santa Maria Formosa, near St. Mark's. The hotel is up a steep flight of stairs, and there's no elevator. *Campo Santa Maria Formosa 5240, tel. 041/522–3507, fax 041/523–5232. 29 rooms, 27 with bath or shower. AE, DC, MC, V.*

Torino. This compact hotel is not for claustrophobics, but its fine location near Santa Maria del Giglio makes it an excellent base for sightseeing. The rooms have all the basics, neatly arranged for maximum efficiency in a small space, and are decorated in pastels. There's a comfortable little sitting room; breakfast is served in your room. *Calle delle Ostreghe 2356, tel. 041/520–5222, fax 041/522–8227. 20 rooms with bath or shower. AE, DC, MC, V.*

Inexpensive **Alboretti.** Redecorated in 1986, this small hotel is simply but attractively furnished. Despite its size and central location, the Alboretti has a little garden courtyard off the breakfast room and a sitting room upstairs from the tiny lobby and bar area. There is no elevator. The hotel restaurant has creative Venetian cuisine. In all, the Alboretti offers good value. *Rio Terrà Sant'Agnese 882, tel. 041/523–0058. 19 rooms with bath or shower. Facilities: restaurant. AE, MC, V.*

La Residenza. A little out of the way, this hotel in a Gothic palace is worth the 10-minute walk from San Marco (or the vaporetto ride to the San Zaccaria stop). Breakfast is served in an authentic Venetian salon, and the rooms are well furnished, especially those on the lower floor. *Campo Bandiera e Moro 3608, tel. 041/528–5315, fax 041/523–8859. 19 rooms, some with bath. AE, DC, MC, V. Closed 2nd week of Jan.–mid-Feb., mid-Nov.–2nd week of Dec.*

San Stefano. Here is a hotel in miniature, from the tiny reception area to the minuscule courtyard and breakfast room and skinny elevator. However, its 11 rooms are well furnished in Venetian style, with optional air-conditioning and TV. It's an excellent value and centrally located, too. *Campo San Stefano 2957, tel. 041/520–0166, fax 041/522–4466. 11 rooms, with bath or shower. No credit cards.*

The Arts and Nightlife

The Arts

You'll find a list of current and upcoming events in the *Guest in Venice* booklet, free at tourist information offices or at your hotel. Keep an eye out for posters announcing concerts and other events. Venice hosts important temporary exhibitions, both in the Doge's Palace and in Palazzo Grassi at San Samuele on the Grand Canal. The **Biennale,** a cultural institution, organizes many events throughout the year, including the film festival, beginning at the end of August. In even-numbered years, the big Biennale international art exhibition is held from the end of June to the end of September.

Concerts A Vivaldi festival is held in September; concerts of classical and contemporary music are performed in the city's theaters and churches throughout the year. Watch for posters, or check with the Venice tourist information office at Piazza San Marco. The **Kele e Teo Agency** (San Marco 4930, tel. 041/520–8722) handles tickets for many musical events.

Opera and Ballet **Teatro La Fenice,** on Campo San Fantin, is one of Italy's oldest opera houses. The opera season lasts from December to May or June. Concerts, ballets, and other musical events are held there throughout the year, except in August. For programs and tickets, write Biglietteria, Teatro La Fenice, Campo San

Fantin, 30124 Venice, or call 041/521–0161. Tickets for opera performances go on sale at the box office about one month in advance. The box office is open Monday–Saturday 9:30–12:30, 4–6. If there is a performance on Sunday, the box office remains open, closing on Monday instead.

Nightlife

Except for the scene at Piazza San Marco in fair weather, when the cafés stay open late and the square is a meeting place for visitors and Venetians, there's practically no nightlife in Venice.

Bars and Nightclubs
The **Martini Scala Club** is an elegant piano bar with restaurant. *Calle delle Veste (Campo San Fantin), tel. 041/522–4121. Open Wed.–Mon. 8 PM (10 PM in summer)–3:30 AM.*

The top hotel bars stay open late if the customers want to linger. **Ai Speci** *(Calle Specchieri 648, tel. 041/520–9088)* is an American-style bar with a relaxing, intimate atmosphere.

Casino
The city-operated gambling casino is open April–September in a modern building on the Lido (Lungomare Marconi 4, tel. 041/526–0626) and in the beautiful Palazzo Vendramin Calergi on the Grand Canal during the other months. Both are open daily 3 PM–about 4:30 AM. ACTV runs a Casino Express (Line 28 from the station and Piazzale Roma) to the casino on the Lido, with a stop at San Zaccaria, during casino hours.

Discos
The disco scene is dismal. **El Souk,** near the Accademia, gets a fairly sophisticated young crowd. *Calle Contarini 1056/A, tel. 041/520–0371. Open daily 10PM–3AM.*

Italian Vocabulary

Words & Phrases

	English	*Italian*	*Pronunciation*
Basics	Yes/no	Sí/No	see/no
	Please	Per favore	pear fa-**vo**-ray
	Yes, please	Sí grazie	see **grah**-tsee-ay
	Thank you	Grazie	**grah**-tsee-ay
	You're welcome	Prego	**pray**-go
	Excuse me, sorry	Scusi	**skoo**-zee
	Sorry!	Mi spiace!	mee spee-**ah**-chay
	Good morning/ afternoon	Buon giorno	bwohn **jor**-no
	Goodevening	Buona sera	**bwoh**-na say-ra
	Goodbye	Arrivederci	a-ree-vah-**dare**-chee
	Mr.(Sir)	Signore	see-**nyo**-ray
	Mrs. (Ma'am)	Signora	see-**nyo**-ra
	Miss	Signorina	see-nyo-**ree**-na
	Pleased to meet you	Piacere	pee-ah-**chair**-ray
	How are you?	Come sta?	**ko**-may **sta**
	Very well, thanks	Bene, grazie	**ben**-ay **grah**-tsee-ay
	And you?	E lei?	ay **lay**-ee
	Hello (over the phone)	Pronto?	**proan**-to
Numbers	one	uno	**oo**-no
	two	due	**doo**-ay
	three	tre	tray
	four	quattro	**kwah**-tro
	five	cinque	**cheen**-kway
	six	sei	say
	seven	sette	**set**-ay
	eight	otto	**oh**-to
	nine	nove	**no**-vay
	ten	dieci	dee-**eh**-chee
	eleven	undici	**oon**-dee-chee
	twelve	dodici	**doe**-dee-chee
	thirteen	tredici	**tray**-dee-chee
	fourteen	quattordici	kwa-**tore**-dee-chee
	fifteen	quindici	**kwin**-dee-chee
	sixteen	sedici	**say**-dee-chee
	seventeen	diciassette	dee-cha-**set**-ay
	eighteen	diciotto	dee-**cho**-to
	nineteen	diciannove	dee-cha-**no**-vay
	twenty	venti	**vain**-tee
	twenty-one	ventuno	vain-**too**-no
	twenty-two	ventidue	vayn-tee-**doo**-ay
	thirty	trenta	**train**-ta
	forty	quaranta	kwa-**rahn**-ta
	fifty	cinquanta	cheen-**kwahn**-ta
	sixty	sessanta	seh-**sahn**-ta
	seventy	settanta	seh-**tahn**-ta
	eighty	ottanta	o-**tahn**-ta
	ninety	novanta	no-**vahn**-ta
	one hundred	cento	**chen**-to

| | ten thousand | diecimila | dee-eh-chee-**mee**-la |
| | one hundred thousand | centomila | chen-to-**mee**-la |

Colors	black	nero	**neh**-ro
	blue	azzurro	a-**tsu**-ro
	brown	bruno	**bru**-no
	green	verde	**vehr**-day
	pink	rosa	**ro**-za
	purple	porpora	**por**-por-a
	orange	arancio	a-**rahn**-cho
	red	rosso	**ros**-so
	white	bianco	bee-**ang**-ko
	yellow	giallo	**ja**-lo

Days of the Week	Monday	lunedì	**loo**-neh-dee
	Tuesday	martedì	**mahr**-teh-dee
	Wednesday	mercoledì	**mare**-co-leh-dee
	Thursday	giovedì	**jo**-veh-dee
	Friday	venerdì	**ven**-air-dee
	Saturday	sabato	**sah**-ba-toe
	Sunday	domenica	doe-**men**-ee-ca

Months	January	gennaio	jeh-**nah**-yo
	February	febbraio	feh-**brah**-yo
	March	marzo	**mahr**-tso
	April	aprile	a-**pree**-lay
	May	maggio	**mah**-jo
	June	giugno	**joon**-yo
	July	luglio	**loo**-lee-o
	August	agosto	**loo**-lee-o
	September	settembre	seh-**tem**-bray
	October	ottobre	o-**toe**-bray
	November	novembre	no-**vem**-bray
	December	dicembre	dee-**chem**-bray
Useful Phrases	Do you speak English?	Parla inglese?	**par**-la een-**glay**-zay
	I don't speak Italian	Non parlo italiano	non **par**-lo ee-tal-**yah**-no
	I don't understand	Non capisco	non ka-**peess**-ko
	Can you please repeat?	Può ripetere?	pwo ree-**pet**-ay-ray
	Slowly!	Lentamente!	**len**-ta-men-tay
	I don't know	Non lo so	noan lo **so**
	I'm American/	Sono americano/a	**so**-no a-may-ree-
	British	Sono inglese	**ka**-no/a **so**-no
			een-**glay**-zay
	What's your name?	Come si chiama?	**ko**-may see kee-**ah**-ma
	My name is . . .	Mi chiamo . . .	mee kee-**ah**-mo
	What time is it?	Che ore sono?	kay **o**-ray **so**-no
	How?	Come?	**ko**-may
	When?	Quando?	**kwan**-doe

Yesterday/today/ tomorrow	Ieri/oggi/ domani	**yer**-ee/**o**-jee/ do-**mah**-nee
This morning/ afternoon	Stamattina/Oggi pomeriggio	sta-ma-**tee**-na/**o**-jee po-mer-**ee**-jo
Tonight	Stasera	sta-**ser**-a
What?	Che cosa?	kay **ko**-za
What is it?	Che cos'è?	kay ko-**zay**
Why?	Perché?	pear-**kay**
Who?	Chi?	kee
Where is . . . the bus stop?	Dov'è . . . la fermata dell'autobus?	doe-**veh** la fer-**ma**-ta del ow-toe-**booss**
the train station?	la stazione?	la sta-tsee-**oh**-nay
the subway station?	la metropolitana?	la may-tro-po-lee- **ta**-na
the terminal?	il terminal?	eel ter-mee-**nahl**
the post office?	l'ufficio postale?	loo-**fee**-cho po-**sta**-lay
the bank?	la banca?	la **bahn**-ka
the . . . hotel?	l'hotel . . . ?	lo-**tel**
the store?	il negozio?	ell nay-**go**-tsee-o
the cashier?	la cassa?	la **ka**-sa
the . . . museum?	il museo . . . ?	eel moo-**zay**-o
the hospital?	l'ospedale?	lo-spay-**dah**-lay
the first aid station?	il pronto soccorso?	eel **pron**-to so-**kor**-so
the elevator?	l'ascensore?	la-shen-**so**-ray
a telephone?	un telefono?	oon tay-**lay**-fo-no
Where are the rest rooms?	Dov'è il bagno?	doe-**vay** eel **bahn**-yo
Here/there Left/right	Qui/là A sinistra/a destra	kwee/la a see-**neess**-tra/ a **des**-tra
Straight ahead	Avanti dritto	a-**vahn**-tee **dree**-to
Is it near/far?	È vicino?/lontano?	ay vee-**chee**-no/ lon-**tah**-no
I'd like . . .	Vorrei . . .	vo-**ray**
a room	una camera	**oo**-na **ka**-may-ra
the key	la chiave	la kee-**ah**-vay
a newspaper	un giornale	oon jor-**na**-lay
a stamp	un francobollo	oon frahn-ko-**bo**-lo
I'd like to buy . . .	Vorrei comprare . . .	vo-**ray** kom-**pra**-ray
a cigar	un sigaro	oon see-**ga**-ro
cigarettes	delle sigarette	day-lay see-ga-**ret**-ay
some matches	dei fiammiferi	day-ee fee-ah-**mee**-fer-ee
some soap	una saponetta	**oo**-na sa-po-**net**-a
a city plan	una pianta della città	**oo**-na **pyahn**-ta day-la chee-**ta**
a road map of . . .	una carta stradale di . . .	**oo**-na **cart**-a stra-**dah**-lay dee

a country map	una carta geografica	**oo**-na **cart**-a jay-o-**grah**-fee-ka
a magazine	una rivista	**oo**-na ree-**veess**-ta
envelopes	delle buste	**day**-lay **booss**-tay
writing paper	della carta da lettere	**day**-la **cart**-a da **let**-air-ay
a postcard	una cartolina	**oo**-na car-toe-**lee**-na
a guidebook	una guida turistica	**oo**-na **gwee**-da too-**reess**-tee-ka
How much is it?	Quanto costa?	**kwahn**-toe **coast**-a
It's expensive/ cheap	È caro/economico	ay **car**-o/ay-ko-**no**-mee-ko
A little/a lot	Poco/tanto	**po**-ko/**tahn**-to
More/less	Più/meno	pee-**oo**/**may**-no
Enough/too (much)	Abbastanza/troppo	a-bas-**tahn**-sa/**tro**-po
I am sick	Sto male	sto **ma**-lay
Please call a doctor	Chiami un dottore	kee-**ah**-mee oon doe-**toe**-ray
Help!	Aiuto!	a-**yoo**-toe
Stop!	Alt!	ahlt
Fire!	Al fuoco!	ahl **fwo**-ko
Caution!/Look out!	Attenzione!	a-ten-**syon**-ay

Dining Out

A bottle of . . .	una bottiglia di . . .	**oo**-na bo-**tee**-lee-ah dee
A cup of . . .	Una tazza di . . .	**oo**-na **tah**-tsa dee
A glass of . . .	Un bicchiere di . . .	oon bee-key-**air**-ay dee
Ashtray	Il portacenere	eel por-ta-**chen**-ay-ray
Bill/check	Il conto	eel **cone**-toe
Bread	Il pane	eel **pa**-nay
Breakfast	La prima colazione	la **pree**-ma ko-la-**tsee**-oh-nay
Cheers!	Cin cin!	cheen cheen
Cocktail/aperitif	L'aperitivo	la-pay-ree-**tee**-vo
Dinner	La cena	la **chen**-a
Enjoy!	Buon appetito	bwone a-pay-**tee**-toe
Fixed-price menu	Menù a prezzo fisso	may-**noo** a **pret**-so **fee**-so
Fork	La forchetta	la for-**ket**-a
I am diabetic	Ho il diabete	o eel dee-a-**bay**-tay
I am on a diet	Sono a dieta	**so**-no a dee-**et**-a

I am vegetarian	Sono vegetariano/a	**so**-no vay-jay-ta-ree-**ah**-no/a
I cannot eat . . .	Non posso mangiare . . .	non **po**-so man-**ja**-ray
I'd like to order	Vorrei ordinare	vo-**ray** or-dee-**nah**-ray
I'd like . . .	Vorrei . . .	vo-**ray**
I'm hungry/thirsty	Ho fame/sete	o **fa**-may/**set**-ay
Is service included?	Il servizio è incluso?	eel ser-**vee**-tzee-o ay een-**kloo**-zo
It's good/bad	È buono/cattivo	ay **bwo**-no/ka-tee-vo
It's hot/cold	È caldo/freddo	ay **kahl**-doe/**fred**-o
Knife	Il coltello	eel kol-**tel**-o
Lunch	Il pranzo	eel **prahnt**-so
Menu	Il menù	eel may-**noo**
Napkin	Il tovagliolo	eel toe-va-lee-**oh**-lo
Please give me . . .	Mi dia . . .	mee **dee**-a
Salt	Il sale	eel **sah**-lay
Spoon	Il cucchiaio	eel koo-kee-**ah**-yo
Sugar	Lo zucchero	lo **tsoo**-ker-o
Waiter/Waitress	Cameriere/cameriera	ka-mare-**yer**-ay/ka-mare-**yer**-a
Wine list	La lista dei vini	la **lee**-sta **day**-ee **vee**-nee

Index

Personal Itinerary

Departure *Date*

Time

Transportation

Arrival *Date*   *Time*

Departure *Date*   *Time*

Transportation

Accommodations

Arrival *Date*   *Time*

Departure *Date*   *Time*

Transportation

Accommodations

Arrival *Date*   *Time*

Departure *Date*   *Time*

Transportation

Accommodations

Addresses

Name _____ | *Name* _____

Address _____ | *Address* _____

_____ | _____

Telephone _____ | *Telephone* _____

Name _____ | *Name* _____

Address _____ | *Address* _____

_____ | _____

Telephone _____ | *Telephone* _____

Name _____ | *Name* _____

Address _____ | *Address* _____

_____ | _____

Telephone _____ | *Telephone* _____

Name _____ | *Name* _____

Address _____ | *Address* _____

_____ | _____

Telephone _____ | *Telephone* _____

Name _____ | *Name* _____

Address _____ | *Address* _____

_____ | _____

Telephone _____ | *Telephone* _____

Name _____ | *Name* _____

Address _____ | *Address* _____

_____ | _____

Telephone _____ | *Telephone* _____

Name _____ | *Name* _____

Address _____ | *Address* _____

_____ | _____

Telephone _____ | *Telephone* _____

Name _____ | *Name* _____

Address _____ | *Address* _____

_____ | _____

Telephone _____ | *Telephone* _____

Fodor's Travel Guides

U.S. Guides

Alaska
Arizona
Boston
California
Cape Cod, Martha's
  Vineyard, Nantucket
The Carolinas & the
  Georgia Coast
The Chesapeake
  Region
Chicago
Colorado
Disney World & the
  Orlando Area
Florida
Hawaii

Las Vegas, Reno,
  Tahoe
Los Angeles
Maine, Vermont,
  New Hampshire
Maui
Miami & the
  Keys
National Parks
  of the West
New England
New Mexico
New Orleans
New York City
New York City
  (Pocket Guide)

Pacific North Coast
Philadelphia & the
  Pennsylvania
  Dutch Country
Puerto Rico
  (Pocket Guide)
The Rockies
San Diego
San Francisco
San Francisco
  (Pocket Guide)
The South
Santa Fe, Taos,
  Albuquerque
Seattle &
  Vancouver

Texas
USA
The U. S. & British
  Virgin Islands
The Upper Great
  Lakes Region
Vacations in
  New York State
Vacations on the
  Jersey Shore
Virginia & Maryland
Waikiki
Washington, D.C.
Washington, D.C.
  (Pocket Guide)

Foreign Guides

Acapulco
Amsterdam
Australia
Austria
The Bahamas
The Bahamas
  (Pocket Guide)
Baja & Mexico's Pacific
  Coast Resorts
Barbados
Barcelona, Madrid,
  Seville
Belgium &
  Luxembourg
Berlin
Bermuda
Brazil
Budapest
Budget Europe
Canada
Canada's Atlantic
  Provinces

Cancun, Cozumel,
  Yucatan Peninsula
Caribbean
Central America
China
Czechoslovakia
Eastern Europe
Egypt
Europe
Europe's Great Cities
France
Germany
Great Britain
Greece
The Himalayan
  Countries
Holland
Hong Kong
India
Ireland
Israel
Italy

Italy 's Great Cities
Jamaica
Japan
Kenya, Tanzania,
  Seychelles
Korea
London
London
  (Pocket Guide)
London Companion
Mexico
Mexico City
Montreal &
  Quebec City
Morocco
New Zealand
Norway
Nova Scotia,
  New Brunswick,
  Prince Edward
  Island
Paris

Paris (Pocket Guide)
Portugal
Rome
Scandinavia
Scandinavian Cities
Scotland
Singapore
South America
South Pacific
Southeast Asia
Soviet Union
Spain
Sweden
Switzerland
Sydney
Thailand
Tokyo
Toronto
Turkey
Vienna & the Danube
  Valley
Yugoslavia

Wall Street Journal Guides to Business Travel

Europe

International Cities

Pacific Rim

USA & Canada

Special-Interest Guides

Bed & Breakfast and
  Country Inn Guides:
Mid-Atlantic Region
New England
The South
The West

Cruises and Ports
  of Call
Healthy Escapes
Fodor's Flashmaps
  New York

Fodor's Flashmaps
  Washington, D.C.
Shopping in Europe
Skiing in the USA &
  Canada

Smart Shopper's
  Guide to London
Sunday in New York
Touring Europe
Touring USA